2/11

W9-BSF-495

Under The Lilacs

Louisa May Alcott

AkashaPublishing.Com

Akasha Classic Series

Akasha Classics is dedicated to the re-publication of cherished works of World Literature. Many of these writings play a special role in recording the history of human kind, who we are and where we have been. If you know of any out-of-print titles that you would like to see back in print, let us know.

Akasha Publishing, LLC
877-745-7317
AkashaPublishing.Com

Under The Lilacs, by Louisa May Alcott

Library of Congress Control Number: 2008941800

ISBN-13: 978-1-60512-305-9 Hardcover
ISBN-13: 978-1-60512-405-6 Paperback

CONTENTS

LOUISA MAY ALCOTT

CHAPTER I

A MYSTERIOUS DOG

The elm-tree avenue was all overgrown, the great gate was never unlocked, and the old house had been shut up for several years.

Yet voices were heard about the place, the lilacs nodded over the high wall as if they said, "We could tell fine secrets if we chose," and the mullein outside the gate made haste to reach the keyhole, that it might peep in and see what was going on. If it had suddenly grown up like a magic bean-stalk, and looked in on a certain June day, it would have seen a droll but pleasant sight, for somebody evidently was going to have a party.

From the gate to the porch went a wide walk, paved with smooth slabs of dark stone, and bordered with the tall bushes which met overhead, making a green roof. All sorts of neglected flowers and wild weeds grew between their stems, covering the walls of this summer parlor with the prettiest tapestry. A board, propped on two blocks of wood, stood in the middle of the walk, covered with a little plaid shawl much the worse for wear, and on it a miniature tea-service was set forth with great elegance. To be sure, the tea-pot had lost its spout, the cream-jug its handle, the sugar-bowl its cover, and the cups and plates were all more or less cracked or nicked; but polite persons would not take notice of these trifling deficiencies, and none but polite persons were invited to this party.

On either side of the porch was a seat, and here a somewhat remarkable sight would have been revealed to any inquisitive eye peering through the aforesaid keyhole. Upon the left-hand seat lay seven dolls, upon the right-hand seat lay six; and so varied were the expressions of their countenances, owing to fractures, dirt, age, and other afflictions, that one would very naturally have thought this a doll's hospital, and these the patients waiting for their tea.

This, however, would have been a sad mistake; for if the wind had lifted the coverings laid over them, it would have disclosed the fact that all were in full dress, and merely reposing before the feast should begin.

There was another interesting feature of the scene which would have puzzled any but those well acquainted with the manners and customs of dolls. A fourteenth rag baby, with a china head, hung by her neck from the rusty knocker in the middle of the door. A sprig of white and one of purple lilac nodded over her, a dress of yellow calico, richly trimmed with red-flannel scallops, shrouded her slender form, a garland of small flowers crowned her glossy curls, and a pair of blue boots touched toes in the friendliest, if not the most graceful, manner. An emotion of grief, as well as of surprise, might well have thrilled any youthful breast at such a spectacle; for why, oh! why, was this resplendent dolly hung up there to be stared at by thirteen of her kindred? Was she a criminal, the sight of whose execution threw them flat upon their backs in speechless horror? Or was she an idol, to be adored in that humble posture? Neither, my friends. She was blonde Belinda, set, or rather hung, aloft, in the place of honor, for this was her seventh birthday, and a superb ball was about to celebrate the great event. All were evidently awaiting a summons to the festive board; but such was the perfect breeding of these dolls, that not a single eye out of the whole twenty-seven (Dutch Hans had lost one of the black beads from his worsted countenance) turned for a moment toward the table, or so much as winked, as they lay in decorous rows, gazing with mute admiration at Belinda. She, unable to repress the joy and pride which swelled her sawdust bosom till the seams gaped, gave an occasional bounce as the wind waved her yellow skirts, or made the blue boots dance a sort of jig upon the door. Hanging was evidently not a painful operation, for she smiled contentedly, and looked as if the red ribbon around her neck was not uncomfortably tight; therefore, if slow suffocation suited her, who else had any right to complain? So a pleasing silence reigned, not even broken by a snore from Dinah, the top of whose turban alone was visible above the coverlet, or a cry from baby Jane, though her bare feet stuck out in a way that would have produced shrieks from a less well-trained infant.

LOUISA MAY ALCOTT

Presently voices were heard approaching, and through the arch which led to a side-path came two little girls, one carrying a small pitcher, the other proudly bearing a basket covered with a napkin. They looked like twins, but were not, for Bab was a year older than Betty, though only an inch taller. Both had on brown calico frocks, much the worse for a week's wear; but clean pink pinafores, in honor of the occasion, made up for that, as well as the gray stockings and thick boots. Both had round, rosy faces rather sunburnt, pug noses somewhat freckled, merry blue eyes, and braided tails of hair hanging down their backs like those of the dear little Kenwigses.

"Don't they look sweet?" cried Bab, gazing with maternal pride upon the left-hand row of dolls, who might appropriately have sung in chorus, "We are seven."

"Very nice; but my Belinda beats them all. I do think she is the splendidest child that ever was!" And Betty set down the basket to run and embrace the suspended darling, just then kicking up her heels with joyful abandon.

"The cake can be cooling while we fix the children. It does smell perfectly delicious!" said Bab, lifting the napkin to hang over the basket, fondly regarding the little round loaf that lay inside.

"Leave some smell for me!" commanded Betty, running back to get her fair share of the spicy fragrance. The pug noses sniffed it up luxuriously, and the bright eyes feasted upon the loveliness of the cake, so brown and shiny, with a tipsy-looking B in pie-crust staggering down one side, instead of sitting properly a-top.

"Ma let me put it on the very last minute, and it baked so hard I couldn't pick it off. We can give Belinda that piece, so it's just as well," observed Betty, taking the lead, as her child was queen of the revel.

"Let's set them round, so they can see too," proposed Bab, going, with a hop, skip, and jump, to collect her young family.

Betty agreed, and for several minutes both were absorbed in seating their dolls about the table; for some of the dear things were so limp they wouldn't sit up, and others so stiff they wouldn't sit down, and all sorts of seats had to be contrived to suit the peculiarities of their spines. This arduous task accomplished, the fond mammas stepped back to enjoy the spectacle, which, I assure you, was an impressive one. Belinda sat with great dignity at the head, her hands genteelly holding a pink cambric pocket-handkerchief in her lap. Josephus, her cousin, took the foot, elegantly arrayed in a new suit of purple and green gingham, with his speaking countenance much obscured by a straw hat several sizes too large for him; while on either side sat guests of every size, complexion, and costume, producing a very gay and varied effect, as all were dressed with a noble disregard of fashion.

"They will like to see us get tea. Did you forget the buns?" inquired Betty, anxiously.

"No; got them in my pocket." And Bab produced from that chaotic cupboard two rather stale and crumbly ones, saved from lunch for the fete. These were cut up and arranged in plates, forming a graceful circle around the cake, still in its basket.

"Ma couldn't spare much milk, so we must mix water with it. Strong tea isn't good for children, she says." And Bab contentedly surveyed the gill of skim-milk which was to satisfy the thirst of the company.

"While the tea draws and the cake cools, let's sit down and rest; I'm so tired!" sighed Betty, dropping down on the door-step and stretching out the stout little legs which had been on the go all day; for Saturday had its tasks as well as its fun, and much business had preceded this unusual pleasure. Bab went and sat beside her, looking idly down the walk toward the gate, where a fine cobweb shone in the afternoon sun.

"Ma says she is going over the house in a day or two, now it is warm and dry after the storm, and we may go with her. You know she wouldn't take us in the fall, cause we had whooping-cough, and it was damp there. Now we shall see all the nice things; won't it be fun?" observed Bab, after a pause.

"Yes, indeed! Ma says there's lots of books in one room, and I can look at 'em while she goes round. May be I'll have time to read some, and then I can tell you," answered Betty, who dearly loved stories, and seldom got any new ones.

"I'd rather see the old spinning-wheel up garret, and the big pictures, and the queer clothes in the blue chest. It makes me mad to have them all shut up there, when we might have such fun with them. I'd just like to bang that old door down!" And Bab twisted round to give it a thump with her boots. "You needn't laugh; you know you'd like it as much as me," she added, twisting back again, rather ashamed of her impatience.

"I didn't laugh."

"You did! Don't you suppose I know what laughing is?"

"I guess I know I didn't."

"You did laugh! How darst you tell such a fib?"

"If you say that again I'll take Belinda and go right home; then what will you do?"

"I'll eat up the cake."

"No, you won't! It's mine, Ma said so; and you are only company, so you'd better behave or I won't have any party at all, so now."

This awful threat calmed Bab's anger at once, and she hastened to introduce a safer subject.

"Never mind; don't let's fight before the children. Do you know, Ma says she will let us play in the coach-house next time it rains, and keep the key if we want to."

"Oh, goody! that's because we told her how we found the little window under the woodbine, and didn't try to go in, though we might have just as easy as not," cried Betty, appeased at once, for, after a ten years' acquaintance, she had grown used to Bab's peppery temper.

"I suppose the coach will be all dust and rats and spiders, but I don't care. You and the dolls can be the passengers, and I shall sit up in front drive."

"You always do. I shall like riding better than being horse all the time, with that old wooden bit in my mouth, and you jerking my arms off," said poor Betty, who was tired of being horse continually.

"I guess we'd better go and get the water now," suggested Bab, feeling that it was not safe to encourage her sister in such complaints.

"It is not many people who would dare to leave their children all alone with such a lovely cake, and know they wouldn't pick at it," said Betty proudly, as they trotted away to the spring, each with a little tin pail in her hand.

Alas, for the faith of these too confiding mammas! They were gone about five minutes, and when they returned a sight met their astonished eyes which produced a simultaneous shriek of horror. Flat upon their faces lay the fourteen dolls, and the cake, the cherished cake, was gone.

For an instant the little girls could only stand motionless, gazing at the dreadful scene. Then Bab cast her water-pail wildly away, and, doubling up her fist, cried out fiercely, -

"It was that Sally! She said she'd pay me for slapping her when she pinched little Mary Ann, and now she has. I'll give it to her! You run that way. I'll run this. Quick! quick!"

Away they went, Bab racing straight on, and bewildered Betty turning obediently round to trot in the opposite direction as fast as

LOUISA MAY ALCOTT

she could, with the water splashing all over her as she ran, for she had forgotten to put down her pail. Round the house they went, and met with a crash at the back door, but no sign of the thief appeared.

"In the lane!" shouted Bab.

"Down by the spring!" panted Betty; and off they went again, one to scramble up a pile of stones and look over the wall into the avenue, the other to scamper to the spot they had just left. Still, nothing appeared but the dandelions' innocent faces looking up at Bab, and a brown bird scared from his bath in the spring by Betty's hasty approach.

Back they rushed, but only to meet a new scare, which made them both cry "Ow!" and fly into the porch for refuge.

A strange dog was sitting calmly among the ruins of the feast, licking his lips after basely eating up the last poor bits of bun, when he had bolted the cake, basket, and all, apparently.

"Oh, the horrid thing!" cried Bab, longing to give battle, but afraid, for the dog was a peculiar as well as a dishonest animal.

"He looks like our China poodle, doesn't he?" whispered Betty, making herself as small as possible behind her more valiant sister.

He certainly did; for, though much larger and dirtier than the well-washed China dog, this live one had the same tassel at the end of his tail, ruffles of hair round his ankles, and a body shaven behind and curly before. His eyes, however, were yellow, instead of glassy black, like the other's; his red nose worked as he cocked it up, as if smelling for more cakes, in the most impudent manner; and never, during the three years he had stood on the parlor mantel-piece, had the China poodle done the surprising feats with which this mysterious dog now proceeded to astonish the little girls almost out of their wits. First he sat up, put his forepaws together, and begged prettily; then he suddenly flung his hind-legs into the air, and walked about with great ease. Hardly had they recovered from this shock, when the hind-legs came down, the fore-legs went up, and he paraded in a soldierly manner to and fro, like a sentinel on guard. But the crowning performance was when he took his tail in his mouth and waltzed down the walk, over the prostrate dolls, to the gate and back again, barely escaping a general upset of the ravaged table.

Bab and Betty could only hold each other tight and squeal with delight, for never had they seen any thing so funny; but, when the gymnastics ended, and the dizzy dog came and stood on the step before them barking loudly, with that pink nose of his sniffing at their feet, and his queer eyes fixed sharply upon them, their amusement turned to fear again, and they dared not stir.

"Whish, go away!" commanded Bab.

"Scat!" meekly quavered Betty.

To their great relief, the poodle gave several more inquiring barks, and then vanished as suddenly as he appeared. With one impulse, the children ran to see what became of him, and, after a brisk scamper through the orchard, saw the tasselled tail disappear under the fence at the far end.

"Where do you s'pose he came from?" asked Betty, stopping to rest on a big stone.

"I'd like to know where he's gone, too, and give him a good beating, old thief!" scolded Bab, remembering their wrongs.

"Oh, dear, yes! I hope the cake burnt him dreadfully if he did eat it," groaned Betty, sadly remembering the dozen good raisins she chopped up, and the "lots of 'lasses" mother put into the dear lost loaf.

"The party's all spoilt, so we may as well go home; and Bab mournfully led the way back. Betty puckered up her face to cry, but burst out laughing in spite of her woe.

"It was so funny to see him spin round and walk on his head! I wish he'd do it all over again; don't you?"

"Yes: but I hate him just the same. I wonder what Ma will say when - why! why!" and Bab stopped short in the arch, with her eyes as round and almost as large as the blue saucers on the tea-tray.

"What is it? oh, what is it?" cried Betty, all ready to run away if any new terror appeared.

"Look! there! it's come back!" said Bab in an awe-stricken whisper, pointing to the table. Betty did look, and her eyes opened even wider, - as well they might, - for there, just where they first put it, was the lost cake, unhurt, unchanged, except that the big B had coasted a little further down the gingerbread hill.

CHAPTER II

WHERE THEY FOUND HIS MASTER

Neither spoke for a minute, astonishment being too great for words; then, as by one impulse, both stole up and touched the cake with a timid finger, quite prepared to see it fly away in some mysterious and startling manner. It remained sitting tranquilly in the basket, however, and the children drew a long breath of relief, for, though they did not believe in fairies, the late performances did seem rather like witchcraft.

"The dog didn't eat it!"

"Sally didn't take it!"

"How do you know?"

"She never would have put it back."

"Who did?"

"Can't tell, but I forgive 'em."

"What shall we do now?" asked Betty, feeling as if it would be very difficult to settle down to a quiet tea-party after such unusual excitement.

"Eat that cake up just as fast as ever we can", and Bab divided the contested delicacy with one chop of the big knife, bound to make sure of her own share at all events.

It did not take long, for they washed it down with sips of milk, and ate as fast as possible, glancing round all the while to see if the queer dog was coming again.

"There! now I'd like to see any one take my cake away," said Bab, defiantly crunching her half of the pie-crust B.

"Or mine either," coughed Betty, choking over a raisin that wouldn't go down in a hurry.

"We might as well clear up, and play there had been an earthquake," suggested Bab, feeling that some such convulsion of Nature was needed to explain satisfactorily the demoralized condition of her family.

"That will be splendid. My poor Linda was knocked right over on her nose. Darlin' child, come to your mother and be fixed," purred Betty, lifting the fallen idol from a grove of chickweed, and tenderly brushing the dirt from Belinda's heroically smiling face.

"She'll have croup to-night as sure as the world. We'd better make up some squills out of this sugar and water," said Bab, who dearly loved to dose the dollies all round.

"P'r'aps she will, but you needn't begin to sneeze yet awhile. I can sneeze for my own children, thank you, ma'am," returned Betty, sharply, for her usually amiable spirit had been ruffled by the late occurrences.

"I didn't sneeze! I've got enough to do to talk and cry and cough for my own poor dears, without bothering about yours," cried Bab, even more ruffled than her sister.

"Then who did? I heard a real live sneeze just as plain as anything," and Betty looked up to the green roof above her, as if the sound came from that direction.

A yellow-bird sat swinging and chirping on the tall lilac-bush, but no other living thing was in sight. Birds don't sneeze, do they?" asked Betty, eying little Goldy suspiciously.

"You goose! of course they don't."

"Well. I should just like to know who is laughing and sneezing round here. "May be it is the dog," suggested Betty looking relieved.

"I never heard of a dog's laughing, except Mother Hubbard's. This is such a queer one, may be he can, though. I wonder where he went to?" and Bab took a survey down both the side-paths, quite longing to see the funny poodle again.

"I know where I 'm going to," said Betty, piling the dolls into her apron with more haste than care. "I'm going right straight home to tell Ma all about it. I don't like such actions, and I 'm afraid to stay."

"I ain't; but I guess it is going to rain, so I shall have to go any way," answered Bab, taking advantage of the black clouds rolling up the sky, for she scorned to own that she was afraid of any thing.

Clearing the table in a summary manner by catching up the four corners of the cloth, Bab put the rattling bundle into her apron, flung her children on the top and pronounced herself ready to depart. Betty lingered an instant to pick up and ends that might be spoilt by the rain, and, when she turned from taking the red halter off the knocker, two lovely pink roses lay on the stone steps.

"Oh, Bab, just see! Here's the very ones we wanted. Wasn't it nice of the wind to blow 'em down?" she called out, picking them up and running after her sister, who had strolled moodily along, still looking about for her sworn foe, Sally Folsom. The flowers soothed the feelings of the little girls, because they had longed for them, and bravely resisted the temptation to climb up the trellis and help themselves, since their mother had forbidden such feats, owing to a fall Bab got trying to reach a honeysuckle from the vine which ran all over the porch.

Home they went and poured out their tale, to Mrs. Moss's great amusement; for she saw in it only some playmate's prank, and was not much impressed by the mysterious sneeze and laugh.

　　　　LOUISA MAY ALCOTT

"We'll have a grand rummage Monday, and find out what is going on over there," was all she said. But Mrs. Moss could not keep her promise, for on Monday it still rained, and the little girls paddled off to school like a pair of young ducks, enjoying every puddle they came to, since India-rubber boots made wading a delicious possibility. They took their dinner, and at noon regaled a crowd of comrades with an account of the mysterious dog, who appeared to be haunting the neighborhood, as several of the other children had seen him examining their back yards with interest. He had begged of them, but to none had he exhibited his accomplishments except Bab and Betty; and they were therefore much set up, and called him "our dog" with an air. The cake transaction remained a riddle, for Sally Folsom solemnly declared that she was playing tag in Mamie Snow's barn at that identical time. No one had been near the old house but the two children, and no one could throw any light upon that singular affair.

It produced a great effect, however; for even "teacher" was interested, and told such amazing tales of a juggler she once saw, that doughnuts were left forgotten in dinner-baskets, and wedges of pie remained suspended in the air for several minutes at a time, instead of vanishing with miraculous rapidity as usual. At afternoon recess, which the girls had first, Bab nearly dislocated every joint of her little body trying to imitate the poodle's antics. She had practised on her bed with great success, but the wood-shed floor was a different thing, as her knees and elbows soon testified.

"It looked just as easy as any thing; I don't see how he did it," she said, coming down with a bump after vainly attempting to walk on her hands.

"My gracious, there he is this very minute!" cried Betty, who sat on a little wood-pile near the door. There was a general rush, - and sixteen small girls gazed out into the rain as eagerly as if to behold Cinderella's magic coach, instead of one forlorn dog trotting by through the mud.

"Oh, do call him in and make him dance!" cried the girls, all chirping at once, till it sounded as if a flock of sparrows had taken possession of the shed.

"I will call him, he knows me," and Bab scrambled up, forgetting how she had chased the poodle and called him names two days ago.

He evidently had not forgotten, however; for, though he paused and looked wistfully at them, he would not approach, but stood dripping in the rain, with his frills much bedraggled, while his tasselled tail wagged slowly, and his pink nose pointed suggestively to the pails and baskets, nearly empty now.

"He's hungry; give him something to eat, and then he'll see that we don't want to hurt him," suggested Sally, starting a contribution with her last bit of bread and butter.

Bab caught up her new pail, and collected all the odds and ends; then tried to beguile the poor beast in to eat and be comforted. But he only came as far as the door, and, sitting up, begged with such imploring eyes that Bab put down the pail and stepped back, saying pitifully, -

"The poor thing is starved; let him eat all he wants, and we won't touch him."

The girls drew back with little clucks of interest and compassion; but I regret to say their charity was not rewarded as they expected, for, the minute the coast was clear, the dog marched boldly up, seized the handle of the pail in his mouth, and was off with it, galloping down the road at a great pace.

Shrieks arose from the children, especially Bab and Betty, basely bereaved of their new dinner-pail; but no one could follow the thief, for the Ben rang, and in they went, so much excited that the boys rushed tumultuously forth to discover the cause. By the time school was over the sun was out, and Bab and Betty hastened home to tell their wrongs and be comforted by mother, who did it most effectually.

LOUISA MAY ALCOTT

"Never mind, dears, I'll get you another pail, if he doesn't bring it back as he did before. As it is too wet for you to play out, you shall go and see the old coach-house as I promised, Keep on your rubbers and come along."

This delightful prospect much assuaged their woe, and away they went, skipping gayly down the gravelled path, while Mrs. Moss followed, with skirts well tucked up, and a great bunch of keys in her hand; for she lived at the Lodge, and had charge of the premises.

The small door of the coach-house was fastened inside, but the large one had a padlock on it; and this being quickly unfastened, one half swung open, and the little girls ran in, too eager and curious even to cry out when they found themselves at last in possession of the long-coveted old carriage. A dusty, musty concern enough; but it had a high seat, a door, steps that let down, and many other charms which rendered it most desirable in the eyes of children.

Bab made straight for the box and Betty for the door; but both came tumbling down faster than they went up, when from the gloom of the interior came a shrill bark, and a low voice saying quickly, "Down, Sancho! down!"

"Who is there?" demanded Mrs. Moss, in a stern tone, backing toward the door with both children clinging to her skirts.

The well-known curly white head was popped out of the broken window, and a mild whine seemed to say, "Don't be alarmed, ladies; we won't hurt you." Come out this minute, or I shall have to come and get you," called Mrs. Moss, growing very brave all of a sudden as she caught sight of a pair of small, dusty shoes under the coach.

"Yes, 'm, I'm coming, as fast as I can," answered a meek voice, as what appeared to be a bundle of rags leaped out of the dark, followed by the poodle, who immediately sat down at the bare feet of his owner with a watchful air, as if ready to assault any one who might approach too near.

"Now, then, who are you, and how did you get here?" asked Mrs. Moss, trying to speak sternly, though her motherly eyes were already full of pity, as they rested on the forlorn little figure before her.

CHAPTER III

BEN

"Please, 'm, my name is Ben Brown, and I'm travellin'."

"Where are you going?"

"Anywheres to get work."

"What sort of work can you do?"

"All kinds. I'm used to horses."

"Bless me! such a little chap as you?

"I'm twelve, ma'am, and can ride any thing on four legs;" and the small boy gave a nod that seemed to say, "Bring on your Cruisers. I'm ready for 'em."

"Haven't you got any folks?" asked Mrs. Moss, amused but still anxious, for the sunburnt face was very thin, the eyes hollow with hunger or pain, and the ragged figure leaned on the wheel as if too weak or weary to stand alone.

"No, 'm, not of my own; and the people I was left with beat me so, I - run away." The last words seemed to bolt out against his will as if the woman's sympathy irresistibly won the child's confidence.

"Then I don't blame you. But how did you get here?"

"I was so tired I couldn't go any further, and I thought the folks up here at the big house would take me in. But the gate was locked, and I was so discouraged, I jest laid down outside and give up."

"Poor little soul, I don't wonder," said Mrs. Moss, while the children looked deeply interested at mention of their gate.

The boy drew a long breath, and his eyes began to twinkle in spite of his forlorn state as he went on, while the dog pricked up his ears at mention of his name: -

"While I was restin' I heard some one come along inside, and I peeked, and saw them little girls playin'. The vittles looked so nice I couldn't help wantin' 'em; but I didn't take nothin', - it was Sancho, and he took the cake for me."

Bab and Betty gave a gasp and stared reproachfully at the poodle, who half closed his eyes with a meek, unconscious look that was very droll.

"And you made him put it back?" cried Bab.

"No; I did it myself. Got over the gate when you was racin' after Sancho, and then clim' up on the porch and hid," said the boy with a grin.

"And you laughed?" asked Bab.

"Yes."

"And sneezed?" added Betty.

"Yes."

"And threw down the roses?" cried both.

"Yes; and you liked 'em, didn't you?"

"Course we did! What made you hide?" said Bab.

"I wasn't fit to be seen," muttered Ben, glancing at his tatters as if he'd like to dive out of sight into the dark coach again.

"How came you here?" demanded Mrs. Moss, suddenly remembering her responsibility.

"I heard 'em talk about a little winder and a shed, and when they'd gone I found it and come in. The glass was broke, and I only pulled the nail out. I haven't done a mite of harm sleepin' here two nights. I was so tuckered out I couldn't go on nohow, though I tried a-Sunday."

"And came back again?

"Yes, 'm; it was so lonesome in the rain, and this place seemed kinder like home, and I could hear 'em talkin' outside, and Sanch he found vittles, and I was pretty comfortable."

"Well, I never!" ejaculated Mrs. Moss, whisking up a corner of her apron to wipe her eyes, for the thought of the poor little fellow alone there for two days and nights with no bed but musty straw, no food but the scraps a dog brought him, was too much for her. "Do you know what I'm going to do with you?" she asked, trying to look calm and cool, with a great tear running down her wholesome red cheek, and a smile trying to break out at the corners of her lips.

"No, ma'am, and I dunno as I care. Only don't be hard on Sanch; he's been real good to me, and we're fond of one another; ain't us, old chap?" answered the boy, with his arm around the dog's neck, and an anxious look which he had not worn for himself.

"I'm going to take you right home, and wash and feed and put you in a good bed; and to-morrow, - well, we'll see what'll happen then," said Mrs. Moss, not quite sure about it herself.

"You're very kind, ma'am, I'll be glad to work for you. Ain't you got a horse I can see to?" asked the boy, eagerly.

"Nothing but hens and a cat."

Bab and Betty burst out laughing when their mother said that, and Ben gave a faint giggle, as if he would like to join in if he only had the strength to do it. But his legs shook under him, and he felt a queer dizziness; so he could only hold on to Sancho, and blink at the light like a young owl.

"Come right along, child. Run on, girls, and put the rest of the broth to warming, and fill the kettle. I'll see to the boy," commanded Mrs. Moss, waving off the children, and going up to feel the pulse of her new charge, for it suddenly occurred to her that he might be sick and not safe to take home.

The hand he gave her was very thin, but clean and cool, and the black eyes were clear though hollow, for the poor lad was half-starved.

"I'm awful shabby, but I ain't dirty. I had a washin' in the rain last night, and I've jest about lived on water lately," he explained, wondering why she looked at him so hard.

"Put out your tongue."

He did so, but took it in again to say quickly, -

"I ain't sick, - I'm only hungry; for I haven't had a mite but what Sanch brought, for three days; and I always go halves, don't I, Sanch?"

The poodle gave a shrill bark, and vibrated excitedly between the door and his master as if he understood all that was going on, and recommended a speedy march toward the promised food and shelter. Mrs. Moss took the hint, and bade the boy follow her at once and bring his "things" with him.

"I ain't got any. Some big fellers took away my bundle, else I wouldn't look so bad. There's only this. I'm sorry Sanch took it, and I'd like to give it back if I knew whose it was," said Ben, bringing the new dinner-pail out from the depths of the coach where he had gone to housekeeping.

"That's soon done; it's mine, and you're welcome to the bits your queer dog ran off with. Come along, I must lock up," and Mrs. Moss clanked her keys suggestively.

Ben limped out, leaning on a broken hoe-handle, for he was stiff after two days in such damp lodgings, as well as worn out with a fortnight's wandering through sun and rain. Sancho was in great spirits, evidently feeling that their woes were over and his foraging expeditions at an end, for he frisked about his master with yelps of pleasure, or made playful darts at the ankles of his benefactress, which caused her to cry, "Whish!" and "Scat!" and shake her skirts at him as if he were a cat or hen.

A hot fire was roaring in the stove under the broth-skillet and tea-kettle, and Betty was poking in more wood, with a great smirch of black on her chubby cheek, while Bab was cutting away at the loaf as if bent on slicing her own fingers off. Before Ben knew what he was about, he found himself in the old rocking-chair devouring bread and butter as only a hungry boy can, with Sancho close by gnawing a mutton-bone like a ravenous wolf in sheep's clothing.

While the new-comers were thus happily employed, Mrs. Moss beckoned the little girls out of the room, and gave them both an errand.

"Bab, you run over to Mrs. Barton's, and ask her for any old duds Billy don't want; and Betty, you go to the Cutters, and tell Miss Clarindy I'd like a couple of the shirts we made at last sewing circle. Any shoes, or a hat, or socks, would come handy, for the poor dear hasn't a whole thread on him."

Away went the children full of anxiety to clothe their beggar; and so well did they plead his cause with the good neighbors, that Ben hardly knew himself when he emerged from the back bedroom half an hour later, clothed in Billy Barton's faded flannel suit, with an unbleached cotton shirt out of the Dorcas basket, and a pair of Milly Cutter's old shoes on his feet.

Sancho also had been put in better trim, for, after his master had refreshed himself with a warm bath, he gave his dog a good scrub while Mrs. Moss set a stitch here and there in the new old clothes; and Sancho reappeared, looking more like the china poodle than ever, being as white as snow, his curls well brushed up, and his tasselly tail waving proudly over his back.

Feeling eminently respectable and comfortable, the wanderers humbly presented themselves, and were greeted with smiles of approval from the little girls and a hospitable welcome from the mother, who set them near the stove to dry, as both were decidedly damp after their ablutions.

"I declare I shouldn't have known you!" exclaimed the good woman, surveying the boy with great satisfaction; for, though still very thin and tired, the lad had a tidy look that pleased her, and a lively way of moving about in his clothes, like an eel in a skin rather too big for him. The merry black eyes seemed to see every thing, the voice had an honest sound, and the sunburnt face looked several years younger since the unnatural despondency had gone out of it.

"It's very nice, and me and Sanch are lots obliged, ma'am," murmured Ben, getting red and bashful under the three pairs of friendly eyes fixed upon him.

Bab and Betty were doing up the tea-things with unusual despatch, so that they might entertain their guest, and just as Ben spoke Bab dropped a cup. To her great surprise no smash followed, for, bending quickly, the boy caught it as it fell, and presented it to her on the back of his hand with a little bow.

"Gracious! how could you do it?" asked Bab, looking as if she thought there was magic about.

"That's nothing; look here," and, taking two plates, Ben sent them spinning up into the air, catching and throwing so rapidly that Bab and Betty stood with their mouths open, as if to swallow the plates should they fall, while Mrs. Moss, with her dish-cloth suspended, watched the antics of her crockery with a housewife's anxiety.

"That does beat all!" was the only exclamation she had time to make; for, as if desirous of showing his gratitude in the only way he could, Ben took clothes-pins from a basket near by, sent several saucers twirling up, caught them on the pins, balanced the pins on chin, nose, forehead, and went walking about with a new and peculiar sort of toadstool ornamenting his countenance.

The children were immensely tickled, and Mrs. Moss was so amused she would have lent her best soup-tureen if he had expressed a wish for it. But Ben was too tired to show all his accomplishments at once, and he soon stopped, looking as if he almost regretted having betrayed that he possessed any.

"I guess you've been in the juggling business," said Mrs. Moss, with a wise nod, for she saw the same look on his face as when he said his name was Ben Brown, - the look of one who was not telling the whole truth.

"Yes, 'm. I used to help Senor Pedro, the Wizard of the World, and I learned some of his tricks," stammered Ben, trying to seem innocent.

"Now, look here, boy, you'd better tell me the whole story, and tell it true, or I shall have to send you up to judge Morris. I wouldn't like to do that, for he is a harsh sort of a man; so, if you haven't done any thing bad, you needn't be afraid to speak out, and I'll do what I can for you," said Mrs. Moss, rather sternly, as she went and sat down in her rocking-chair, as if about to open the court.

"I haven't done any thing bad, and I ain't afraid, only I don't want to go back; and if I tell, may be you'll let 'em know where I be," said Ben, much distressed between his longing to confide in his new friend and his fear of his old enemies.

"If they abused you, of course I wouldn't. Tell the truth, and I'll stand by you. Girls, you go for the milk."

"Oh, Ma, do let us stay! We'll never tell, truly, truly!" cried Bab and Betty, full of dismay being sent off when secrets were about to be divulged.

"I don't mind 'em," said Ben handsomely.

"Very well, only hold your tongues. Now, boy where did you come from?" said Mrs. Moss, as the little girls hastily sat down together on their private and particular bench opposite their mother, brimming with curiosity and beaming with satisfaction at the prospect before them.

CHAPTER IV

HIS STORY

"I ran away from a circus," began Ben, but got no further, for Bab and Betty gave a simultaneous bounce of delight, and both cried out at once, -

"We've been to one! It was splendid!"

"You wouldn't think so if you knew as much about it as I do," answered Ben, with a sudden frown and wriggle, as if he still felt the smart of the blows he had received. "We don't call it splendid; do we, Sancho?" he added, making a queer noise, which caused the poodle to growl and bang the floor irefully with his tail, as he lay close to his master's feet, getting acquainted with the new shoes they wore.

"How came you there?" asked Mrs. Moss, rather disturbed at the news.

"Why, my father was the 'Wild Hunter of the Plains.' Didn't you ever see or hear of him?" said Ben, as if surprised at her ignorance.

"Bless your heart, child, I haven't been to a circus this ten years, and I'm sure I don't remember what or who I saw then," answered Mrs. Moss, amused, yet touched by the son's evident admiration for his father.

"Didn't you see him?" demanded Ben, turning to the little girls.

"We saw Indians and tumbling men, and the Bounding Brothers of Borneo, and a clown and monkeys, and a little mite of a pony with blue eyes. Was he any of them?" answered Betty, innocently.

"Pooh! he didn't belong to that lot. He always rode two, four, six, eight horses to oncet, and I used to ride with him till I got too big. My father was A No. 1, and didn't do any thing but break horses and ride 'em," said Ben, with as much pride as if his parent had been a President.

"Is he dead?" asked Mrs. Moss.

"I don't know. Wish I did," - and poor Ben gave a gulp as if something rose in his throat and choked him.

"Tell us all about it, dear, and may be we can find out where he is," said Mrs. Moss, leaning forward to pat the shiny dark head that was suddenly bent over the dog.

"Yes, ma'am. I will, thank y'," and with an effort the boy steadied his voice and plunged into the middle of his story.

"Father was always good to me, and I liked bein' with him after granny died. I lived with her till I was seven; then father took me, and I was trained for rider. You jest oughter have seen me when I was a little feller all in white tights, and a gold belt, and pink riggin', standing' on father's shoulder, or hangin' on to old General's tail, and him gallopin' full pelt; or father ridin' three horses with me on his head wavin' flags, and every one clapping like fun."

"Oh, weren't you scared to pieces?" asked Betty, quaking at the mere thought.

"Not a bit. I liked it."

"So should I!" cried Bab enthusiastically.

"Then I drove the four ponies in the little chariot, when we paraded," continued Ben, "and I sat on the great ball up top of the grand car drawed by Hannibal and Nero. But I didn't like that, 'cause it was awful high and shaky, and the sun was hot, and the trees slapped my face, and my legs ached holdin' on."

"What's hanny bells and neroes?" demanded Betty.

"Big elephants. Father never let 'em put me up there, and they didn't darst till he was gone; then I had to, else they'd 'a' thrashed me."

"Didn't any one take your part?" asked Mrs. Moss.

"Yes, 'm, 'most all the ladies did; they were very good to me, 'specially 'Melia. She vowed she wouldn't go on in the Tunnymunt act if they didn't stop knockin' me round when I wouldn't help old Buck with the bears. So they had to stop it, 'cause she led first rate, and none of the other ladies rode half as well as 'Melia."

"Bears! oh, do tell about them!" exclaimed Bab, in great excitement, for at the only circus she had seen the animals were her delight.

"Buck had five of 'em, cross old fellers, and he showed 'em off. I played with 'em once, jest for fun, and he thought it would make a hit to have me show off instead of him. But they had a way of clawin' and huggin' that wasn't nice, and you couldn't never tell whether they were good-natured or ready to bite your head off. Buck was all over scars where they'd scratched and bit him, and I wasn't going to do it; and I didn't have to, owin' to Miss St. John's standin' by me like a good one."

"Who was Miss St. John?" asked Mrs. Moss, rather confused by the sudden introduction of new names and people.

"Why she was 'Melia, - Mrs. Smithers, the ringmaster's wife. His name wasn't Montgomery any more'n hers was St. John. They all change 'em to something fine on the bills, you know. Father used to be Senor Jose Montebello; and I was Master Adolphus Bloomsbury, after I stopped bein' a flyin' Coopid and a infant Progidy."

Mrs. Moss leaned back in her chair to laugh at that, greatly to the surprise of the little girls, who were much impressed with the elegance of these high-sounding names.

"Go on with your story, Ben, and tell why you ran away and what became of your Pa," she said, composing herself to listen, really interested in the child.

"Well, you see, father had a quarrel with old Smithers, and went off sudden last fall, just before tenting season' was over. He told me he was goin' to a great ridin' school in New York and when he was fixed he'd send for me. I was to stay in the museum and help Pedro with the trick business. He was a nice man and I liked him, and 'Melia was goin' to see to me, and I didn't mind for awhile. But father didn't send for me, and I began to have horrid times. If it hadn't been for 'Melia and Sancho I would have cut away long before I did."

"What did you have to do?"

"Lots of things, for times was dull and I was smart. Smithers said so, any way, and I had to tumble up lively when he gave the word. I didn't mind doin' tricks or showin' off Sancho, for father trained him, and he always did well with me. But they wanted me to drink gin to keep me small, and I wouldn't, 'cause father didn't like that kind of thing. I used to ride tip-top, and that just suited me till I got a fall and hurt my back; but I had to go on all the same, though I ached dreadful, and used to tumble off, I was so dizzy and weak."

"What a brute that man must have been! Why didn't 'Melia put a stop to it?" asked Mrs. Moss, indignantly.

"She died, ma'am, and then there was no one left but Sanch; so I run away."

Then Ben fell to patting his dog again, to hide the tears he could not keep from coming at the thought of the kind friend he had lost.

"What did you mean to do?"

"Find father; but I couldn't, for he wasn't at the ridin' school, and they told me he had gone out West to buy mustangs for a man who wanted a lot. So then I was in a fix, for I couldn't go to father,

LOUISA MAY ALCOTT

didn't know jest where he was, and I wouldn't sneak back to Smithers to be abused. Tried to make 'em take me at the ridin' school, but they didn't want a boy, and I travelled along and tried to get work. But I'd have starved if it hadn't been for Sanch. I left him tied up when I ran off, for fear they'd say I stole him. He's a very valuable dog, ma'am, the best trick dog I ever see, and they'd want him back more than they would me. He belongs to father, and I hated to leave him; but I did. I hooked it one dark night, and never thought I'd see him ag'in. Next mornin' I was eatin' breakfast in a barn miles away, and dreadful lonesome, when he came tearin' in, all mud and wet, with a great piece of rope draggin'. He'd gnawed it and come after me, and wouldn't go back or be lost; and I'll never leave him again, will I, dear old feller?"

Sancho had listened to this portion of the tale with intense interest, and when Ben spoke to him he stood straight up, put both paws on the boy's shoulders, licked his face with a world of dumb affection in his yellow eyes, and gave a little whine which said as plainly as words, -

"Cheer up, little master; fathers may vanish and friends die, but I never will desert you."

Ben hugged him close and smiled over his curly, white head at the little girls, who clapped their hands at the pleasing tableau, and then went to pat and fondle the good creature, assuring him that they entirely forgave the theft of the cake and the new dinner-pail. Inspired by these endearments and certain private signals given by Ben, Sancho suddenly burst away to perform all his best antics with unusual grace and dexterity.

Bab and Betty danced about the room with rapture, while Mrs. Moss declared she was almost afraid to have such a wonderfully intelligent animal in the house. Praises of his dog pleased Ben more than praises of himself, and when the confusion had subsided he entertained his audience with a lively account of Sancho's cleverness, fidelity, and the various adventures in which he had nobly borne his part.

While he talked, Mrs. Moss was making up her mind about him, and when he came to an end of his dog's perfections, she said, gravely, -

"If I can find something for you to do, would you like to stay here awhile?"

"Oh, yes, ma'am, I'd be glad to!" answered Ben, eagerly; for the place seemed home-like already, and the good woman almost as motherly as the departed Mrs. Smithers.

"Well, I'll step over to the Squire's to-morrow to see what he says. Shouldn't wonder if he'd take you for a chore-boy, if you are as smart as you say. He always has one in the summer, and I haven't seen any round yet. Can you drive cows?"

"Hope so;" and Ben gave a shrug, as if it was a very unnecessary question to put to a person who had driven four calico ponies in a gilded chariot.

"It mayn't be as lively as riding elephants and playing with bears, but it is respectable; and I guess you'll be happier switching Brindle and Buttercup than being switched yourself," said Mrs. Moss, shaking her head at him with a smile.

"I guess I will, ma'am," answered Ben, with sudden meekness, remembering the trials from which he had escaped.

Very soon after this, he was sent off For a good night's sleep in the back bedroom, with Sancho to watch over him. But both found it difficult to slumber till the racket overhead subsided; for Bab insisted on playing she was a bear and devouring poor Betty, in spite of her wails, till their mother came up and put an end to it by threatening to send Ben and his dog away in the morning, if the girls "didn't behave and be as still as mice."

This they solemnly promised; and they were soon dreaming of gilded cars and mouldy coaches, runaway boys and dinner-pails, dancing dogs and twirling teacups.

LOUISA MAY ALCOTT

CHAPTER V

BEN GETS A PLACE

When Ben awoke next morning, he looked about him for a moment half bewildered, because there was neither a canvas tent, a barn roof, nor the blue sky above him, but a neat white ceiling, where several flies buzzed sociably together, while from without came, not the tramping of horses, the twitter of swallows, or the chirp of early birds, but the comfortable cackle of hens and the sound of two little voices chanting the multiplication table.

Sancho sat at the open window, watching the old cat wash her face, and trying to imitate her with his great ruffled paw, so awkwardly that Ben laughed; and Sanch, to hide his confusion at being caught, made one bound from chair to bed, and licked his master's face so energetically that the boy dived under the bedclothes to escape from the rough tongue. A rap on the floor from below made both jump up, and in ten minutes a shiny-faced lad and a lively dog went racing downstairs, - one to say, "Good-mornin', ma'am," the other to wag his tail faster than ever tail wagged before, for ham frizzled on the stove, and Sancho was fond of it.

"Did you rest well?" asked Mrs. Moss, nodding at him, fork in hand.

"Guess I did! Never saw such a bed. I'm used to hay and a horse-blanket, and lately nothin' but sky for a cover and grass for my feather-bed," laughed Ben, grateful for present comforts and making light of past hardships.

"Clean, sweet corn-husks ain't bad for young bones, even if they haven't got more flesh on them than yours have," answered Mrs. Moss, giving the smooth head a motherly stroke as she went by.

"Fat ain't allowed in our profession, ma'am. The thinner the better for tight-ropes and tumblin'; likewise bareback ridin' and spry jugglin'. Muscle's the thing, and there you are."

Ben stretched out a wiry little arm with a clenched fist at the end of it, as if he were a young Hercules, ready to play ball with the stove if she gave him leave. Glad to see him in such good spirits, she pointed to the well outside, saying pleasantly, -

"Well, then, just try your muscle by bringing in some fresh water."

Ben caught up a pail and ran off, ready to be useful; but, while he waited for the bucket to fill down among the mossy stones, he looked about him, well pleased with all he saw, - the small brown house with a pretty curl of smoke rising from its chimney, the little sisters sitting in the sunshine, green hills and newly-planted fields far and near, a brook dancing through the orchard, birds singing in the elm avenue, and all the world as fresh and lovely as early summer could make it.

"Don't you think it's pretty nice here?" asked Bab, as his eye came back to them after a long look, which seemed to take in every thing, brightening as it roved.

"Just the nicest place that ever was. Only needs a horse round somewhere to be complete," answered Ben, as the long well-sweep came up with a dripping bucket at one end, an old grindstone at the other.

"The judge has three, but he's so fussy about them he won't even let us pull a few hairs out of old Major's tail to make rings of," said Betty, shutting her arithmetic, with an injured expression.

"Mike lets me ride the white one to water when the judge isn't round. It's such fun to go jouncing down the lane and back. I do love horses!" cried Bab, bobbing up and down on the blue bench to imitate the motion of white Jenny.

"I guess you are a plucky sort of a girl," and Ben gave her an approving look as he went by, taking care to slop a little water on Mrs. Puss, who stood curling her whiskers and humping up her back at Sancho.

"Come to breakfast!" called Mrs. Moss; and for about twenty minutes little was said, as mush and milk vanished in a way that would have astonished even Jack the Giant-killer with his leather bag.

"Now, girls, fly round and get your chores done up; Ben, you go chop me some kindlings; and I'll make things tidy. Then we can all start off at once," said Mrs. Moss, as the last mouthful vanished, and Sancho licked his lips over the savory scraps that fell to his share.

Ben fell to chopping so vigorously that chips flew wildly all about the shed; Bab rattled the cups into her dish-pan with dangerous haste, and Betty raised a cloud of dust "sweeping-up;" while mother seemed to be everywhere at once. Even Sanch, feeling that his fate was at stake, endeavored to help in his own somewhat erratic way, - now frisking about Ben at the risk of getting his tail chopped off, then trotting away to poke his inquisitive nose into every closet and room whither he followed Mrs. Moss in her "flying round" evolutions; next dragging off the mat so Betty could brush the door-steps, or inspecting Bab's dish-washing by standing on his hind-legs to survey the table with a critical air. When they drove him out he was not the least offended, but gayly barked Puss up a tree, chased all the hens over the fence, and carefully interred an old shoe in the garden, where the remains of the mutton-bone were already buried.

By the time the others were ready, he had worked off his superfluous spirits, and trotted behind the party like a well-behaved dog accustomed to go out walking with ladies. At the cross-roads they separated, the little girls running on to school, while Mrs. Moss and Ben went up to the Squire's big house on the hill.

"Don't you be scared, child. I'LL make it all right about your running away; and if the Squire gives you a job, just thank him for it, and do your best to be steady and industrious; then you'll get on, I haven't a doubt," she whispered, ringing the Ben at a side-door, on which the word "Morris" shone in bright letters.

"Come in!" called a gruff voice; and, feeling very much as if he were going to have a tooth out, Ben meekly followed the good woman, who put on her pleasantest smile, anxious to make the best possible impression.

A white-headed old gentleman sat reading a paper, and peered over his glasses at the new-comers with a pair of sharp eyes, saying in a testy tone, which would have rather daunted any one who did not know what a kind heart he had under his capacious waistcoat, -

"Good-morning, ma'am. What's the matter now? Young tramp been stealing your chickens?"

"Oh, dear no, sir!" exclaimed Mrs. Moss, as if shocked at the idea. Then, in a few words, she told Ben's story, unconsciously making his wrongs and destitution so pathetic by her looks and tones, that the Squire could not help being interested, and even Ben pitied himself as if he were somebody else.

"Now, then, boy, what can you do?" asked the old gentleman, with an approving nod to Mrs. Moss as she finished, and such a keen glance from under his bushy brows that Ben felt as if be was perfectly transparent.

"'Most any thing, sir, to get my livin'."

"Can you weed?"

"Never did, but I can learn, sir."

"Pull up all the beets and leave the pigweed, hey? Can you pick strawberries?"

LOUISA MAY ALCOTT

"Never tried any thing but eatin' 'em, sir,"

"Not likely to forget that part of the job. Can you ride a horse to plow?"

"Guess I could, sir!" - and Ben's eyes began to sparkle, for he dearly loved the noble animals who had been his dearest friends lately.

"No antics allowed. My horse is a fine fellow, and I'm very particular about him." The Squire spoke soberly, but there was a twinkle in his eye, and Mrs. Moss tried not to smile; for the Squire's horse was a joke all over the town, being about twenty years old, and having a peculiar gait of his own, lifting his fore-feet very high, with a great show of speed, though never going out of a jog-trot. The boys used to say he galloped before and walked behind, and made all sorts of fun of the big, Roman-nosed beast, who allowed no liberties to be taken with him.

"I'm too fond of horses to hurt 'em, Sir. As for ridin', I ain't afraid of any thing on four legs. The King of Morocco used to kick and bite like fun, but I could manage him first-rate."

"Then you'd be able to drive cows to pasture, perhaps?"

"I've drove elephants and camels, ostriches and grizzly bears, and mules, and six yellow ponies all to oncet. May be I could manage cows if I tried hard," answered Ben, endeavoring to be meek and respectful when scorn filled his soul at the idea of not being able to drive a cow.

The Squire liked him all the better for the droll mixture of indignation and amusement betrayed by the fire in his eyes and the sly smile round his lips; and being rather tickled by Ben's list of animals, he answered gravely, -

"Don't raise elephants and camels much round here. Bears used to be plenty, but folks got tired of them. Mules are numerous, but we have the two-legged kind; and as a general thing prefer Shanghae fowls to ostriches."

He got no farther, for Ben laughed out so infectiously that both the others joined him; and somehow that jolly laugh seemed to settle matters than words. As they stopped, the Squire tapped on the window behind him, saying, with an attempt at the former gruffness, -

"We'll try you on cows awhile. My man will show you where to drive them, and give you some odd jobs through the day. I'll see what you are good for, and send you word to-night, Mrs. Moss. The boy can sleep at your house, can't he?"

"Yes, indeed, sir. He can go on doing it, and come up to his work just as well as not. I can see to him then, and he won't be a care to any one," said Mrs. Moss, heartily.

"I'll make inquiries concerning your father, boy; meantime mind what you are about, and have a good report to give when he comes for you," returned the Squire, with a warning wag of a stern fore-finger.

"Thanky', sir. I will, sir. Father'll come just as soon as he can, if he isn't sick or lost," murmured Ben, inwardly thanking his stars that he had not done any thing to make him quake before that awful finger, and resolved that he never would.

Here a red-headed Irishman came to the door, and stood eying the boy with small favor while the Squire gave his orders.

"Pat, this lad wants work. He's to take the cows and go for them. Give him any light jobs you have, and let me know if he's good for any thing."

"Yis, your honor. Come out o' this, b'y, till I show ye the bastes," responded Pat; and, with a hasty good-by to Mrs. Moss, Ben followed his new leader, sorely tempted to play some naughty trick upon him in return for his ungracious reception.

But in a moment he forgot that Pat existed, for in the yard stood the Duke of Wellington, so named in honor of his Roman nose. If

Ben had known any thing about Shakespeare, he would have cried, "A horse, a horse! my kingdom for a horse!" for the feeling was in his heart, and he ran up to the stately animal without a fear. Duke put back his ears and swished his tail as if displeased for a moment; but Ben looked straight in his eyes, gave a scientific stroke to the iron-gray nose, and uttered a chirrup which made the ears prick up as if recognizing a familiar sound.

"He'll nip ye, if ye go botherin' that way. Leave him alone, and attend to the cattle as his honor told ye," commanded Pat, who made a great show of respect toward Duke in public, and kicked him brutally in private.

"I ain't afraid! You won't hurt me, will you, old feller? See there now! - he knows I 'm a friend, and takes to me right off," said Ben, with an arm around Duke's neck, and his own cheek confidingly laid against the animal's; for the intelligent eyes spoke to him as plainly as the little whinny which he under-stood and accepted as a welcome.

The Squire saw it all from the open window, and suspecting from Pat's face that trouble was brewing, called out, -
"Let the lad harness Duke, if he can. I'm going out directly, and he may as well try that as any thing."

Ben was delighted, and proved himself so brisk and handy that the roomy chaise stood at the door in a surprisingly short time, with a smiling little ostler at Duke's head when the Squire came out.

His affection for the horse pleased the old gentleman, and his neat way of harnessing suited as well; but Ben got no praise, except a nod and a brief "All right, boy," as the equipage went creaking and jogging away.

Four sleek cows filed out of the barnyard when Pat opened the gate, and Ben drove them down the road to a distant pasture where the early grass awaited their eager cropping. By the school they went, and the boy looked pityingly at the black, brown, and yellow heads bobbing past the windows as a class went up to recite; for it seemed a hard thing to the liberty-loving lad to be shut up there so many hours on a morning like that.

But a little breeze that was playing truant round the steps did Ben a service without knowing it, for a sudden puff blew a torn leaf to his feet, and seeing a picture he took it up. It evidently had fallen from some ill-used history, for the picture showed some queer ships at anchor, some oddly dressed men just landing, and a crowd of Indians dancing about on the shore. Ben spelt out all be could about these interesting personages, but could not discover what it meant, because ink evidently had deluged the page, to the new reader's great disappointment.

"I'll ask the girls; may be they will know," said Ben to himself as, after looking vainly for more stray leaves, he trudged on, enjoying the bobolink's song, the warm sunshine, and a comfortable sense of friendliness and safety, which soon set him to whistling as gayly as any blackbird in the meadow.

LOUISA MAY ALCOTT

CHAPTER VI

A CIRCULATING LIBRARY

After supper that night, Bab and Betty sat in the old porch playing with Josephus and Belinda, and discussing the events of the day; for the appearance of the strange boy and his dog had been a most exciting occurrence in their quiet lives. They had seen nothing of him since morning, as he took his meals at the Squire's, and was at work with Pat in a distant field when the children passed. Sancho had stuck closely to his master, evidently rather bewildered by the new order of things, and bound to see that no harm happened to Ben.

"I wish they'd come. It's sundown, and I heard the cows mooing, so I know they have gone home," said Betty, impatiently; for she regarded the new-comer in the light of an entertaining book, and wished to read on as fast as possible.

"I'm going to learn the signs he makes when he wants Sancho to dance; then we can have fun with him whenever we like. He's the dearest dog I ever saw!" answered Bab, who was fonder of animals than her sister.

"Ma said - Ow, what's that?" cried Betty with a start, as something bumped against the gate outside; and in a moment Ben's head peeped over the top as he swung himself up to the iron arch, in the middle of which was the empty lantern frame.

"Please to locate, gentlemen; please to locate. The performance is about to begin with the great Flyin' Coopid act, in which Master Bloomsbury has appeared before the crowned heads of Europe. Pronounced by all beholders the most remarkable youthful progidy agoin'. Hooray! here we are!"

Having rattled off the familiar speech in Mr. Smithers's elegant manner, Ben begin to cut up such capers that even a party of dignified hens, going down the avenue to bed, paused to look on with clucks of astonishment, evidently fancying that salt had set him to fluttering and tumbling as it did them. Never had the old gate beheld such antics, though it had seen gay doings in its time; for of all the boys who had climbed over it, not one had ever stood on his head upon each of the big balls which ornamented the posts, hung by his heels from the arch, gone round and round like a wheel with the bar for an axis, played a tattoo with his toes while holding on by his chin, walked about the wall on his hands, or closed the entertainment by festooning himself in an airy posture over the side of the lantern frame, and kissing his hand to the audience as a well-bred Cupid is supposed to do on making his bow.

The little girls clapped and stamped enthusiastically, while Sancho, who had been calmly surveying the show, barked his approval as he leaped up to snap at Ben's feet.

"Come down and tell what you did up at the Squire's. Was he cross? Did you have to work hard? Do you like it?" asked Bab, when the noise had subsided.

"It's cooler up here," answered Ben, composing himself in the frame, and fanning his hot face with a green spray broken from the tall bushes rustling odorously all about him. "I did all sorts of jobs. The old gentleman wasn't cross; he gave me a dime, and I like him first-rate. But I just hate 'Carrots; ' he swears at a feller, and fired a stick of wood at me. Guess I'll pay him off when I get a chance."

Fumbling in his pocket to show the bright dime, he found the torn page, and remembered the thirst for information which had seized him in the morning. "Look here, tell me about this, will you? What are these chaps up to? The ink has spoilt all but the picture and this bit of reading. I want to know what it means. Take it to 'em, Sanch."

The dog caught the leaf as it fluttered to the ground, and carrying it carefully in his mouth, deposited it at the feet of the little girls, seating himself before them with an air of deep interest. Bab and Betty picked it up and read it aloud in unison, while Ben leaned from his perch to listen and learn.

"'When day dawned, land was visible. A pleasant land it was. There were gay flowers, and tall trees with leaves and fruit, such as they had never seen before. On the shore were unclad copper-colored men, gazing with wonder at the Spanish ships. They took them for great birds, the white sails for their wings, and the Spaniards for superior beings brought down from heaven on their backs.'"

"Why, that's Columbus finding San Salvador. Don't you know about him?" demanded Bab, as if she were one of the "superior beings," and intimately acquainted with the immortal Christopher.

"No, I don't. Who was he any way? I s'pose that's him paddlin' ahead; but which of the Injuns is Sam Salvindoor?" asked Ben, rather ashamed of his ignorance, but bent on finding out now he had begun.

"My gracious! twelve years old and not know your Quack-enbos!" laughed Bab, much amused, but rather glad to find that she could teach the "whirligig boy" something, for she considered him a remarkable creature.

"I don't care a bit for your quackin' boss, whoever he is. Tell about this fine feller with the ships; I like him," persisted Ben.

So Bab, with frequent interruptions and hints from Betty, told the wonderful tale in a simple way, which made it easy to understand; for she liked history, and had a lively tongue of her own.

"I'd like to read some more. Would my ten cents buy a book?" asked Ben, anxious to learn a little since Bab laughed at him.

"No, indeed! I'll lend you mine when I'm not using it, and tell you all about it," promised Bab; forgetting that she did not know "all about it" herself yet.

"I don't have any time only evenings, and then may be you'll want it," begun Ben, in whom the inky page had roused a strong curiosity.

"I do get my history in the evening, but you could have it mornings before school."

"I shall have to go off early, so there won't be any chance. Yes, there will, - I'LL tell you how to do it. Let me read while I drive up the cows. Squire likes 'em to eat slow along the road, so's to keep the grass short and save mowin'. Pat said so, and I could do history instead of loafin' round!" cried Ben full of this bright idea.

"How will I get my book back in time to recite?" asked Bab, prudently.

"Oh, I'll leave it on the window-sill, or put it inside the door as I go back. I'll be real careful, and just as soon as I earn enough, I'll buy you a new one and take the old one. Will you?"

"Yes; but I'll tell you a nicer way to do. Don't put the book on the window, 'cause teacher will see you; or inside the door, 'cause some one may steal it. You put it in my cubby-house, right at the corner of the wall nearest the big maple. You'll find a cunning place between the roots that stick up under the flat stone. That's my closet, and I keep things there. It's the best cubby of all, and we take turns to have it."

"I'll find it, and that'll be a first-rate place," said Ben, much gratified.

"I could put my reading-book in sometimes, if you'd like it. There's lots of pretty stories in it and pictures," proposed Betty, rather timidly; for she wanted to share the benevolent project, but had little to offer, not being as good a scholar as Bab.

"I'd like a 'rithmetic better. I read tip-top, but I ain't much on 'rithmetic"; so, if you can spare yours, I might take a look at it. Now I'm goin' to earn wages, I ought to know about addin' 'em up, and so on," said Ben, with the air of a Vanderbilt oppressed with the care of millions.

"I'll teach you that. Betty doesn't know much about sums. But she spells splendidly, and is always at the head of her class. Teacher is real proud of her, 'cause she never misses, and spells hard, fussy words, like chi-rog-ra-phy and bron-chi-tis as easy as any thing."

Bab quite beamed with sisterly pride, and Betty smoothed down her apron with modest satisfaction, for Bab seldom praised her, and she liked it very much.

"I never went to school, so that's the reason I ain't smart. I can write, though, better 'n some of the boys up at school. I saw lots of names on the shed door. See here, now," - and scrambling down, Ben pulled out a cherished bit of chalk, and flourished off ten letters of the alphabet, one on each of the dark stone slabs that paved the walk.

"Those are beautiful! I can't make such curly ones. Who taught you to do it?" asked Bab, as she and Betty walked up and down admiring them.

"Horse blankets," answered Ben, soberly.

"What!" cried both girls, stopping to stare.

"Our horses all had their names on their blankets, and I used to copy 'em. The wagons had signs, and I learned to read that way after father taught me my letters off the red and yellow posters. First word I knew was lion, 'cause I was always goin' to see old Jubal in his cage. Father was real proud when I read it right off. I can draw one, too."

Ben proceeded to depict an animal intended to represent his lost friend; but Jubal would not have recognized his portrait, since it looked much more like Sancho than the king of the forest. The children admired it immensely, however, and Ben gave them a lesson in natural history which was so interesting that it kept them busy and happy till bedtime; for the boy described what he had seen in such lively language, and illustrated in such a droll way, it was no wonder they were charmed.

LOUISA MAY ALCOTT

CHAPTER VII

NEW FRIENDS TROT IN

Next day Ben ran off to his work with Quackenbos's "Elementary History of the United States" in his pocket, and the Squire's cows had ample time to breakfast on way-side grass before they were put into their pasture. Even then the pleasant lesson was not ended, for Ben had an errand to town; and all the way he read busily, tumbling over the hard words, and leaving bits which he did not understand to be explained at night by Bab.

At "The First Settlements" he had to stop, for the schoolhouse was reached, and the book must be returned. The maple-tree closet was easily found, and a little surprise hidden under the flat stone; for Ben paid two sticks of red and white candy for the privilege of taking books from the new library.

When recess came, great was the rejoicing of the children over their unexpected treat, for Mrs. Moss had few pennies to spare for sweets, and, somehow, this candy tasted particularly nice, bought out of grateful Ben's solitary dime. The little girls shared their goodies with their favorite mates, but said nothing about the new arrangement, fearing it would be spoilt if generally known. They told their mother, however, and she gave them leave to lend their books and encourage Ben to love learning all they could. She also proposed that they should drop patch-work, and help her make some blue shirts for Ben. Mrs. Barton had given her the materials, and she thought it would be an excellent lesson in needle-work as well as a useful gift to Ben, - who, boy-like, never troubled himself as to what he should wear when his one suit of clothes gave out.

Wednesday afternoon was the sewing time; so the two little B's worked busily at a pair of shirt-sleeves, sitting on their bench in the doorway, while the rusty needles creaked in and out, and the childish voices sang school-songs, with frequent stoppages for lively chatter.

For a week, Ben worked away bravely, and never shirked nor complained, although Pat put many a hard or disagreeable job upon him, and chores grew more and more distasteful. His only comfort was the knowledge that Mrs. Moss and the Squire were satisfied with him; his only pleasure the lessons he learned while driving the cows, and recited in the evening when the three children met under the lilacs to "play school."

He had no thought of studying when he began, and hardly knew that he was doing it as he pored over the different books he took from the library. But the little girls tried him with all they Possessed, and he was mortified to find how ignorant he was. He never owned it in words, but gladly accepted all the bits of knowledge they offered from their small store; getting Betty to hear him spell "just for fun;" agreeing to draw Bab all the bears and tigers she wanted if she would show him how to do sums on the flags, and often beguiled his lonely labors by trying to chant the multiplication table as they did. When Tuesday night came round, the Squire paid him a dollar, said he was "a likely boy," and might stay another week if he chose. Ben thanked him and thought he would; but the next morning, after he had put up the bars, he remained sitting on the top rail to consider his prospects, for he felt uncommonly reluctant to go back to the society of rough Pat. Like most boys, he hated work, unless it was of a sort which just suited him; then he could toil like a beaver and never tire. His wandering life had given him no habits of steady industry; and, while he was an unusually capable lad of his age, he dearly loved to "loaf" about and have a good deal of variety and excitement in his life.

Now he saw nothing before him but days of patient and very uninteresting labor. He was heartily sick of weeding; even riding Duke before the cultivator had lost its charms, and a great pile of wood lay in the Squire's yard which he knew he would be set to piling up in the shed. Strawberry-picking would soon follow the asparagus cultivation; then haying; and so on all the long bright summer, without any fun, unless his father came for him.

On the other hand, he was not obliged to stay a minute longer unless he liked. With a comfortable suit of clothes, a dollar in his pocket, and a row of dinner-baskets hanging in the school-house entry to supply him with provisions if he didn't mind stealing them, what was easier than to run away again? Tramping has its charms in fair weather, and Ben had lived like a gypsy under canvas for years; so he feared nothing, and began to look down the leafy road with a restless, wistful expression, as the temptation grew stronger and stronger every minute.

Sancho seemed to share the longing, for he kept running off a little way and stopping to frisk and bark; then rushed back to sit watching his master with those intelligent eyes of his, which seemed to say, "Come on, Ben, let us scamper down this pleasant road and never stop till we are tired." Swallows darted by, white clouds fled before the balmy west wind, a squirrel ran along the wall, and all things seemed to echo the boy's desire to leave toil behind and roam away as care-free as they. One thing restrained him, the thought of his seeming ingratitude to good Mrs. Moss, and the disappointment of the little girls at the loss of their two new play-fellows. While he paused to think of this, something happened which kept him from doing what he would have been sure to regret afterward.

Horses had always been his best friends, and one came trotting up to help him now; though he did not know how much he owed it till long after. Just in the act of swinging himself over the bars to take a shortcut across the fields, the sound of approaching hoofs, unaccompanied by the roll of wheels, caught his ear; and, pausing, he watched eagerly to see who was coming at such a pace.

At the turn of road, however, the quick trot stopped, and in a moment a lady on a bay mare came pacing slowly into sight, - a young and pretty lady, all in dark blue, with a bunch of dandelions like yellow stars in her button-hole, and a silver-handled whip hanging from the pommel of her saddle, evidently more for ornament than use. The handsome mare limped a little, and shook her head as if something plagued her; while her mistress leaned down to see what was the matter, saying, as if she expected an answer of some sort, -

"Now, Chevalita, if you have got a stone in your foot, I shall have to get off and take it out. Why don't you look where you step, and save me all this trouble?"

"I'll look for you, ma'am; I'd like to!" said an eager voice so unexpectedly, that both horse and rider started as a boy came down the bank with a jump.

"I wish you would. You need not be afraid; Lita is as gentle as a lamb," answered the young lady, smiling, as if amused by the boy's earnestness.

"She's a beauty, any way," muttered Ben, lifting one foot after another till he found the stone, and with some trouble got it out.

"That was nicely done, and I'm much obliged. Can you tell me if that cross-road leads to the Elms?" asked the lady, as she went slowly on with Ben beside her.

"No, ma'am; I'm new in these parts, and I only know where Squire Morris and Mrs. Moss live."

"I want to see both of them, so suppose you show me the way. I was here long ago, and thought I should remember how to find the old house with the elm avenue and the big gate, but I don't."

"I know it; they call that place the Laylocks now, 'cause there's a hedge of 'em all down the path and front wall. It's a real pretty place; Bab and Betty play there, and so do I."

Ben could not restrain a chuckle at the recollection of his first appearance there, and, as if his merriment or his words interested her, the lady said pleasantly,

"Tell me all about it. Are Bab and Betty your sisters?" Quite forgetting his intended tramp, Ben plunged into a copious history of himself and new-made friends, led on by a kind look, an inquiring word, and sympathetic smile, till he had told every thing. At the school-house corner he stopped and said, spreading his arms like a sign-post, -

"That's the way to the Laylocks, and this is the way to the Squire's."

"As I'm in a hurry to see the old house, I'll go this way first, if you will be kind enough to give my love to Mrs. Morris, and tell the Squire Miss Celia is coming to dine with him. I won't say good-by, because I shall see you again."

With a nod and a smile, the young lady cantered away, and Ben hurried up the hill to deliver his message, feeling as if something pleasant was going to happen; so it would be wise to defer running away, for the present at least.

At one o'clock Miss Celia arrived, and Ben had the delight of helping Pat stable pretty Chevalita; then, his own dinner hastily eaten, he fell to work at the detested wood-pile with sudden energy; for as he worked he could steal peeps into the dining-room, and see the curly brown head between the two gay ones, as the three sat round the table. He could not help hearing a word now and then, as the windows were open, and these bits of conversation filled him with curiosity for the names "Thorny," "Celia," and "George" were often repeated, and an occasional merry laugh from the young lady sounded like music in that usually quiet place.

When dinner was over, Ben's industrious fit left him, and he leisurely trundled his barrow to and fro till the guest departed. There was no chance for him to help now, since Pat, anxious to get whatever trifle might be offered for his services, was quite devoted in his attentions to the mare and her mistress, till she was mounted and off. But Miss Celia did not forget her little guide, and, spying a wistful face behind the wood-pile, paused at the gate and beckoned with that winning smile of hers. If ten Pats had stood scowling in the way, Ben would have defied them all; and, vaulting over the fence, he ran up with a shining face, hoping she wanted some last favor of him. Leaning down, Miss Celia slipped a new quarter into his hand, saying,

"Lita wants me to give you this for taking the stone out of her foot."

"Thank y', ma'am; I liked to do it, for I hate to see 'em limp, 'specially such a pretty one as she is," answered Ben, stroking the glossy neck with a loving touch.

"The Squire says you know a good deal about horses, so I suppose you understand the Houyhnhnm language? I'm learning it, and it is very nice," laughed Miss Celia, as Chevalita gave a little whinny and snuffled her nose into Ben's pocket.

"No, miss, I never went to school."

"That is not taught there. I'll bring you a book all about it when I come back. Mr. Gulliver went to the horse-country and heard the dear things speak their own tongue."

"My father has been on the prairies, where there's lots of wild ones, but he didn't hear 'em speak. I know what they want without talkin'," answered Ben, suspecting a joke, but not exactly seeing what it was.

"I don't doubt it, but I won't forget the book. Good-by, my lad, we shall soon meet again," and away went Miss Celia as if she were in a hurry to get back.

"If she only had a red habit and a streamin' white feather, she'd look as fine as 'Melia used to. She is 'most as kind and rides 'most as well. Wonder where she's goin' to. Hope she will come soon," thought Ben, watching till the last flutter of the blue habit vanished round the corner; and then he went back to his work with his head full of the promised book, pausing now and then to chink the two silver halves and the new quarter together in his pocket, wondering what he should buy with this vast sum.

Bab and Betty meantime had had a most exciting day; for when they went home at noon they found the pretty lady there, and she had talked to them like an old friend, given them a ride on the little horse, and kissed them both good-by when they went back to school. In the afternoon the lady was gone, the old house all open, and their mother sweeping, airing, in great spirits. So they had a splendid frolic tumbling on feather-beds, beating bits of carpet, opening closets, and racing from garret to cellar like a pair of distracted kittens.

Here Ben found them, and was at once overwhelmed with a burst of news which excited him as much as it did them. Miss Celia owned the house, was coming to liver there, and things were to be made ready as soon as possible. All thought the prospect a charming one: Mrs. Moss, because life had been dull for her during the year she had taken charge of the old house; the little girls had heard rumors of various pets who were coming; and Ben, learning that a boy and a donkey were among them, resolved that nothing but the arrival of his father should tear him from this now deeply interesting spot.

"I'm in such a hurry to see the peacocks and hear them scream. She said they did, and that we'd laugh when old Jack brayed," cried Bab, hopping about on one foot to work off her impatience.

"Is a faytun a kind of a bird? I heard her say she could keep it in the coach-house," asked Betty, inquiringly.

"It's a little carriage," and Ben rolled in the grass, much tickled at poor Betty's ignorance.

"Of course it is. I looked it out in the dic., and you mustn't call it a payton, though it is spelt with a p," added Bab, who liked to lay down the law on all occasions, and did not mention that she had looked vainly among the Vs till a school-mate set her right.

"You can't tell me much about carriages. But what I want to know is where Lita will stay?" said Ben.

"Oh, she's to be up at the Squire's till things are fixed, and you are to bring her down. Squire came and told Ma all about it, and said you were a boy to be trusted, for he had tried you."

Ben made no answer, but secretly thanked his stars that he had not proved himself untrustworthy by running away, and so missing all this fun.

"Won't it be fine to have the house open all the time? We can run over and see the pictures and books whenever we like. I know we can, Miss Celia is so kind," began Betty, who cared for these things more than for screaming peacocks and comical donkeys.

"Not unless you are invited," answered their mother, locking the front door behind her. "You'd better begin to pick up your duds right away, for she won't want them cluttering round her front yard. If you are not too tired, Ben, you might rake round a little while I shut the blinds. I want things to look nice and tidy."

Two little groans went up from two afflicted little girls as they looked about them at the shady bower, the dear porch, and the winding walks where they loved to run "till their hair whistled in the wind," as the fairy-books say.

"Whatever shall we do! Our attic is so hot and the shed so small, and the yard always full of hens or clothes. We shall have to pack all our things away, and never play any more," said Bab, tragically.

"May be Ben could build us a little house in the orchard," proposed Betty, who firmly believed that Ben could do any thing.

"He won't have any time. Boys don't care for baby-houses," returned Bab, collecting her homeless goods and chattels with a dismal face.

"We sha'n't want these much when all the new things come; see if we do," said cheerful little Betty, who always found out a silver lining to every cloud.

LOUISA MAY ALCOTT

CHAPTER VIII

MISS CELIA'S MAN

Ben was not too tired, and the clearing-up began that very night. None too soon, for in a day or two things arrived, to the great delight of the children, who considered moving a most interesting play. First came the phaeton, which Ben spent all his leisure moments in admiring; wondering with secret envy what happy boy would ride in the little seat up behind, and beguiling his tasks by planning how, when he got rich, he would pass his time driving about in just such an equipage, and inviting all the boys he met to have a ride.

Then a load of furniture came creaking in at the lodge gate, and the girls had raptures over a cottage piano, several small chairs, and a little low table, which they pronounced just the thing for them to play at. The live stock appeared next, creating a great stir in the neighborhood, for peacocks were rare birds there; the donkey's bray startled the cattle and convulsed the people with laughter; the rabbits were continually getting out to burrow in the newly made garden; and Chevalita scandalized old Duke by dancing about the stable which he had inhabited for years in stately solitude.

Last but by no means least, Miss Celia, her young brother, and two maids arrived one evening so late that only Mrs. Moss went over to help them settle. The children were much disappointed, but were appeased by a promise that they should all go to pay their respects in the morning.

They were up so early, and were so impatient to be off, that Mrs. Moss let them go with the warning that they would find only the servants astir. She was mistaken, however, for, as the procession approached, a voice from the porch called out, "Good-morning little neighbors!" so unexpectedly, that Bab nearly spilt the new milk she carried, Betty gave such a start that the fresh-laid eggs quite skipped in the dish, and Ben's face broke into a broad grin over the armful of clover which he brought for the bunnies, as he bobbed his head, saying briskly, -

"She's all right, miss, Lita is; and I can bring her over any minute you say."

"I shall want her at four o'clock. Thorny will be too tired to drive, but I must hear from the post-office, rain or shine;" and Miss Celia's pretty color brightened as she spoke, either from some happy thought or because she was bashful, for the honest young faces before her plainly showed their admiration of the white-gowned lady under the honeysuckles.

The appearance of Miranda, the maid, reminded the children of their errand; and having delivered their offerings, they were about to retire in some confusion, when Miss Celia said pleasantly, -

"I want to thank you for helping put things in such nice order. I see signs of busy hands and feet both inside the house and all about the grounds, and I am very much obliged."

"I raked the beds," said Ben, proudly eying the neat ovals and circles.

"I swept all the paths," added Bab, with a reproachful glance at several green sprigs fallen from the load of clover on the smooth walk.

"I cleared up the porch," and Betty's clean pinafore rose and fell with a long sigh, as she surveyed the late summer residence of her exiled family. Miss Celia guessed the meaning of that sigh, and made haste to turn it into a smile by asking anxiously, -

"What has become of the playthings? I don't see them anywhere."

LOUISA MAY ALCOTT

"Ma said you wouldn't want our duds round, so we took them all home," answered Betty, with a wistful face.

"But I do want them round. I like dolls and toys almost as much as ever, and quite miss the little 'duds' from porch and path. Suppose you come to tea with me to-night and bring some of them back? I should be very sorry to rob you of your pleasant play-place."

"Oh, yes, 'm, we'd love to come! and we'll bring our best things."

"Ma always lets us have our shiny pitchers and the china poodle when we go visiting or have company at home," said Bab and Betty, both speaking at once.

"Bring what you like, and I'll hunt up my toys, too. Ben is to come also, and his poodle is especially invited," added Miss Celia, as Sancho came and begged before her, feeling that some agreeable project was under discussion.

"Thank you, miss. I told them you'd be willing they should come sometimes. They like this place ever so much, and so do I," said Ben, feeling that few spots combined so many advantages in the way of climbable trees, arched gates, half-a-dozen gables, and other charms suited to the taste of an aspiring youth who had been a flying Cupid at the age of seven.

"So do I," echoed Miss Celia, heartily. "Ten years ago I came here a little girl, and made lilac chains under these very bushes, and picked chickweed over there for my bird, and rode Thorny in his baby-wagon up and down these paths. Grandpa lived here then, and we had fine times; but now they are all gone except us two."

"We haven't got any father, either," said Bab, for something in Miss Celia's face made her feel as if a cloud had come over the sun.

"I have a first-rate father, if I only knew where he'd gone to," said Ben, looking down the path as eagerly as if one waited for him behind the locked gate.

"You are a rich boy, and you are happy little girls to have so good a mother; I've found that out already," and the sun shone again as the young lady nodded to the neat, rosy children before her.

"You may have a piece of her if you want to, 'cause you haven't got any of your own," said Betty with a pitiful look which made her blue eyes as sweet as two wet violets.

"So I will! and you shall be my little sisters. I never had any, and I'd love to try how it seems;" and Celia took both the chubby hands in hers, feeling ready to love every one this first bright morning in the new home, which she hoped to make a very happy one.

Bab gave a satisfied nod, and fell to examining the rings upon the white hand that held her own. But Betty put her arms about the new friend's neck, and kissed her so softly that the hungry feeling in Miss Celia's heart felt better directly; for this was the food it wanted, and Thorny had not learned yet to return one half of the affection he received. Holding the child close, she played with the yellow braids while she told them about the little German girls in their funny black-silk caps, short-waisted gowns, and wooden shoes, whom she used to see watering long webs of linen bleaching on the grass, watching great flocks of geese, or driving pigs to market, knitting or spinning as they went.

Presently "Randa," as she called her stout maid, came to tell her that "Master Thorny couldn't wait another minute;" and she went in to breakfast with a good appetite, while the children raced home to bounce in upon Mrs. Moss, talking all at once like little lunatics.

"The phaeton at four, - so sweet in a beautiful white gown, - going to tea, and Sancho and all the baby things invited. Can't we wear our Sunday frocks? A splendid new net for Lita. And she likes dolls. Goody, goody, won't it be fun!"

With much difficulty their mother got a clear account of the approaching festivity out of the eager mouths, and with still more difficulty, got breakfast into them, for the children had few pleasures, and this brilliant prospect rather turned their heads.

Bab and Betty thought the day would never end, and cheered the long hours by expatiating on the pleasures in store for them, till their playmates were much afflicted because they were not going also. At noon their mother kept them from running over to the old house lest they should be in the way; so they consoled themselves by going to the syringa bush at the corner and sniffing the savory odors which came from the kitchen, where Katy, the cook, was evidently making nice things for tea.

Ben worked as if for a wager till four; then stood over Pat while he curried Lita till her coat shone like satin, then drove her gently down to the coach-house, where he had the satisfaction of harnessing her "all his own self".

"Shall I go round to the great gate and wait for you there, miss?" he asked, when all was ready, looking up at the porch, where the young lady stood watching him as she put on her gloves.

"No, Ben, the great gate is not to be opened till next October. I shall go in and out by the lodge, and leave the avenue to grass and dandelions, meantime," answered Miss Celia, as she stepped in and took the reins, with a sudden smile.

But she did not start, even when Ben had shaken out the new duster and laid it neatly over her knees.

"Isn't it all right now?" asked the boy, anxiously.

"Not quite; I need one thing more. Can't you guess what it is?" and Miss Celia watched his anxious face as his eyes wandered from the tips of Lita's ears to the hind-wheel of the phaeton, trying to discover what had been omitted.

"No, miss, I don't see - " he began, much mortified to think he had forgotten any thing.

"Wouldn't a little groom up behind improve the appearance of my turnout?" she said, with a look which left no doubt in his mind that he was to be the happy boy to occupy that proud perch.

He grew red with pleasure, but stammered, as he hesitated, looking down at his bare feet and blue shirt, -

"I ain't fit, miss; and I haven't got any other clothes."

Miss Celia only smiled again more kindly than before, and answered, in a tone which he understood better than her words, - "A great man said his coat-of-arms was a pair of shirt-sleeves, and a sweet poet sang about a barefooted boy; so I need not be too proud to ride with one. Up with you, Ben, my man, and let us be off, or we shall be late for our party."

With one bound the new groom was in his place, sitting very erect, with his legs stiff, arms folded, and nose in the air, as he had seen real grooms sit behind their masters in fine dog-carts or carriages. Mrs. Moss nodded as they drove past the lodge, and Ben touched his torn hat-brim in the most dignified manner, though he could not suppress a broad grin of delight, which deepened into a chuckle when Lita went off at a brisk trot along the smooth road toward town.

It takes so little to make a child happy, it is a pity grown people do not oftener remember it and scatter little bits of pleasure before the small people, as they throw crumbs to the hungry sparrows. Miss Celia knew the boy was pleased, but he had no words in which to express his gratitude for the great contentment she had given him. He could only beam at all he met, smile when the floating ends of the gray veil blew against his face, and long in his heart to give the new friend a boyish hug, as he used to do his dear 'Melia when she was very good to him.

School was just out as they passed; and it was a spectacle, I assure you, to see the boys and girls stare at Ben up aloft in such state; also to see the superb indifference with which that young man regarded the vulgar herd who went afoot. He couldn't resist an affable nod to Bab and Betty, for they stood under the maple-tree,

LOUISA MAY ALCOTT

and the memory of their circulating library made him forget his dignity in his gratitude.

"We will take them next time, but now I want to talk to you," began Miss Celia, as Lita climbed the hill. "My brother has been ill, and I have brought him here to get well. I want to do all sorts of things to amuse him, and I think you can help me in many ways. Would you like to work for me instead of the Squire?

"I guess I would!" ejaculated Ben, so heartily that no further assurances were needed, and Miss Celia went on, well pleased: -

"You see, poor Thorny is weak and fretful, and does not like to exert himself, though he ought to be out a great deal, and kept from thinking of his little troubles. He cannot walk much yet, so I have a wheeled chair to push him in; and the paths are so hard, it will be easy to roll him about. That will be one thing you can do. Another is to take care of his pets till he is able to do it himself. Then you can tell him your adventures, and talk to him as only a boy can talk to a boy. That will amuse him when I want to write or go out; but I never leave him long, and hope he will soon be running about as well as the rest of us. How does that sort of work look to you?"

"First-rate! I'll take real good care of the little feller, and do every thing I know to please him, and so will Sanch; he's fond of children," answered Ben, heartily, for the new place looked very inviting to him. Miss Celia laughed, and rather damped his ardor by her next words.

"I don't know what Thorny would say to hear you call him 'little.' He is fourteen, and appears to get taller and taller every day. He seems like a child to me, because I am nearly ten years older than he is; but you needn't be afraid of his long legs and big eyes, he is too feeble to do any harm; only you mustn't mind if he orders you about."

"I'm used to that. I don't mind it if he won't call me a 'spalpeen,' and fire things at me," said Ben, thinking of his late trials with Pat.

"I can promise that; and I am sure Thorny will like you, for I told him your story, and he is anxious to see 'the circus boy' as he called you. Squire Allen says I may trust you, and I am glad to do so, for it saves me much trouble to find what I want all ready for me. You shall be well fed and clothed, kindly treated and honestly paid, if you like to stay with me."

"I know I shall like it - till father comes, anyway. Squire wrote to Smithers right off, but hasn't got any answer yet. I know they are on the go now, so may be we won't hear for ever so long," answered Ben, feeling less impatient to be off than before this fine proposal was made to him.

"I dare say; meantime, we will see how we get on together, and perhaps your father will be willing leave you for the summer if he is away. Now show me the baker's, the candy-shop, and the post-office," said Miss Celia, as they rattled down the main street of the village.

Ben made himself useful; and when all the other errands were done, received his reward in the shape of a new pair of shoes and a straw hat with a streaming blue ribbon, on the ends of which shone silvery anchors. He was also allowed to drive home, while his new mistress read her letters. One particularly long one, with a queer stamp on the envelope, she read twice, never speaking a word till they got back. Then Ben was sent off with Lita and the Squire's letters, promising to get his chores done in time for tea.

CHAPTER IX

A HAPPY TEA

Exactly five minutes before six the party arrived in great state, for Bab and Betty wore their best frocks and hair-ribbons, Ben had a new blue shirt and his shoes on as full-dress, and Sancho's curls were nicely brushed, his frills as white as if just done up.

No one was visible to receive them, but the low table stood in the middle of the walk, with four chairs and a foot-stool around it. A pretty set of green and white china caused the girls to cast admiring looks upon the little cups and plates, while Ben eyed the feast longingly, and Sancho with difficulty restrained himself from repeating his former naughtiness. No wonder the dog sniffed and the children smiled, for there was a noble display of little tarts and cakes, little biscuits and sandwiches, a pretty milk-pitcher shaped like a white calla rising out of its green leaves, and a jolly little tea-kettle singing away over the spirit-lamp as cosily as you please.

"Isn't it perfectly lovely?" whispered Betty, who had never seen any thing like it before.

"I just wish Sally could see us now," answered Bab, who had not yet forgiven her enemy.

"Wonder where the boy is," added Ben, feeling as good as any one, but rather doubtful how others might regard him.

Here a rumbling sound caused the guests to look toward the garden, and in a moment Miss Celia appeared, pushing a wheeled chair, in which sat her brother. A gay afghan covered the long legs, a broad-brimmed hat half hid the big eyes, and a discontented expression made the thin face as unattractive as the fretful voice, which said, complainingly, -

"If they make a noise, I'll go in. Don't see what you asked them for."

"To amuse you, dear. I know they will, if you will only try to like them," whispered the sister, smiling, and nodding over the chair-back as she came on, adding aloud, "Such a punctual party! I am all ready, however, and we will sit down at once. This is my brother Thornton, and we are all going to be very good friends by-and-by. Here's the droll dog, Thorny; isn't he nice and curly?"

Now, Ben had heard what the other boy said, and made up his mind that he shouldn't like him; and Thorny had decided beforehand that he wouldn't play with a tramp, even if he cut capers; go both looked decidedly cool and indifferent when Miss Celia introduced them. But Sancho had better manners and no foolish pride; he, therefore, set them a good example by approaching the chair, with his tail waving like a flag of truce, and politely presented his ruffled paw for a hearty shake.

Thorny could not resist that appeal, and patted the white head, with a friendly look into the affectionate eyes of the dog, saying to his sister as he did so, -

"What a wise old fellow he is! It seems as if he could almost speak, doesn't it?"

"He can. Say 'How do you do,' Sanch," commanded Ben, relenting at once, for he saw admiration in Thorny's face.

"Wow, wow, wow!" remarked Sancho, in a mild and conversational tone, sitting up and touching one paw to his head, as if he saluted by taking off his hat. Thorny laughed in spite of himself, and Miss Celia seeing that the ice was broken, wheeled him to his place at the foot of the table. Then, seating the little girls on one side, Ben and the dog on the other, took the head herself and told her guests to begin. Bab and Betty were soon chattering away to their pleasant hostess as freely as if they had

LOUISA MAY ALCOTT

known her for months; but the boys were still rather shy, and made Sancho the medium through which they addressed one another. The excellent beast behaved with wonderful propriety, sitting upon his cushion in an attitude of such dignity that it seemed almost a liberty to offer him food. A dish of thick sandwiches had been provided for his especial refreshment; and, as Ben from time to time laid one on his plate, he affected entire unconsciousness of it till the word was given, when it vanished at one gulp, and Sancho again appeared absorbed in deep thought.

But, having once tasted of this pleasing delicacy, it was very hard to repress his longing for more; and, in spite of all his efforts, his nose would work, his eye kept a keen watch upon that particular dish, and his tail quivered with excitement as it lay like a train over the red cushion. At last, a moment came when temptation proved too strong for him. Ben was listening to something Miss Celia said; a tart lay unguarded upon his plate; Sanch looked at Thorny who was watching him; Thorny nodded, Sanch gave one wink, bolted the tart, and then gazed pensively up at a sparrow swinging on a twig overhead.

The slyness of the rascal tickled the boy so much that he pushed back his hat, clapped his hands, and burst out laughing as he had not done before for weeks. Every one looked round surprised, and Sancho regarded them with a mildly inquiring air, as if he said, "Why this unseemly mirth, my friends?"

Thorny forgot both sulks and shyness after that, and suddenly began to talk. Ben was flattered by his interest in the dear dog, and opened out so delightfully that he soon charmed the other by his lively tales of circus-life. Then Miss Celia felt relieved, and every thing went splendidly, especially the food; for the plates were emptied several times, the little tea-pot ran dry twice, and the hostess was just wondering if she ought to stop her voracious guests, when something occurred which spared her that painful task.

A small boy was suddenly discovered standing in the path behind them, regarding the company with an air of solemn interest. A pretty, well-dressed child of six, with dark hair cut short across the brow, a rosy face, a stout pair of legs, left bare by the socks which had slipped down over the dusty little shoes. One end of a wide sash trailed behind him, a straw hat hung at his back, his right hand firmly grasped a small turtle, and his left a choice collection of sticks. Before Miss Celia could speak, the stranger calmly announced his mission.

"I have come to see the peacocks."

"You shall presently -" began Miss Celia, but got no further, for the child added, coming a step nearer, -

"And the wabbits."

"Yes, but first won't you -"

"And the curly dog," continued the small voice, as another step brought the resolute young personage nearer.

"There he is."

A pause, a long look; then a new demand with the same solemn tone, the same advance.

"I wish to hear the donkey bray."

"Certainly, if he will."

"And the peacocks scream."

"Any thing more, sir?"
Having reached the table by this time, the insatiable infant surveyed its ravaged surface, then pointed a fat little finger at the last cake, left for manners, and said, commandingly, -

"I will have some of that."

"Help yourself; and sit upon the step to eat it, while you tell me whose boy you are," said Miss Celia, much amused at his proceedings.

Deliberately putting down his sticks, the child took the cake, and, composing himself upon the step, answered with his rosy mouth full, -

"I am papa's boy. He makes a paper. I help him a great deal."

"What is his name?"

"Mr. Barlow. We live in Springfield," volunteered the new guest, unbending a trifle, thanks to the charms of the cake.

"Have you a mamma, dear?"

"She takes naps. I go to walk then."

"Without leave, I suspect. Have you no brothers or sisters to go with you?" asked Miss Celia, wondering where the little runaway belonged.

"I have two brothers, Thomas Merton Barlow and Harry Sanford Barlow. I am Alfred Tennyson Barlow. We don't have any girls in our house, only Bridget."

"Don't you go to school?"

"The boys do. I don't learn any Greeks and Latins yet. I dig, and read to mamma, and make poetrys for her."

"Couldn't you make some for me? I'm very fond of poetrys," proposed Miss Celia, seeing that this prattle amused the children.

"I guess I couldn't make any now; I made some coming along. I will say it to you." And, crossing his short legs, the inspired babe half said, half sung the following poem: (1)

> "Sweet are the flowers of life,
> Swept o'er my happy days at home;
> Sweet are the flowers of life
> When I was a little child.

"Sweet are the flowers of life
That I spent with my father at home;
Sweet are the flowers of life
When children played about the house.

"Sweet are the flowers of life
When the lamps are lighted at night;
Sweet are the flowers of life
When the flowers of summer bloomed.

"Sweet are the flowers of life
Dead with the snows of winter;
Sweet are the flowers of life
When the days of spring come on.

(1) These lines were actually composed by a six-year old child.

"That's all of that one. I made another one when I digged after the turtle. I will say that. It is a very pretty one," observed the poet with charming candor; and, taking a long breath, he tuned his little lyre afresh:

Sweet, sweet days are passing
O'er my happy home.
Passing on swift wings through the valley of life.
Cold are the days when winter comes again.
When my sweet days were passing at my happy home,
Sweet were the days on the rivulet's green brink ;
Sweet were the days when I read my father's books;
Sweet were the winter days when bright fires are blazing."

"Bless the baby! where did he get all that?" exclaimed Miss Celia, amazed; while the children giggled as Tennyson, Jr., took a bite at the turtle instead of the half-eaten cake, and then, to prevent further mistakes, crammed the unhappy creature into a diminutive pocket in the most business-like way imaginable.

"It comes out of my head. I make lots of them," began the imperturbable one, yielding more and more to the social influences of the hour.

"Here are the peacocks coming to be fed," interrupted Bab, as the handsome birds appeared with their splendid plumage glittering in the sun.

Young Barlow rose to admire; but his thirst for knowledge was not yet quenched, and he was about to request a song from Juno and Jupiter, when old Jack, pining for society, put his head over the garden wall with a tremendous bray.

This unexpected sound startled the inquiring stranger half out of his wits; for a moment the stout legs staggered and the solemn countenance lost its composure, as he whispered, with an astonished air,

"Is that the way peacocks scream?"

The children were in fits of laughter, and Miss Celia could hardly make herself heard as she answered merrily, -

"No, dear; that is the donkey asking you to come and see him: will you go?

"I guess I couldn't stop now. Mamma might want me."

And, without another word, the discomfited poet precipitately retired, leaving his cherished sticks behind him.

Ben ran after the child to see that he came to no harm, and presently returned to report that Alfred had been met by a servant, and gone away chanting a new verse of his poem, in which peacocks, donkeys, and "the flowers of life" were sweetly mingled.

"Now I'll show you my toys, and we';; have a little play before it gets too late for Thorny to stay with us," said Miss Celia, as Randa carried away the tea-things and brought back a large tray full of picture-books, dissected maps, puzzles, games, and several pretty models of animals, the whole crowned with a large doll dressed as a baby.

At sight of that, Betty stretched out her arms to receive it with a cry of delight. Bab seized the games, and Ben was lost in admiration of the little Arab chief prancing on the white horse, - all saddled and bridled and fit for the fight. Thorny poked about to find a certain curious puzzle which he could put together without a mistake after long study. Even Sancho found something to interest him; and, standing on his hind-legs, thrust his head between the boys to paw at several red and blue letters on square blocks.

"He looks as if he knew them," said Thorny, amused at the dog's eager whine and scratch.

"He does. Spell your name, Sanch;" and Ben put all the gay letters down upon the flags with a chirrup which set the dog's tail to wagging as he waited till the alphabet was spread before him. Then, with great deliberation, he pushed the letters about till he had picked out six; these he arranged with nose and paw till the word "Sancho" lay before him correctly spelt.

"Isn't that clever? Can he do any more?" cried Thorny, delighted.

"Lots; that's the way he gets his livin', and mine too," answered Ben; and proudly put his poodle through his well-learned lessons sith Such success that even Miss Celia was surprised.

"He has been carefully trained. Do you know how it was done?" she asked, when Sancho lay down to rest and be caressed by the children.

"No, 'm, father did it when I was a little chap, and never told me how. I used to help teach him to dance, and that was easy enough, he is so smart. Father said the middle of the night was the best time to give him his lessons; it was so still then, and nothing disturbed Sanch and made him forget. I can't do half the tricks, but I'm goin' to learn when father comes back. He'd rather have me show off Sanch than ride, till I'm older."

"I have a charming book about animals, and in it an interesting account of some trained poodles who could do the most wonderful things. Would you like to hear it while you put your maps and puzzles together?" asked Miss Celia, glad to keep her brother interested in their four-footed guest at least.

"Yes,'m, yes,'m," answered the children; and, fetching the book, she read the pretty account, shortening and simplifying it here and there to suit her hearers.

"I invited the two dogs to dine and spend the evening; and they came with their master, who was a Frenchman. He had been a teacher in a deaf and dumb school, and thought he would try the same plan with dogs. He had also been a conjurer, and now was supported by Blanche and her daughter Lyda. These dogs behaved at dinner just like other dogs; but when I gave Blanche a bit of cheese and asked if she knew the word for it, her master said she could spell it. So a table was arranged with a lamp on it, and round the table were laid the letters of the alphabet painted on cards. Blanche sat in the middle, waiting till her master told her to spell cheese, which she at once did in French, F R O M A G E. Then she translated a word for us very cleverly. Some one wrote pferd, the German for horse, on a slate. Blanche looked at it and pretended to read it, putting by the slate with her paw when she had done. 'Now give us the French for that word,' said the man; and she instantly brought CHEVAL. 'Now, as you are at an Englishman's house, give it to us in English;' and she brought me HORSE. Then we spelt some words wrong, and she corrected them with wonderful accuracy. But she did not seem to like it, and whined and growled and looked so worried, that she was allowed to go and rest and eat cakes in a corner.

"Then Lyda took her place on the table, and did sums on the slate with a set of figures. Also mental arithmetic, which was very pretty. 'Now, Lyda,' said her master, 'I want to see if you understand division. Suppose you had ten bits of sugar, and you met ten Prussian dogs, how many lumps would you, a French dog, give to each of the Prussians?' Lyda very decidedly replied to this with a cipher. 'But, suppose you divided your sugar with me, how many lumps would you give me?' Lyda took up the figure five and politely presented it to her master."

"Wasn't she smart? Sanch can't do that," exclaimed Ben, forced to own that the French doggie beat his cherished pet.

"He is not too old to learn. Shall I go on?" asked Miss Celia, seeing that the boys liked it, though Betty was absorbed with the doll, and Bab deep in a puzzle.

"Oh, yes! What else did they do?"

"They played a game of dominoes together, sitting in chairs opposite each other, and touched the dominoes that were wanted; but the man placed them and kept telling how the game went. Lyda was beaten, and hid under the sofa, evidently feeling very badly about it. Blanche was then surrounded with playing-cards, while her master held another pack and told us to choose a card; then he asked her what one had been chosen, and she always took up the right one in her teeth. I was asked to go into another room, put a light on the floor with cards round it, and leave the doors nearly shut. Then the man begged some one to whisper in the dog's ear what card she was to bring, and she went at once and fetched it, thus showing that she understood their names. Lyda did many tricks with the numbers, so curious that no dog could possibly understand them; yet what the secret sign was I could not discover, but suppose it must have been in the tones of the master's voice, for he certainly made none with either head or hands.

"It took an hour a day for eighteen months to educate a dog enough to appear in public, and (as you say, Ben) the night was the best time to give the lessons. Soon after this visit, the master died; and these wonderful dogs were sold because their mistress did not know how to exhibit them."

"Wouldn't I have liked to see 'em and find out how they were taught! Sanch, you'll have to study up lively, for I'm not going to have you beaten by French dogs," said Ben, shaking his finger so sternly that Sancho grovelled at his feet and put both paws over his eyes in the most abject manner.

"Is there a picture of those smart little poodles?" asked Ben, eying the book, which Miss Celia left open before her.

"Not of them, but of other interesting creatures; also anecdotes about horses, which will please you, I know," and she turned the pages for him, neither guessing how much good Mr. Hamerton's charming "Chapters on Animals" were to do the boy when he needed comfort for a sorrow which was very near.

CHAPTER X

A HEAVY TROUBLE

"Thank you, ma'am, that's a tip-top book, 'specially the pictures. But I can't bear to see these poor fellows;" and Ben brooded over the fine etching of the dead and dying horses on a battle-field, one past all further pain, the other helpless, but lifting his head from his dead master to neigh a farewell to the comrades who go galloping away in a cloud of dust.

"They ought to stop for him, some of 'em," muttered Ben, hastily turning back to the cheerful picture of the three happy horses in the field, standing knee-deep among the grass as they prepare to drink at the wide stream.

"Ain't that black one a beauty? Seems as if I could see his mane blow in the wind, and hear him whinny to that small feller trotting down to see if he can't get over and be sociable. How I'd like to take a rousin' run round that meadow on the whole lot of 'em!" and Ben swayed about in his chair as if he was already doing it in imagination.

"You may take a turn round my field on Lita any day. She would like it, and Thorny's saddle will be here next week," said Miss Celia, pleased to see that the boy appreciated the fine pictures, and felt such hearty sympathy with the noble animals whom she dearly loved herself.

"Needn't wait for that. I'd rather ride bareback. Oh, I say, is this the book you told about, where the horses talked?" asked Ben, suddenly recollecting the speech he had puzzled over ever since he heard it.

"No; I brought the book, but in the hurry of my tea-party forgot to unpack it. I'll hunt it up to-night. Remind me, Thorny."

"There, now, I've forgotten something, too! Squire sent you a letter; and I'm having such a jolly time, I never thought of it."

Ben rummaged out the note with remorseful haste, protesting that he was in no hurry for Mr. Gulliver, and very glad to save him for another day. Leaving the young folks busy with their games, Miss Celia sat in the porch to read her letters, for there were two; and as she read her face grew so sober, then so sad, that if any one had been looking he would have wondered what bad news had chased away the sunshine so suddenly. No one did look; no one saw how pitifully her eyes rested on Ben's happy face when the letters were put away, and no one minded the new gentleness in her manner as she came back, to the table. But Ben thought there never was so sweet a lady as the one who leaned over him to show him how the dissected map went together and never smiled at his mistakes.

So kind, so very kind was she to them all, that when, after an hour of merry play, she took her brother in to bed, the three who remained fell to praising her enthusiastically as they put things to rights before taking leave.

"She's like the good fairies in the books, and has all sorts of nice, pretty things in her house," said Betty, enjoying a last hug of the fascinating doll whose lids would shut so that it was a pleasure to Sing, "Bye, sweet baby, bye," with no staring eyes to Spoil the illusion.

"What heaps she knows! More than Teacher, I do believe; and she doesn't mind how many questions we ask. I like folks that will tell me things," added Bab, whose inquisitive mind was always hungry.

"I like that boy first-rate, and I guess he likes me, though I didn't know where Nantucket ought to go. He wants me to teach him to ride when he's on his pins again, and Miss Celia says I may. She knows how to make folks feel good, don't she?" and Ben gratefully surveyed the Arab chief, now his own, though the best of all the collection.

"Won't we have splendid times? She Says we may come over every night and play with her and Thorny."

"And she's goin', to have the seats in the porch lift up, so we can put our things in there all day and have 'em handy."

"And I'm going to be her boy, and stay here all the time. I guess the letter I brought was a recommend from the Squire."

"Yes, Ben; and if I had not already made up my mind to keep you before, I certainly would now, my boy."

Something in Miss Celia's voice, as she said the last two words with her hand on Ben's shoulder, made him look up quickly and turn red with pleasure, wondering what the Squire had written about him.

"Mother must have some of the party; so you shall take her these, Bab, and Betty may carry Baby home for the night. She is so nicely asleep, it is a pity to wake her. Good by till to-morrow, little neighbors," continued Miss Celia, and dismissed the girls with a kiss.

"Is Ben coming, too?" asked Bab, as Betty trotted off in a silent rapture with the big darling bobbing over her shoulder.

"Not yet; I've several things to settle with my new man. Tell mother he will come by-and-by."

Off rushed Bab with the plateful of goodies; and, drawing Ben down beside her on the wide step, Miss Celia took out the letters, with a shadow creeping over her face as softly as the twilight was stealing over the world, while the dew fell, and every thing grew still and dim.

LOUISA MAY ALCOTT

"Ben, dear, I've something to tell you," she began, slowly; and the boy waited with a happy face, for no one had called him so since 'Melia died.

"The Squire has heard about your father, and this is the letter Mr. Smithers sends."

"Hooray! where is he, please?" cried Ben, wishing she would hurry up; for Miss Celia did not even offer him the letter, but sat looking down at Sancho on the lower step, as if she wanted him to come and help her. "He went after the mustangs, and sent some home, but could not come himself."

"Went further on, I s'pose. Yes, he said he might go as far as California, and if he did he'd send for me. I'd like to go there; it's a real splendid place, they say."

"He has gone further away than that, to a lovelier country than California, I hope." And Miss Celia's eyes turned to the deep sky, where early stars were shining.

"Didn't he send for me? Where's he gone? When 's he coming back?" asked Ben, quickly; for there was a quiver in her voice, the meaning of which he felt before he understood.

Miss Celia put her arms about him, and answered very tenderly, - "Ben, dear, if I were to tell you that he was never coming back, could you bear it?"

"I guess I could, - but you don't mean it? Oh, ma'am, he isn't dead?" cried Ben, with a cry that made her heart ache, and Sancho leap up with a bark.

"My poor little boy, I wish I could say no."

There was no need of any more words, no need of tears or kind arms around him. He knew he was an orphan now, and turned instinctively to the old friend who loved him best. Throwing himself down beside his dog, Ben clung about the curly neck, sobbing bitterly, -

"Oh, Sanch, he's never coming back again; never, never any more!"

Poor Sancho could only whine and lick away the tears that wet the half-hidden face, questioning the new friend meantime with eyes so full of dumb love and sympathy and sorrow that they seemed almost human. Wiping away her own tears, Miss Celia stooped to pat the white head, and to stroke the black one lying so near it that the dog's breast was the boy's pillow. Presently the sobbing ceased, and Ben whispered, without looking up, -

"Tell me all about it; I'll be good."

Then, as kindly as she could, Miss Celia read the brief letter which told the hard news bluntly; for Mr. Smithers was obliged to confess that he had known the truth months before, and never told the boy, lest he should be unfitted for the work they gave him. Of Ben Brown the elder's death there was little to tell, except that he was killed in some wild place at the West, and a stranger wrote the fact to the only person whose name was found in Ben's pocket-book. Mr. Smithers offered to take the boy back and "do well by him," averring that the father wished his son to remain where he left him, and follow the profession to which he was trained.

"Will you go, Ben?" asked Miss Celia, hoping to distract his mind from his grief by speaking of other things.

"No, no; I'd rather tramp and starve. He's awful hard to me and Sanch; and he'd be worse, now father's gone. Don't send me back! Let me stay here; folks are good to me; there's nowhere else to go." And the head Ben had lifted up with a desperate sort of look, went down again on Sancho's breast as if there were no other refuge left.

"You shall stay here, and no one shall take you away against your will. I called you 'my boy' in play, now you shall be my boy in earnest; this shall be your home, and Thorny your brother. We are orphans, too; and we will stand by one another till a stronger friend comes to help us," said Miss Celia, with such a mixture of resolution and tenderness in her voice, that Ben felt comforted at once, and thanked her by laying his cheek against the pretty slipper that rested on the step beside him, as if he had no words in which to swear loyalty to the gentle mistress whom be meant henceforth to serve with grateful fidelity.

Sancho felt that he must follow suit; and gravely put his paw upon her knee, with a low whine, as if he said, "Count me in, and let me help to pay my master's debt if I can."

Miss Celia shook the offered paw cordially, and the good creature crouched at her feet like a small lion, bound to guard her and her house for evermore.

"Don't lie on that cold stone, Ben; come here and let me try to comfort you," she said, stooping to wipe away the great drops that kept rolling down the brown cheek half hidden in her dress. But Ben put his arm over his face, and sobbed out with a fresh burst of grief, -

"You can't, you didn't know him! Oh, daddy! daddy! if I'd only seen you jest once more!"

No one could grant that wish; but Miss Celia did comfort him, for presently the sound of music floated out from the parlor, - music so soft, so sweet, that involuntarily the boy stopped his crying to listen; then quieter tears dropped slowly, seeming to soothe his pain as they fell, while the sense of loneliness passed away, and it grew possible to wait till it was time to go to father in that far-off country lovelier than golden California.

How long she played Miss Celia never minded; but, when she stole out to see if Ben had gone, she found that other friends, even kinder than herself, had taken the boy into their gentle keeping. The wind had sung a lullaby among the rustling lilacs, the moon's mild face looked through the leafy arch to kiss the heavy eyelids, and faithful Sancho still kept guard beside his little master, who, with his head pillowed on his arm, lay fast asleep, dreaming, happily, that Daddy had come home again.

CHAPTER XI

SUNDAY

Mrs. Moss woke Ben with a kiss next morning, for her heart yearned over the fatherless lad as if he had been her own, and she had no other way of showing her sympathy. Ben had forgotten his troubles in sleep; but the memory of them returned as soon as he opened his eyes, heavy with the tears they had shed. He did not cry any more, but felt strange and lonely till he called Sancho and told him all about it, for he was shy even with kind Mrs. Moss, and glad when she went away.

Sancho seemed to understand that his master was in trouble, and listened to the sad little story with gurgles of interest, whines of condolence, and intelligent barks whenever the word "daddy" was uttered. He was only a brute, but his dumb affection comforted the boy more than any words; for Sanch had known and loved "father" almost as long and well as his son, and that seemed to draw them closely together, now they were left alone.

"We must put on mourning, old feller. It's the proper thing, and there's nobody else to do it now," said Ben, as he dressed, remembering how all the company wore bits of crape somewhere about them at 'Melia's funeral.

It was a real sacrifice of boyish vanity to take the blue ribbon with its silver anchors off the new hat, and replace it with the dingy black band from the old one; but Ben was quite sincere in doing this, though doubtless his theatrical life made him think of the effect more than other lads would have done. He could find nothing in his limited wardrobe with which to decorate Sanch except a black cambric pocket. It was already half torn out of his trousers with the weight of nails, pebbles, and other light trifles; so he gave it a final wrench and tied it into the dog's collar, saying to himself, as he put away his treasures, with a sigh, -

LOUISA MAY ALCOTT

"One pocket is enough; I sha'n't want anything but a han'k'chi'f to-day."

Fortunately, that article of dress was clean, for he had but one; and, with this somewhat ostentatiously drooping from the solitary pocket, the serious hat upon his head, the new shoes creaking mournfully, and Sanch gravely following, much impressed with his black bow, the chief mourner descended, feeling that he had done his best to show respect to the dead.

Mrs. Moss's eyes filled as she saw the rusty band, and guessed why it was there; but she found it difficult to repress a smile when she beheld the cambric symbol of woe on the dog's neck. Not a word was said to disturb the boy's comfort in these poor attempts, however; and he went out to do his chores, conscious that he was an object of interest to his friends, especially so to Bab and Betty, who, having been told of Ben's loss, now regarded him with a sort of pitying awe very grateful to his feelings.

"I want you to drive me to church by-and-by. It is going to be pretty warm, and Thorny is hardly strong enough to venture yet," said Miss Celia, when Ben ran over after breakfast to see if she had any thing for him to do; for he considered her his mistress now, though he was not to take possession of his new quarters till the morrow.

"Yes, 'm, I'd like to, if I look well enough," answered Ben, pleased to be asked, but impressed with the idea that people had to be very fine on such occasions.

"You will do very well when I have given you a touch. God doesn't mind our clothes, Ben, and the poor are as welcome as the rich to him. You have not been much, have you?" asked Miss Celia, anxious to help the boy, and not quite sure how to begin.

"No, 'm; our folks didn't hardly ever go, and father was so tired he used to rest Sundays, or go off in the woods with me."

A little quaver came into Ben's voice as he spoke, and a sudden motion made his hat-brim hide his eyes, for the thought of the happy times that would never come any more was almost too much for him.

"That was a pleasant way to rest. I often do so, and we will go to the grove this afternoon and try it. But I have to go to church in the morning,; it seems to start me right for the week; and if one has a sorrow that is the place where one can always find comfort. Will you come and try it, Ben, dear?"

"I'd do any thing to please you," muttered Ben, without looking up; for, though he felt her kindness to the bottom of his heart, he did wish that no one would talk about father for a little while; it was so hard to keep from crying, and he hated to be a baby.

Miss Celia seemed to understand, for the next thing she said, in a very cheerful tone, was, "See what a pretty sight that is. When I was a little girl I used to think spiders spun cloth for the fairies, and spread it on the grass to bleach."

Ben stopped digging a hole in the ground with his toe, and looked up, to see a lovely cobweb like a wheel, circle within circle, spun across a corner of the arch over the gate. Tiny drops glittered on every thread as the light shone through the gossamer curtain, and a soft breath of air made it tremble as if about to blow it away.

"It's mighty pretty, but it will fly off. just as the others did. I never saw such a chap as that spider is. He keeps on spinning a new one every day, for they always get broke. and he don't seem to be discouraged a mite," said Ben, glad to change the subject, as she knew he would be.

"That is the way he gets his living. he spins his web and waits for his daily bread, - or fly, rather; and it always comes, I fancy. By-and-by you will see that pretty trap full of insects, and Mr. Spider will lay up his provisions for the day. After that he doesn't care how soon his fine web blows away."

"I know him; he's a handsome feller, all black and yellow, and lives up in that corner where the shiny sort of hole is. He dives down the minute I touch the gate, but comes up after I've kept still a minute. I like to watch him. But he must hate me, for I took away a nice green fly and some little millers one day."

"Did you ever hear the story of Bruce and his spider? Most children know and like that," said Miss Celia, seeing that he seemed interested.

"No, 'm ; I don't know ever so many things most children do," answered Ben, soberly; for, since he had been among his new friends, he had often felt his own deficiencies.

"Ah, but you also know many things which they do not. Half the boys in town would give a great deal to be able to ride and run and leap as you do; and even the oldest are not as capable of taking care of themselves as you are. Your active life has done much in some ways to make a man of you; but in other ways it was bad, as I think you begin to see. Now, suppose you try to forget the harmful part, and remember only the good, while learning to be more like our boys, who go to school and church, and fit themselves to become industrious, honest men." Ben had been looking straight up in Miss Celia's face as she spoke, feeling that every word was true, though he could not have expressed it if he had tried; and, when she paused, with her bright eyes inquiringly fixed on his, he answered heartily, -

"I'd like to stay here and be respectable; for, since I came, I've found out that folks don't think much of circus riders, though they like to go and see 'em. I didn't use to care about school and such things, but I do now; and I guess he'd like it better than to have me knockin' round that way without him to look after me."

"I know he would; so we will try, Benny. I dare say it will seem dull and hard at first, after the gay sort of life you have led, and you will miss the excitement. But it was not good for you, and we will do our best to find something safer. Don't be discouraged; and, when things trouble you, come to me as Thorny does, and I'll try to straighten them out for you. I've got two boys now, and I want to do my duty by both."

Before Ben had time for more than a grateful look, a tumbled head appeared at an upper window, and a sleepy voice drawled out, -

"Celia! I can't find a bit of a shoe-string, and I wish you'd come and do my neck-tie."

"Lazy boy, come down here, and bring one of your black ties with you. Shoe-strings are in the little brown bag on my bureau," called back Miss Celia; adding, with a laugh, as the tumbled head disappeared mumbling something about "bothering old bags", "Thorny has been half spoiled since he was ill. You mustn't mind his fidgets and dawdling ways. He'll get over them soon, and then I know you two will be good friends."

Ben had his doubts about that, but resolved to do his best for her sake; so, when Master Thorny presently appeared, with a careless "How are you, Ben?" that young person answered respectfully, - "Very well, thank you," though his nod was as condescending as his new master's; because he felt that a boy who could ride bareback and turn a double somersault in the air ought not to "knuckle under" to a fellow who had not the strength of a pussy-cat.

"Sailor's knot, please; keeps better so," said Thorny, holding up his chin to have a blue-silk scarf tied to suit him, for he was already beginning to be something of a dandy.

"You ought to wear red till you get more color, dear;" and his sister rubbed her blooming cheek against his pale one, as if to lend him some of her own roses.

"Men don't care how they look," said Thorny, squirming out of her hold, for he hated to be "cuddled" before people.

"Oh, don't they? Here's a vain boy who brushes his hair a dozen times a day, and quiddles over his collar till he is so tired he can hardly stand," laughed Miss Celia, with a little tweak of his ear.

LOUISA MAY ALCOTT

"I should like to know what this is for?" demanded Thorny, in a dignified tone, presenting a black tie.

"For my other boy. He is going to church with me," and Miss Celia tied a second knot for this young gentleman, with a smile that seemed to brighten up even the rusty hat-band.

"Well, I like that -" began Thorny, in a tone that contradicted his words.

A look from his sister reminded him of what she had told him half an hour ago, and he stopped short, understanding now why she was "extra good to the little tramp."

"So do I, for you are of no use as a driver yet, and I don't like to fasten Lita when I have my best gloves on," said Miss Celia, in a tone that rather nettled Master Thorny.

"Is Ben going to black my boots before he goes? with a glance at the new shoes which caused them to creak uneasily.

"No; he is going to black mine, if he will be so kind. You won't need boots for a week yet, so we won't waste any time over them. You will find every thing in the shed, Ben; and at ten you may go for Lita."

With that, Miss Celia walked her brother off to the dining-room, and Ben retired to vent his ire in such energetic demonstrations with the blacking-brush that the little boots shone splendidly.

He thought he had never seen any thing as pretty as his mistress when, an hour later, she came out of the house in her white shawl and bonnet, holding a book and a late lily-of-the-valley in the pearl-colored gloves, which he hardly dared to touch as he helped her into the carriage. He had seen a good many fine ladies in his life; and those he had known had been very gay in the colors of their hats and gowns, very fond of cheap jewelry, and much given to feathers, lace, and furbelows; so it rather puzzled him to discover why Miss Celia looked so sweet and elegant in such a simple suit. He did not then know that the charm was in the woman, not the clothes; or that merely living near such a person would do more to give him gentle manners, good principles, and pure thoughts, than almost any other training he could have had. But he was conscious that it was pleasant to be there, neatly dressed, in good company, and going to church like a respectable boy. Somehow, the lonely feeling got better as be rolled along between green fields, with the June sunshine brightening every thing, a restful quiet in the air, and a friend beside him who sat silently looking out at the lovely world with what he afterward learned to call her "Sunday face," - a soft, happy look, as if all the work and weariness of the past week were forgotten, and she was ready to begin afresh when this blessed day was over.

"Well, child, what is it?" she asked, catching his eye as he stole a shy glance at her, one of many which she had not seen.

"I was only thinking, you looked as if -"

"As if what? Don't be afraid," she said, for Ben paused and fumbled at the reins, feeling half ashamed to tell his fancy.

"You were saying prayers," he added, wishing she had not caught him.

"So I was. Don't you, when you are happy?

"No,'m. I'm glad, but I don't say any thing."

"Words are not needed; but they help, sometimes, if they are sincere and sweet. Did you never learn any prayers, Ben?"

"Only 'Now I lay me.' Grandma taught me that when I was a little mite of a boy."

"I will teach you another, the best that was ever made, because it says all we need ask."

"Our folks wasn't very pious; they didn't have time, I s'pose."

"I wonder if you know just what it means to be pious?"

"Goin' to church, and readin' the Bible, and sayin' prayers and hymns, ain't it?"

"Those things are a part of it; but being kind and cheerful, doing one's duty, helping others, and loving God, is the best way to show that we are pious in the true sense of the word."

"Then you are!" and Ben looked as if her acts had been a better definition than her words.

"I try to be, but I very often fail; so every Sunday I make new resolutions, and work hard to keep them through the week. That is a great help, as you will find when you begin to try it."

"Do you think if I said in meetin', ' I won't ever swear any more,' that I wouldn't do it again?" asked Ben, soberly; for that was his besetting sin just now.

"I'm afraid we can't get rid of our faults quite so easily; I wish we could: but I do believe that if you keep saying that, and trying to stop, you will cure the habit sooner than you think."

"I never did swear very bad, and I didn't mind much till I came here; but Bab and Betty looked so scared when I said 'damn,' and Mrs. Moss scolded me so, I tried to leave off. It's dreadful hard, though, when I get mad. 'Hang it!' don't seem half so good if I want to let off steam."

"Thorny used to 'confound!' every thing, so I proposed that he should whistle instead; and now he sometimes pipes up so suddenly and shrilly that it makes me jump. How would that do, instead of swearing?" proposed Miss Celia, not the least surprised at the habit of profanity, which the boy could hardly help learning among his former associates.

Ben laughed, and promised to try it, feeling a mischievous satisfaction at the prospect of out-whistling Master Thorny, as he knew he should; for the objectionable words rose to his lips a dozen times a day.

The Ben was ringing as they drove into town; and, by the time Lita was comfortably settled in her shed, people were coming up from all quarters to cluster around the steps of the old meeting-house like bees about a hive. Accustomed to a tent, where people kept their hats on, Ben forgot all about his, and was going down the aisle covered, when a gentle hand took it off, and Miss Celia whispered, as she gave it to him, -

"This is a holy place; remember that, and uncover at the door."

Much abashed, Ben followed to the pew, where the Squire and his wife soon joined them.

"Glad to see him here," said the old gentleman with an approving nod, as he recognized the boy and remembered his loss.

"Hope he won't nestle round in meeting-time," whispered Mrs. Allen, composing herself in the corner with much rustling of black silk.

"I'll take care that he doesn't disturb you," answered Miss Celia, pushing a stool under the short legs, and drawing a palm-leaf fan within reach.

Ben gave an inward sigh at the prospect before him; for an hour's captivity to an active lad is hard to bear, and he really did want to behave well. So he folded his arms and sat like a statue, with nothing moving but his eyes. They rolled to and fro, up and down, from the high red pulpit to the worn hymnbooks in the rack, recognizing two little faces under blue-ribboned hats in a distant pew, and finding it impossible to restrain a momentary twinkle in return for the solemn wink Billy Barton bestowed upon him across the aisle. Ten minutes of this decorous demeanor made it absolutely necessary for him to stir; so he unfolded his arms and crossed his legs as cautiously as a mouse moves in the presence of a cat; for Mrs. Allen's eye was on him, and he knew by experience that it was a very sharp one.

The music which presently began was a great relief to him, for under cover of it he could wag his foot and no one heard the creak thereof; and when they stood up to sing, he was so sure that all the boys were looking at him, he was glad to sit down again. The good old minister read the sixteenth chapter of Samuel, and then proceeded to preach a long and somewhat dull sermon. Ben listened with all his ears, for he was interested in the young shepherd, "ruddy and of a beautiful countenance," who was chosen to be Saul's armor-bearer. He wanted to hear more about him, and how he got on, and whether the evil spirits troubled Saul again after David had harped them out. But nothing more came; and the old gentleman droned on about other things till poor Ben felt that he must either go to sleep like the Squire, or tip the stool over by accident, since "nestling" was forbidden, and relief of some sort he must have.

Mrs. Allen gave him a peppermint, and he dutifully ate it, though it was so hot it made his eyes water. Then she fanned him, to his great annoyance, for it blew his hair about; and the pride of his life was to have his head as smooth and shiny as black satin. An irrepressible sigh of weariness attracted Miss Celia's attention at last; for, though she seemed to be listening devoutly, her thoughts had flown over the sea, with tender prayers for one whom she loved even more than David did his Jonathan. She guessed the trouble in a minute, and had provided for it, knowing by experience that few small boys can keep quiet through sermon-time. Finding a certain place in the little book she had brought, she put it into his hands, with the whisper, "Read if you are tired."

Ben clutched the book and gladly obeyed, though the title, "Scripture Narratives," did not look very inviting. Then his eye fell on the picture of a slender youth cutting a large man's head off, while many people stood looking on.

"Jack, the giant-killer," thought Ben, and turned the page to see the words "David and Goliath", which was enough to set him to reading the story with great interest; for here was the shepherd boy turned into a hero. No more fidgets now; the sermon was no longer heard, the fan flapped unfelt, and Billy Barton's spirited sketches in the hymnbook were vainly held up for admiration. Ben was quite absorbed in the stirring history of King David, told in a way that fitted it for children's reading, and illustrated with fine pictures which charmed the boy's eye.

Sermon and story ended at the same time; and, while he listened to the prayer, Ben felt as if he understood now what Miss Celia meant by saying that words helped when they were well chosen and sincere. Several petitions seemed as if especially intended for him; and he repeated them to himself that he might remember them, they sounded so sweet and comfortable heard for the first time just when he most needed comfort. Miss Celia saw a new expression in the boy's face as she glanced down at him, and heard a little humming at her side when all stood up to sing the cheerful hymn with which they were dismissed.

"How do you like church?" asked the young lady, as they drove away.

"First-rate!" answered Ben, heartily.

"Especially the sermon?"

Ben laughed, and said, with an affectionate glance at the little book in her lap, -

"I couldn't understand it; but that story was just elegant. There's more; and I'd admire to read 'em, if I could."

"I'm glad you like them; and we will keep the rest for another sermon-time. Thorny used to do so, and always called this his 'pew book.' I don't expect you to understand much that you hear yet awhile; but it is good to be there, and after reading these stories you will be more interested when you hear the names of the people mentioned here."

"Yes, 'm. Wasn't David a fine feller? I liked all about the kid and the corn and the ten cheeses, and killin' the lion and bear, and slingin' old Goliath dead first shot. I want to know about Joseph next time, for I saw a gang of robbers puttin' him in a hole, and it looked real interesting."

Miss Celia could not help smiling at Ben's way of telling things; but she was pleased to see that he was attracted by the music and the stories, and resolved to make church-going so pleasant that he would learn to love it for its own sake.

"Now, you have tried my way this morning, and we will try yours this afternoon. Come over about four and help me roll Thorny down to the grove. I am going to put one of the hammocks there, because the smell of the pines is good for him, and you can talk or read or amuse yourselves in any quiet way you like."

"Can I take Sanch along? He doesn't like to be left, and felt real bad because I shut him up, for fear he'd follow and come walkin' into meetin' to find me."

"Yes, indeed; let the clever Bow-wow have a good time and enjoy Sunday as much as I want my boys to."

Quite content with this arrangement, Ben went home to dinner, which he made very lively by recounting Billy Barton's ingenious devices to beguile the tedium of sermon time. He said nothing of his conversation with Miss Celia, because he had not quite made up his mind whether he liked it or not; it was so new and serious, he felt as if he had better lay it by, to think over a good deal before he could understand all about it. But he had time to get dismal again, and long for four o'clock; because he had nothing to do except whittle. Mrs. Moss went to take a nap; Bab and Betty sat demurely on their bench reading Sunday books; no boys were allowed to come and play; even the hens retired under the currant-bushes, and the cock stood among them, clucking drowsily, as if reading them a sermon.

"Dreadful slow day!" thought Ben; and, retiring to the recesses of his own room, he read over the two letters which seemed already old to him. Now that the first shock was over, he could not make it true that his father was dead, and he gave up trying; for he was an honest boy, and felt that it was foolish to pretend to be more unhappy than he really was. So he put away his letters, took the black pocket off Sanch's neck, and allowed himself to whistle softly as he packed up his possessions, ready to move next day, with few regrets and many bright anticipations for the future.

"Thorny, I want you to be good to Ben, and amuse him in some quiet way this afternoon. I must stay and see the Morrises, who are coming over; but you can go to the grove and have a pleasant time," said Miss Celia to her brother.

"Not much fun in talking to that horsey fellow. I'm sorry for him, but I can't do anything to amuse him," objected Thorny, pulling himself up from the sofa with a great yawn.

You can be very agreeable when you like; and Ben has had enough of me for this time. To-morrow he will have his work, and do very well; but we must try to help him through to-day, because he doesn't know what to do with himself. Besides, it is just the time to make a good impression on him, while grief for his father softens him, and gives us a chance. I like him, and I'm sure he wants to do well; so it is our duty to help him, as there seems to be no one else."

"Here goes, then! Where is he?" and Thorny stood up, won by his sister's sweet earnestness, but very doubtful of his own success with the "horsey fellow."

"Waiting with the chair. Randa has gone on with the hammock. Be a dear boy, and I'll do as much for you some day."

"Don't see how you can be a dear boy. You're the best sister that ever was; so I'lllove all the scallywags you ask me to."

With a laugh and a kiss, Thorny shambled off to ascend his chariot, good-humoredly saluting his pusher, whom he found sitting on the high rail behind, with his feet on Sanch.

"Drive on, Benjamin. I don't know the way, so I can't direct. Don't spill me out, - that's all I've got to say."

"All right, sir," - and away Ben trundled down the long walk that led through the orchard to a little grove of seven pines.

A pleasant spot; for a soft rustle filled the air, a brown carpet of pine needles, with fallen cones for a pattern, lay under foot; and over the tops of the tall brakes that fringed the knoll one had glimpses of hill and valley, farm-houses and winding river, like a silver ribbon through the low, green meadows.

"A regular summer house!" said Thorny, surveying it with approval. "What's the matter, Randa? Won't it do?" he asked, as the stout maid dropped her arms with a puff, after vainly trying to throw the hammock rope over a branch.

"That end went up beautiful, but this one won't; the branches is so high, I can't reach 'em; and I'm no hand at flinging ropes round."

"I'll fix it;" and Ben went up the pine like a squirrel, tied a stout knot, and swung himself down again before Thorny could get out of the chair.

"My patience, what a spry boy!" exclaimed Randa, admiringly.

"That's nothing; you ought to see me shin up a smooth tent-pole," said Ben, rubbing the pitch off his hands, with a boastful wag of the head.

"You can go, Randa. just hand me my cushion and books, Ben; then you can sit in the chair while I talk to you," commanded Thorny, tumbling into the hammock.

"What's he goin' to say to me?" wondered Ben to himself, as he sat down with Sanch sprawling among the wheels.

"Now, Ben, I think you'd better learn a hymn; I always used to when I was a little chap, and it is a good thing to do Sundays," began the new teacher, with a patronizing air, which ruffled his pupil as much as the opprobrious term "little chap."

"I'll be - whew - if I do! " whistled Ben, stopping an oath just in time.

"It is not polite to whistle in company," said Thorny, with great dignity.

"Miss Celia told me to. I'll say 'confound it,' if you like that better," answered Ben, as a sly smile twinkled in his eyes.

"Oh, I see! She's told you about it? Well, then, if you want to please her, you'll learn a hymn right off. Come, now, she wants me to be clever to you, and I'd like to do it; but if you get peppery, how can I?"

Thorny spoke in a hearty, blunt way, which suited Ben much better than the other, and he responded pleasantly, -

"If you won't be grand I won't be peppery. Nobody is going to boss me but Miss Celia; so I'll learn hymns if she wants me to."

"'In the soft season of thy youth' is a good one to begin with. I learned it when I was six. Nice thing; better have it." And Thorny offered the book like a patriarch addressing an infant.

Ben surveyed the yellow page with small favor, for the long s in the old-fashioned printing bewildered him; and when he came to the last two lines, he could not resist reading them wrong, -

"The earth affords no lovelier fight Than a religious youth."

"I don't believe I could ever get that into my head straight. Haven't you got a plain one any where round?" he asked, turning over the leaves with some anxiety.

"Look at the end, and see if there isn't a piece of poetry pasted in. You learn that, and see how funny Celia will look when you say it to her. She wrote it when she was a girl, and somebody had it printed for other children. I like it best, myself."

Pleased by the prospect of a little fun to cheer his virtuous task, Ben whisked over the leaves, and read with interest the lines Miss Celia had written in her girlhood:

"MY KINGDOM

A little kingdom I possess,
Where thoughts and feelings dwell;
And very hard I find the task
Of governing it well.
For passion tempts and troubles me,
A wayward will misleads,
And selfishness its shadow casts
On all my words and deeds.

"How can I learn to rule myself,
To be the child I should, -
Honest and brave, - nor ever tire
Of trying to be good?
How can I keep a sunny soul
To shine along life's way?
How can I tune my little heart
To sweetly sing all day?

"Dear Father, help me With the love
That casteth out my fear!
Teach me to lean on thee, and feel
That thou art very near;
That no temptation is unseen,
No childish grief too small,
Since Thou, with patience infinite,
Doth soothe and comfort all.

"I do not ask for any crown,
But that which all may will
Nor seek to conquer any world
Except the one within.
Be then my guide until I find,
Led by a tender hand,
Thy happy kingdom in myself,
And dare to take command."

"I like that!" said Ben, emphatically, when he had read the little hymn. "I understand it, and I'll learn it right away. Don't see how she could make it all come out so nice and pretty."

"Celia can do any thing!" and Thorny gave an all-embracing wave of the hand, which forcibly expressed his firm belief in his sister's boundless powers.

"I made some poetry once. Bab and Betty thought it was first-rate, I didn't," said Ben, moved to confidence by the discovery of Miss Celia's poetic skill.

"Say it," commanded Thorny, adding with tact, I can't make any to save my life, - never could but I'm fond of it."

"Chevalita,
Pretty cretr,
I do love her
Like a brother;
Just to ride
Is my delight,
For she does not
Kick or bite,"

recited Ben, with modest pride, for his first attempt had been inspired by sincere affection, and pronounced "lovely" by the admiring girls.

"Very good! You must say them to Celia, too. She likes to hear Lita praised. You and she and that little Barlow boy ought to try for a prize, as the poets did in Athens. I'll tell you all about it some time. Now, you peg away at your hymn."

Cheered by Thorny's commendation, Ben fell to work at his new task, squirming about in the chair as if the process of getting words into his memory was a very painful one. But he had quick wits, and had often learned comic songs; so he soon was able to repeat the four verses without mistake, much to his own and Thorny's satisfaction.

"Now we'll talk," said the well-pleased preceptor; and talk they did, one swinging in the hammock, the other rolling about on the pine-needles, as they related their experiences boy fashion. Ben's were the most exciting; but Thorny's were not without interest, for he had lived abroad for several years, and could tell all sorts of droll stories of the countries he had seen.

Busied with friends, Miss Celia could not help wondering how the lads got on; and, when the tea-Ben rang, waited a little anxiously for their return, knowing that she could tell at a glance if they had enjoyed themselves.

"All goes well so far," she thought, as she watched their approach with a smile; for Sancho sat bolt upright in the chair which Ben pushed, while Thorny strolled beside him, leaning on a stout cane newly cut. Both boys were talking busily, and Thorny laughed from time to time, as if his comrade's chat was very amusing.

"See what a jolly cane Ben cut for me! He's great fun if you don't stroke him the wrong way", said the elder lad, flourishing his staff as they came up.

"What have you been doing down there? You look so merry, I suspect mischief," asked Miss Celia, surveying them front the steps.

"We've been as good as gold. I talked, and Ben learned a hymn to please you. Come, young man, say your piece," said Thorny, with an expression of virtuous content.

Taking off his hat, Ben soberly obeyed, much enjoying the quick color that came up in Miss Celia's face as she listened, and feeling as if well repaid for the labor of learning by the pleased look with which She said, as he ended with a bow, -

"I feel very proud to think you chose that, and to hear you say it as if it meant something to you. I was only fourteen when I wrote it; but it came right out of my heart, and did me good. I hope it may help you a little."

Ben murmured that he guessed it would; but felt too shy to talk about such things before Thorny, so hastily retired to put the chair away, and the others went in to tea. But later in the evening, when Miss Celia was singing like a nightingale, the boy slipped away from sleepy Bab and Betty to stand by the syringa bush and listen, with his heart full of new thoughts and happy feelings; for never before had he spent a Sunday like this. And when he went to bed, instead of saying "Now I lay me," he repeated the third verse of Miss Celia's hymn; for that was his favorite, because his longing for the father whom he had seen made it seem sweet and natural now to love and lean, without fear upon the Father whom he had not seen.

LOUISA MAY ALCOTT

CHAPTER XII

GOOD TIMES

Every one was very kind to Ben when his loss was known. The Squire wrote to Mr. Smithers that the boy had found friends and would stay where he was. Mrs. Moss consoled him in her motherly way, and the little girls did their very best to "be good to poor Benny." But Miss Celia was his truest comforter, and completely won his heart, not only by the friendly words she said and the pleasant things she did, but by the unspoken sympathy which showed itself just at the right minute, in a look, a touch, a smile, more helpful than any amount of condolence. She called him "my man," and Ben tried to be one, bearing his trouble so bravely that she respected him. although he was only a little boy, because it promised well for the future.

Then she was so happy herself, it was impossible for those about her to be sad, and Ben soon grew cheerful again in spite of the very tender memory of his father laid quietly away in the safest corner of his heart. He would have been a very unboyish boy if he had not been happy, for the new place was such a pleasant one, he soon felt as if, for the first time, he really had a home. No more grubbing now, but daily tasks which never grew tiresome, they were so varied and so light. No more cross Pats to try his temper, but the sweetest mistress that ever was, since praise was oftener on her lips than blame, and gratitude made willing service a delight.

At first, it seemed as if there was going to be trouble between the two boys; for Thorny was naturally masterful, and illness had left him weak and nervous, so he was often both domineering and petulant. Ben had been taught instant obedience to those older than him self, and if Thorny had been a man Ben would have made no complaint; but it was hard to be "ordered round" by a boy, and an unreasonable one into the bargain.

A word from Miss Celia blew away the threatening cloud, however; and for her sake her brother promised to try to be patient; for her sake Ben declared he never would "get mad" if Mr. Thorny did fidget; and both very soon forgot all about master and man and lived together like two friendly lads, taking each other's ups and downs good-naturedly, and finding mutual pleasure and profit in the new companionship.

The only point on which they never could agree was legs, and many a hearty laugh did they give Miss Celia by their warm and serious discussion of this vexed question. Thorny insisted that Ben was bowlegged; Ben resented the epithet, and declared that the legs of all good horsemen must have a slight curve, and any one who knew any thing about the matter would acknowledge both its necessity and its beauty. Then Thorny Would observe that it might be all very well in the saddle, but it made a man waddle like a duck when afoot; whereat Ben would retort that, for his part, he would rather waddle like a duck than tumble about like a horse with the staggers. He had his opponent there, for poor Thorny did look very like a weak-kneed colt when he tried to walk; but he would never own it, and came down upon Ben with crushing allusions to centaurs, or the Greeks and Romans, who were famous both for their horsemanship and fine limbs. Ben could not answer that, except by proudly referring to the chariot-races copied from the ancients, in which he had borne a part, which was more than some folks with long legs could say. Gentlemen never did that sort of thing, nor did they twit their best friends with their misfortunes, Thorny would remark; casting a pensive glance at his thin hands, longing the while to give Ben a good shaking. This hint would remind the other of his young master's late sufferings and all he owed his dear mistress; and he usually ended the controversy by turning a few lively somersaults as a vent for his swelling wrath, and come up with his temper all right again. Or, if Thorny happened to be in the wheeled chair, he would trot him round the garden at a pace which nearly took his breath away, thereby proving that if "bow-legs" were not beautiful to some benighted beings they were "good to go."

Thorny liked that, and would drop the subject for the time by politely introducing some more agreeable topic; so the impending quarrel would end in a laugh over some boyish joke, and the word "legs" be avoided by mutual consent till accident brought it up again.

The spirit of rivalry is hidden in the best of us, and is a helpful and inspiring power if we know how to use it. Miss Celia knew this, and tried to make the lads help one another by means of it, - not in boastful or ungenerous comparison of each other's gifts, but by interchanging them, giving and taking freely, kindly, and being glad to love what was admirable wherever they found it. Thorny admired Ben's strength, activity, and independence; Ben envied Thorny's learning, good manners, and comfortable surroundings; and, when a wise word had set the matter rightly before them, both enjoyed the feeling that there was a certain equality between them, since money could not buy health, and practical knowledge was as useful as any that can be found in books. So they interchanged their small experiences, accomplishments, and pleasures, and both were the better, as well as the happier, for it; because in this way only can we truly love our neighbor as ourself, and get the real sweetness out of life.

There was no end to the new and pleasant things Ben had to do, from keeping paths and flower-beds neat, feeding the pets, and running errands, to waiting on Thorny and being right-hand man to Miss Celia. He had a little room in the old house, newly papered with hunting scenes, which he was never tired of admiring. In the closet hung several out-grown suits of Thorny's, made over for his valet; and, what Ben valued infinitely more, a pair of boots, well blacked and ready for grand occasions, when he rode abroad, with one old spur, found in the attic, brightened up and merely worn for show, since nothing would have induced him to prick beloved Lita with it.

Many pictures, cut from illustrated papers, of races, animals, and birds, were stuck round the room, giving it rather the air of a circus and menagerie. This, however, made it only the more home-like to its present owner, who felt exceedingly rich and respectable as he surveyed his premises; almost like a retired showman who still fondly remembers past successes, though now happy in the more private walks of life.

In one drawer of the quaint little bureau which he used, were kept the relics of his father; very few and poor, and of no interest to any one but himself, - only the letter telling of his death, a worn-out watch-chain, and a photograph of Senor Jose Montebello, with his youthful son standing on his head, both airily attired, and both smiling with the calmly superior expression which gentlemen of their profession usually wear in public. Ben's other treasures had been stolen with his bundle; but these he cherished and often looked at when he went to bed, wondering what heaven was like, since it was lovelier than California, and usually fell asleep with a dreamy impression that it must be something like America when Columbus found it, - "a pleasant land, where were gay flowers and tall trees, with leaves and fruit such as they had never seen before." And through this happy hunting-ground "father" was for ever riding on a beautiful white horse with wings, like the one of which Miss Celia had a picture.

Nice times Ben had in his little room poring over his books, for he soon had several of his own; but his favorites were Hamerton's "Animals" and "Our Dumb Friends," both full of interesting pictures and anecdotes such as boys love. Still nicer times working about the house, helping get things in order; and best of all were the daily drives with Miss Celia and Thorny, when weather permitted, or solitary rides to town through the heaviest rain, for certain letters must go and come, no matter how the elements raged. The neighbors soon got used to the "antics of that boy," but Ben knew that he was an object of interest as he careered down the main street in a way that made old ladies cry out and brought people flying to the window, sure that some one was being run away with. Lita enjoyed the fun as much as he, and apparently did her best to send him heels over head, having rapidly earned to understand the signs he gave her by the touch of hand and foot, or the tones of his voice.

These performances caused the boys to regard Ben Brown with intense admiration, the girls with timid awe, all but Bab, who burned to imitate him, and tried her best whenever she got a

LOUISA MAY ALCOTT

chance, much to the anguish and dismay of poor Jack, for that long-suffering animal was the only steed she was allowed to ride. Fortunately, neither she nor Betty had much time for play just now, as school was about to close for the long vacation, and all the little people were busy finishing up, that they might go to play with free minds. So the "lilac-parties," as they called them, were deferred till later, and the lads amused themselves in their own way, with Miss Celia to suggest and advise.

It took Thorny a long time to arrange his possessions, for he could only direct while Ben unpacked, wondering and admiring as he worked, because he had never seen so many boyish treasures before. The little printing-press was his especial delight, and leaving every thing else in confusion, Thorny taught him its and planned a newspaper on the spot, with Ben for printer, himself for editor, and "Sister" for chief contributor, while Bab should be carrier and Betty office-boy. Next came a postage-stamp book, and a rainy day was happily spent in pasting a new collection where each particular one belonged, with copious explanations from Thorny as they went along. Ben did not feel any great interest in this amusement after one trial of it, but when a book containing patterns of the flags of all nations turned up, he was seized with a desire to copy them all, so that the house could be fitly decorated on gala occasions. Finding that it amused her brother, Miss Celia generously opened her piece-drawer and rag-bag, and as the mania grew till her resources were exhausted, she bought bits of gay cambric and many-colored papers, and startled the store-keeper by purchasing several bottles of mucilage at once. Bab and Betty were invited to sew the bright strips of stars, and pricked their little fingers assiduously, finding this sort of needle-work much more attractive than piecing bed-quilts.

Such a snipping and pasting, planning and stitching as went on in the big back room, which was given up to them, and such a noble array of banners and petitions as soon decorated its walls, would have caused the dullest eye to brighten with amusement, if not with admiration. Of course, the Stars and Stripes hung highest, with the English lion ramping on the royal standard close by; then followed a regular picture-gallery, for there was the white elephant of Siam, the splendid peacock of Burmah, the double-headed

Russian eagle, and black dragon of China, the winged lion of Venice, and the prancing pair on the red, white, and blue flag of Holland. The keys and mitre of the Papal States were a hard job, but up they went at last, with the yellow crescent of Turkey on one side and the red full moon of Japan on the other; the pretty blue and white flag of Greece hung below and the cross of free Switzerland above. If materials had held out, the flags of all the United States would have followed; but paste and patience were exhausted, so the busy workers rested awhile before they "flung their banner to the breeze," as the newspapers have it.

A spell of ship-building and rigging followed the flag fit; for Thorny, feeling too old now for such toys, made over his whole fleet to "the children," condescending, however, to superintend a thorough repairing of the same before he disposed of all but the big man-of-war, which continued to ornament his own room, with all sail set and a little red officer perpetually waving his sword on the quarter-deck.

These gifts led to out-of-door water-works, for the brook had to be dammed up, that a shallow ocean might be made, where Ben's piratical "Red Rover," with the black flag, might chase and capture Bab's smart frigate, "Queen," while the "Bounding Betsey," laden with lumber, safely sailed from Kennebunkport to Massachusetts Bay. Thorny, from his chair, was chief-engineer, and directed his gang of one how to dig the basin, throw up the embankment, and finally let in the water till the mimic ocean was full; then regulate the little water-gate, lest it should overflow and wreck the pretty squadron or ships, boats, canoes, and rafts, which soon rode at anchor there.

Digging and paddling in mud and water proved such a delightful pastime that the boys kept it up, till a series of water-wheels, little mills and cataracts made the once quiet brook look as if a manufacturing town was about to spring up where hitherto minnows had played in peace and the retiring frog had chanted his serenade unmolested.

Miss Celia liked all this, for any thing which would keep Thorny happy out-of-doors in the sweet June weather found favor in her eyes, and when the novelty had worn off from home affairs, she planned a series of exploring expeditions which filled their boyish souls with delight. As none of them knew much about the place, it really was quite exciting to start off on a bright morning with a roll of wraps and cushions, lunch, books, and drawing materials packed into the phaeton, and drive at random about the shady roads and lanes, pausing when and where they liked. Wonderful discoveries were made, pretty places were named, plans were drawn, and all sorts of merry adventures befell the pilgrims.

Each day they camped in a new spot, and while Lita nibbled the fresh grass at her ease, Miss Celia sketched under the big umbrella, Thorny read or lounged or slept on his rubber blanket, and Ben made himself generally useful. Unloading, filling the artist's water-bottle, piling the invalid's cushions, setting out the lunch, running to and fro for a Bower or a butterfly, climbing a tree to report the view, reading, chatting, or frolicking with Sancho, - any sort of duty was in Ben's line, and he did them all well, for an out-of-door life was natural to him and he liked it.

"Ben, I want an amanuensis," said Thorny, dropping book and pencil one day after a brief interval of silence, broken only by the whisper of the young leaves overhead and the soft babble of the brook close by.

"A what?" asked Ben, pushing back his hat with such an air of amazement that Thorny rather loftily inquired:

"Don't you know what an amanuensis is?"

"Well, no; not unless it's some relation to an anaconda. Shouldn't think you'd want one of them, anyway."

Thorny rolled over with a hoot of derision, and his sister, who sat close by, sketching an old gate, looked up to see what was going on.

"Well, you needn't laugh at a feller. You didn't know what a wombat was when I asked you, and I didn't roar," said Ben, giving his hat a slap, as nothing else was handy.

"The idea of wanting an anaconda tickled me so, I couldn't help it. I dare say you'd have got me one if I had asked for it, you are such an obliging chap,"

"Of course I would if I could. Shouldn't be surprised if you did some day, you want such funny things," answered Ben, appeased by the compliment.

"I'll try the amanuensis first. It's only some one to write for me; I get so tired doing it without a table. You write well enough, and it will be good for you to know something about botany. I intend to teach you, Ben," said Thorny, as if conferring a great favor.

"It looks pretty hard," muttered Ben, with a doleful Glance at the book laid open upon a strew of torn leaves and flowers.

"No, it isn't; it's regularly jolly; and you'd be no end of a help if you only knew a little. Now, suppose I say, 'Bring me a "ranunculus bulbosus,"' how would you know what I wanted?" demanded Thorny, waving his microscope with a learned air.

"Shouldn't."

"There are quantities of them all round us; and I want to analyze one. See if you can't guess."

Ben stared vaguely from earth to sky, and was about to give it up, when a buttercup fell at his feet, and he caught sight of Miss Celia smiling at him from behind her brother, who did not see the flower.

"S'pose you mean this? I don't call 'em rhinocerus bulburses, so I wasn't sure." And, taking the hint as quickly as it was given, Ben presented the buttercup as if he knew all about it.

"You guessed that remarkably well. Now bring me a 'leonto-don taraxacum,'" said Thorny, charmed with the quickness of his pupil, and glad to display his learning.

Again Ben gazed, but the field was full of early flowers; and, if a long pencil had not pointed to a dandelion close by, he would have been lost.

"Here you are, sir," he answered with a chuckle and Thorny took his turn at being astonished now.

"How the dickens did you know that?"

"Try it again, and may be you'll find out," laughed Ben.

Diving hap-hazard into his book, Thorny demanded a "trifolium pratense."

The clever pencil pointed, and Ben brought a red clover, mightily enjoying the joke, and thinking that their kind of botany wasn't bad fun.

"Look here, no fooling!" and Thorny sat up to investigate the matter, so quickly that his sister had not time to sober down. "Ah, I've caught you! Not fair to tell, Celia. Now, Ben, you've got to learn all about this buttercup, to pay for cheating."

"Werry good, sir; bring on your rhinoceriouses," answered Ben, who couldn't help imitating his old friend the clown when he felt particularly jolly.

"Sit there and write what I tell you," ordered Thorny, with all the severity of a strict schoolmaster. Perching himself on the mossy stump, Ben obediently floundered through the following analysis, with constant help in the spelling, and much private wonder what would come of it: -

"Phaenogamous. Exogenous. Angiosperm. Polypetalous. Stamens, more than ten. Stamens on the receptacle. Pistils, more than one and separate. Leaves without stipules. Crowfoot family. Genus ranunculus. Botanical name, Ranunculus bulbosus."

"Jerusalem! what a flower! Pistols and crows' feet, and Polly put the kettles on, and Angy sperms and all the rest of 'em! If that's your botany, I won't take any more, thank you," said Ben, as he paused as hot and red as if he had been running a race.

"Yes, you Will; you'll learn that all by heart, and then I shall give you a dandelion to do. You'll like that, because it means dent de lion, or lion's tooth; and I'll show them to you through my glass. You've no idea how interesting it is, and what heaps of pretty things you'll see," answered Thorny, who had already discovered how charming the study was, and had found great satisfaction in it, since he had been forbidden more active pleasures.

"What's the good of it, anyway?" asked Ben, who would rather have been set to mowing the big field than to the task before him.

"It tells all about it in my book here, - 'Gray's Botany for Young People.' But I can tell you what use it is to us," continued Thorny, crossing his legs in the air and preparing to argue the matter, comfortably lying flat on his back. "We are a Scientific Exploration Society, and we must keep an account of all the plants, animals, minerals, and so on, as we come across them. Then, suppose we get lost, and have to hunt for food, how are we to know what is safe and what isn't? Come, now, do you know the difference between a toadstool and a mushroom?"

"No, I don't."

"Then I'll teach you some day. There is sweet flag and poisonous flag, and all sorts of berries and things; and you'd better look out when you are in the woods, or you'll touch ivy and dogwood, and have a horrid time, if you don't know your botany."

"Thorny learned much of his by sad experience; and you will be wise to take his advice," said Miss Celia, recalling her brother's various mishaps before the new fancy came on.

"Didn't I have a time of it, though, when I had to go round for a week with plantain leaves and cream stuck all over my face! Just picked some pretty red dogwood, Ben; and then I was a regular guy, with a face like a lobster, and my eyes swelled out of sight.

Come along, and learn right away, and never get into scrapes like most fellows."

Impressed by this warning, and attracted by Thorny's enthusiasm, Ben cast himself down upon the blanket, and for an hour the two heads bobbed to and fro, from microscope to book, the teacher airing his small knowledge, the pupil more and more interested in the new and curious things he saw or heard, - though it must be confessed that Ben infinitely preferred to watch ants and bugs, queer little worms and gauzy-winged flies, rather than "putter" over plants with long names. He did not dare to say so, however; but, when Thorny asked him if it wasn't capital fun, he dodged cleverly by proposing to hunt up the flowers for his master to study, offering to learn about the dangerous ones, but pleading want of time to investigate this pleasing science very deeply.

As Thorny had talked himself hoarse, he was very ready to dismiss his class of one to fish the milk-bottle out of the brook; and recess was prolonged till next day. But both boys found a new pleasure in the pretty pastime they made of it; for active Ben ranged the woods and fields with a tin box slung over his shoulder, and feeble Thorny had a little room fitted up for his own use, where he pressed flowers in newspaper books, dried herbs on the walls, had bottles and cups, pans and platters, for his treasures, and made as much litter as he liked.

Presently, Ben brought such lively accounts of the green nooks where jacks-in-the-pulpit preached their little sermons; brooks, beside which grew blue violets and lovely ferns; rocks, round which danced the columbines like rosy elves, or the trees where birds built, squirrels chattered, and woodchucks burrowed, that Thorny was seized with a desire to go and see these beauties for himself. So Jack was saddled, and went plodding, scrambling, and wandering into all manner of pleasant places, always bringing home a stronger, browner rider than he carried away.

This delighted Miss Celia; and she gladly saw them ramble off together, leaving her time to stitch happily at certain dainty bits of sewing, write voluminous letters, or dream over others quite as long, swinging in her hammock under the lilacs.

CHAPTER XIII

SOMEBODY RUNS AWAY

> "'School is done,
> Now we'll have fun,"

Sung Bab and Betty, slamming down their books as if they never meant to take them up again, when they came home on the last day of June.

Tired teacher had dismissed them for eight whole weeks, and gone away to rest; the little school-house was shut up, lessons were over, spirits rising fast, and vacation had begun. The quiet town seemed suddenly inundated with children, all in such a rampant state that busy mothers wondered how they ever should be able to keep their frisky darlings out of mischief; thrifty fathers planned how they could bribe the idle hands to pick berries or rake hay; and the old folks, while wishing the young folks well, secretly blessed the man who invented schools.

The girls immediately began to talk about picnics, and have them, too; for little hats sprung up in the fields like a new sort of mushroom, - every hillside bloomed with gay gowns, looking as if the flowers had gone out for a walk; and the woods were full of featherless birds chirping away as blithely as the thrushes, robins, and wrens.

The boys took to base-ball like ducks to water, and the common was the scene of tremendous battles, waged with much tumult, but little bloodshed. To the uninitiated, it appeared as if these young men had lost their wits; for, no matter how warm it was, there they were, tearing about in the maddest mannet, jackets off, sleeves rolled up, queer caps flung on any way, all batting shabby leather balls, and catching the same, as if their lives depended on it. Every one talking in his gruffest tone, bawling at the top of his voice, squabbling over every point of the game, and seeming to enjoy himself immensely, in spite of the heat, dust, uproar, and imminent danger of getting eyes or teeth knocked out.

Thorny was an excellent player, but, not being strong enough to show his prowess, he made Ben his proxy; and, sitting on the fence, acted as umpire to his heart's content. Ben was a promising pupil, and made rapid progress; for eye, foot, and hand had been so well trained, that they did him good service now; and Brown was considered a first-rate "catcher".

Sancho distinguished himself by his skill in hunting up stray balls, and guarding jackets when not needed, with the air of one of the Old Guard on duty at the tomb of Napoleon. Bab also longed to join in the fun, which suited her better than "stupid picnics" or "fussing over dolls;" but her heroes would not have her at any price; and she was obliged to content herself with sitting by Thorny, and watching with breathless interest the varying fortunes of "our side."

A grand match was planned for the Fourth of July; but when the club met, things were found to be unpropitious. Thorny had gone out of town with his sister to pass the day, two of the best players did not appear, and the others were somewhat exhausted by the festivities, which began at sunrise for them. So they lay about on the grass in the shade of the big elm, languidly discussing their various wrongs and disappointments.

"It's the meanest Fourth I ever saw. Can't have no crackers, because somebody's horse got scared last year," growled Sam Kitteridge, bitterly resenting the stern edict which forbade free-born citizens to burn as much gunpowder as they liked on that glorious day.

"Last year Jimmy got his arm blown off when they fired the old cannon. Didn't we have a lively time going for the doctors and getting him home?" asked another boy, looking as if he felt defrauded of the most interesting part of the anniversary, because no accident had occurred.

"Ain't going to be fireworks either, unless somebody's barn burns up. Don't I just wish there would,: gloomily responded another youth who had so rashly indulged in pyrotechnics on a former occasion that a neighbor's cow had been roasted whole.

"I wouldn't give two cents for such a slow old place as this. Why, last Fourth at this time, I was rumbling though Boston streets on top of our big car, all in my best toggery. Hot as pepper, but good fun looking in at the upper windows and hearing the women scream when the old thing waggled round and I made believe I was going to tumble off, said Ben, leaning on his bat with the air of a man who had seen the world and felt some natural regret at descending from so lofty a sphere.

"Catch me cuttin' away if I had such a chance as that!" answered Sam, trying to balance his bat on his chin and getting a smart rap across the nose as he failed to perform the feat.

"Much you know about it, old chap. It's hard work, I can tell you, and that wouldn't suit such a lazy-bones. Then you are too big to begin, though you might do for a fat boy if Smithers wanted one," said Ben, surveying the stout youth, with calm contempt.

"Let's go in swimming, not loaf round here, if we can't play," proposed a red and shiny boy, panting for a game of leap-frog in Sandy pond.

"May as well; don't see much else to do," sighed Sam, rising like a young elephant.

The others were about to follow, when a shrill "Hi, hi, boys, hold on!" made them turn about to behold Billy Barton tearing down the street like a runaway colt, waving a long strip of paper as he ran.

"Now, then, what's the matter?" demanded Ben, as the other came up grinning and puffing, but full of great news.

LOUISA MAY ALCOTT

"Look here, read it! I'm going; come along, the whole of you," panted Billy, putting the paper into Sam's hand, and surveying the crowd with a face as beaming as a full moon.

"Look out for the big show," read Sam. "Van Amburgh & Co.'s New Great Golden Menagerie, Circus and Colosseum, will exhibit at Berryville, July 4th, at 1 and 7 precisely. Admission 50 cents, children half-price. Don't forget day and date. H. Frost, Manager."

While Sam read, the other boys had been gloating over the enticing pictures which covered the bill. There was the golden car, filled with noble beings in helmets, all playing on immense trumpets; the twenty-four prancing steeds with manes, tails, and feathered heads tossing in the breeze; the clowns, the tumblers, the strong men, and the riders flying about in the air as if the laws of gravitation no longer existed. But, best of all, was the grand conglomeration of animals where the giraffe appears to stand on the elephant's back, the zebra to be jumping over the seal, the hippopotamus to be lunching off a couple of crocodiles, and lions and tigers to be raining down in all directions with their mouths, wide open and their tails as stiff as that of the famous Northumberland House lion.

"Cricky! wouldn't I like to see that," said little Cyrus Fay, devoutly hoping that the cage, in which this pleasing spectacle took place, was a very strong one.

"You never would, it's only a picture! That, now, is something like," and Ben, who had pricked up his ears at the word "circus," laid his finger on a smaller cut of a man hanging by the back of his neck with a child in each hand, two men suspended from his feet, and the third swinging forward to alight on his head.

"I 'm going," said Sam, with calm decision, for this superb array of unknown pleasures fired his soul and made him forget his weight.

"How will you fix it?" asked Ben, fingering the bill with a nervous thrill all through his wiry limbs, just as he used to feel it when his father caught him up to dash into the ring.

"Foot it with Billy. It's only four miles, and we've got lots of time, so we can take it easy. Mother won't care, if I send word by Cy," answered Sam, producing half a dollar, as if such magnificent sums were no strangers to his pocket.

"Come on, Brown; you'll be a first-rate fellow to show us round, as you know all the dodges," said Billy, anxious to get his money's worth.

"Well, I don't know," began Ben, longing to go, but afraid Mrs. Moss would say "No!" if he asked leave.

"He's afraid," sneered the red-faced boy, who felt bitterly toward all mankind at that instant, because he knew there was no hope of his going.

"Say that again, and I'll knock your head off," and Ben faced round with a gesture which caused the other to skip out of reach precipitately.

"Hasn't got any money, more likely," observed a shabby youth, whose pockets never had any thing in them but a pair of dirty hands.

Ben calmly produced a dollar bill and waved it defiantly before this doubter, observing with dignity:

"I've got money enough to treat the whole crowd, if I choose to, which I don't."

"Then come along and have a jolly time with Sam and me. We can buy some dinner and get a ride home, as like as not," said the amiable Billy, with a slap on the shoulder, and a cordial grin which made it impossible for Ben to resist.

"What are you stopping for?" demanded Sam, ready to be off, that they might "take it easy."

"Don't know what to do with Sancho. He'll get lost or stolen if I take him, and it's too far to carry him home if you are in a hurry," began Ben, persuading himself that this was the true reason of his delay.

"Let Cy take him back. He'll do it for a cent; won't you, Cy?" proposed Billy, smoothing away all objections, for he liked Ben, and saw that he wanted to go.

"No, I won't; I don't like him. He winks at me, and growls when I touch him," muttered naughty Cy, remembering how much reason poor Sanch had to distrust his tormentor.

"There 's Bab; she'll do it. Come here, sissy; Ben wants you," called Sam, beckoning to a small figure just perching on the fence.

Down it jumped and Came fluttering up, much elated at being summoned by the captain of the sacred nine.

"I want you to take Sanch home, and tell your mother I'm going to walk, and may be won't be back till sundown. Miss Celia said I Might do what I pleased, all day. You remember, now."

Ben spoke without looking up, and affected to be very busy buckling a strap into Sanch's collar, for the two were so seldom parted that the dog always rebelled. It was a mistake on Ben's part, for while his eyes were on his work Bab's were devouring the bill which Sam still held, and her suspicions were aroused by the boys' faces.

"Where are you going? Ma will want to know," she said, as curious as a magpie all at once.

"Never you mind; girls can't know every thing. You just catch hold of this and run along home. Lock Sanch up for an hour, and tell your mother I'm all right," answered Ben, bound to assert his manly supremacy before his mates.

"He's going to the circus," whispered Fay, hoping to make mischief.

"Circus! Oh, Ben, do take me!" cried Bab, falling into a state of great excitement at the mere thought of such delight.

"You couldn't walk four miles," began Ben.

"Yes, I could, as easy as not."

"You haven't got any money."

"You have; I saw you showing your dollar, and you could pay for me, and Ma would pay it back."

"Can't wait for you to get ready."

"I'll go as I am. I don't care if it is my old hat," and Bab jerked it on to her head.

"Your mother wouldn't like it."

"She won't like your going, either."

"She isn't my missis now. Miss Celia wouldn't care, and I'm going, any way."

"Do, do take me, Ben! I'll be just as good as ever was, and I'll take care of Sanch all the way," pleaded Bab, clasping her hands and looking round for some sign of relenting in the faces of the boys.

"Don't you bother; we don't want any girls tagging after us," said Sam, walking off to escape the annoyance.

"I'll bring you a roll of chickerberry lozengers, if you won't tease," whispered kind-hearted Billy, with a consoling pat on the crown of the shabby straw hat.

"When the circus comes here you shall go, certain sure, and Betty too," said Ben, feeling mean while he proposed what he knew was a hollow mockery.

"They never do come to such little towns; you said so, and I think you are very cross, and I won't take care of Sanch, so, now!" cried Bab, getting into a passion, yet ready to cry, she was so disappointed.

"I Suppose it wouldn't do -" hinted Billy, with a look from Ben to the little girl, who stood winking hard to keep the tears back.

"Of Course it wouldn't. I'd like to see her walking eight miles. I don't mind paying for her; it's getting her there and back. Girls are such a bother when you want to knock round. No, Bab, you can't go. Travel right home and don't make a fuss. Come along, boys; it's most eleven, and we don't want to walk fast."

Ben spoke very decidedly; and, taking Billy's arm, away they went, leaving poor Bab and Sanch to watch them out of sight, one sobbing, the other whining dismally.

Somehow those two figures seemed to go before Ben all along the pleasant road, and half spoilt his fun; for though he laughed and talked, cut canes, and seemed as merry as a grig, he could not help feeling that he ought to have asked leave to go, and been kinder to Bab.

"Perhaps Mrs. Moss would have planned somehow so we could all go, if I'd told her, I'd like to show her round, and she's been real good to me. No use now. I'll take the girls a lot of candy and make it all right."

He tried to settle it in that way and trudged gayly off, hoping Sancho wouldn't feel hurt at being left, wondering if any of "Smithers's lot" would be round, and planning to do the honors handsomely to the boys.

It was very warm; and just outside of the town they paused by a wayside watering-trough to wash their dusty faces, and cool off before plunging into the excitements of the afternoon. As they stood refreshing themselves, a baker's cart came jingling by; and Sam proposed a hasty lunch while they rested. A supply of gingerbread was soon bought; and, climbing the green bank above, they lay on the grass under a wild cherry-tree, munching luxuriously, while they feasted their eyes at the same time on the splendors awaiting them; for the great tent, with all its flags flying, was visible from the hill.

"We'll cut across those fields, - it's shorter than going by the road, - and then we can look round outside till it's time to go in. I want to have a good go at every thing, especially the lions," said Sam, beginning on his last cookie.

"I heard 'em roar just now;" and Billy stood up to gaze with big eyes at the flapping canvas which hid the king of beasts from his longing sight.

"That was a cow mooing. Don't you be a donkey, Bill. When you hear a real roar, you'll shake in your boots," said Ben, holding up his handkerchief to dry, after it had done double duty as towel and napkin.

"I wish you'd hurry up, Sam. Folks are going in now. I see 'em!" and Billy pranced with impatience; for this was his first circus, and he firmly believed that he was going to behold all that the pictures promised.

"Hold on a minute, while I get one more drink. Buns are dry fodder," said Sam, rolling over to the edge of the bank and preparing to descend with as little trouble as possible.

He nearly went down head first, however; for, as he looked before he leaped, he beheld a sight which caused him to stare with all his might for an instant, then turn and beckon, saying in an eager whisper, "Look here, boys, - quick!"

Ben and Billy peered over, and both suppressed an astonished "Hullo!" for there stood Bab, waiting for Sancho to lap his fill out of the overflowing trough.

Such a shabby, tired-looking couple as they were! Bab with a face as red as a lobster and streaked with tears, shoes white with dust, Playfrock torn at the gathers, something bundled up in her apron, and one shoe down at the heel as if it hurt her. Sancho lapped eagerly, with his eyes shut; all his ruffles were gray with dust, and his tail hung wearily down, the tassel at half mast, as if in mourning for the master whom be had come to find. Bab still held the strap, intent on keeping her charge safe, though she lost herself; but her courage seemed to be giving out, as she looked anxiously up and down the road, seeing no sign of the three familiar figures she had been following as steadily as a little Indian on the war-trail.

"Oh, Sanch, what shall I do if they don't come along? We must have gone by them somewhere, for I don't see any one that way, and there isn't any other road to the circus, seems to me."

Bab spoke as if the dog could understand and answer; and Sancho looked as if he did both, for he stopped drinking, pricked up his cars, and, fixing his sharp eyes on the grass above him, gave a suspicious bark.

"It's only squirrels; don't mind, but come along and be good; for I 'm so tired, I don't know what to do!" sighed Bab, trying to pull him after her as she trudged on, bound to see the outside of that wonderful tent, even if she never got in.

But Sancho had heard a soft chirrup; and, with a sudden bound, twitched the strap away, sprang up the bank, and landed directly on Ben's back as he lay peeping over. A peal of laughter greeted him; and, having got the better of his master in more ways than one, he made the most of the advantage by playfully worrying him as he kept him down, licking his face in spite of his struggles, burrowing in his neck with a ticklish nose, snapping at his buttons, and yelping joyfully, as if it was the best joke in the world to play hide-and-seek for four long miles.

Before Ben could quiet him, Bab came climbing up the bank, with such a funny mixture of fear, fatigue, determination, and relief in her dirty little face, that the boys could not look awful if they tried.

"How dared you come after us, miss?" demanded Sam, as she looked calmly about her, and took a seat before she was asked.

"Sanch would come after Ben; I couldn't make him go home, so I had to hold on till he was safe here, else he'd be lost, and then Ben would feel bad."

The cleverness of that excuse tickled the boys immensely; and Sam tried again, while Ben was getting the dog down and sitting on him.

"Now you expect to go to the circus, I suppose."

"Course I do. Ben said he didn't mind paying, if I could get there without bothering him, and I have; and I'll go home alone. I ain't afraid. Sanch will take care of me, if you won't," answered Bab, stoutly.

"What do you suppose your mother will say to you?" asked Ben, feeling much reproached by her last words.

"I guess she'll say you led me into mischief; and the sharp child nodded, as if she defied him to deny the truth of that.

"You'll catch it when you get home, Ben; so you'd better have a good time while you can," advised Sam. thinking Bab great fun, since none of the blame of her pranks would fall on him. "What would you have done if you hadn't found us?" asked Billy, forgetting his impatience in his admiration for this plucky young lady.

"I'd have gone on and seen the circus, and then I'd have gone home again and told Betty all about it," was the prompt answer.

"But you haven't any money."

"Oh, I'd ask somebody to pay for me. I 'm so little, it wouldn't be much."

"Nobody would do it; so you'd have to stay outside, you see."

"No, I wouldn't. I thought of that, and planned how I'd fix it if I didn't find Ben. I'd make Sanch do his tricks, and get a quarter that way; so, now! answered Bab, undaunted by any obstacle.

"I do believe she would! You are a smart child, Bab; and if I had enough I'd take you in myself," said Billy, heartily; for, having sisters of his own, he kept a soft place in his heart for girls, especially enterprising ones.

"I'll take care of her. It was very naughty to come, Bab; but, so long as you did, you needn't worry about any thing. I'll see to you; and you shall have a real good time," said Ben, accepting his responsibilities without a murmur, and bound to do the handsome thing by his persistent friend.

"I thought you would;" and Bab folded her arms, as if she had nothing further to do but enjoy herself.

"Are you hungry?" asked Billy, fishing out several fragments of gingerbread.

"Starving!" and Bab ate them with such a relish that Sam added a small contribution; and Ben caught some water for her in his hand, where the little spring bubbled up beside a stone.

"Now, you wash your face and spat down your hair, and put your hat on straight, and then we'll go," commanded Ben, giving Sanch a roll on the grass to clean him.

Bab scrubbed her face till it shone; and, pulling down her apron to wipe it, scattered a load of treasures collected in her walk. Some of the dead flowers, bits of moss, and green twigs fell near Ben, and one attracted his attention, - a spray of broad, smooth leaves, with a bunch of whitish berries on it.

"Where did you get that?" he asked, poking it with his foot.

"In a swampy place, coming along. Sanch saw something down there; and I went with him, 'cause I thought may be it was a musk-rat, and you'd like one if we could get him."

"Was it?" asked the boys all at once, and with intense interest.

"No; only a snake, and I don't care for snakes. I picked some of that, it was so green and pretty. Thorny likes queer leaves and berries, you know," answered Bab, "spatting," down her rough locks.

"Well, he won't like that, nor you either; it's poisonous, and I shouldn't wonder if you'd got poisoned, Bab. Don't touch it! Swamp-sumach is horrid stuff, - Miss Celia said so;" and Ben looked anxiously at Bab, who felt her chubby face all over, and examined her dingy hands with a solemn air, asking, eagerly, -

"Will it break out on me 'fore I get to the circus?"

"Not for a day or so, I guess; but it's bad when it does come."

"I don't care, if I see the animals first. Come quick, and never mind the old weeds and things," said Bab, much relieved; for present bliss was all she had room for now in her happy little heart.

CHAPTER XIV

SOMEBODY GETS LOST

Putting all care behind them, the young folks ran down the hill, with a very lively dog gambolling beside them, and took a delightfully tantalizing survey of the external charms of the big tent. But people were beginning to go in, and it was impossible to delay when they came round to the entrance.

Ben felt that now "his foot was on his native heath," and the superb air of indifference with which he threw down his dollar at the ticket-office, carelessly swept up the change, and strolled into the tent with his hands in his pockets, was so impressive that even big Sam repressed his excitement and meekly followed their leader, as he led them from cage to cage, doing the honors as if he owned the whole concern. Bab held tight to the flap of his jacket, staring about her with round eyes, and listening with little gasps of astonishment or delight to the roaring of lions, the snarling of tigers, the chatter of the monkeys, the groaning of camels, and the music of the very brass band shut up in a red bin.

Five elephants were tossing their hay about in the middle of the menagerie, and Billy's legs shook under him as he looked up at the big beasts whose long noses and small, sagacious eyes filled him with awe. Sam was so tickled by the droll monkeys that the others left him before the cage and went on to see the zebra, "striped just like Ma's muslin gown," Bab declared. But the next minute she forgot all about him in her raptures over the ponies and their tiny colts; especially one mite of a thing who lay asleep on the hay, such a miniature copy of its little mouse-colored mamma that one could hardly believe it was alive.

"Oh, Ben, I must feel of it! - the cunning baby horse!" and down went Bab inside the rope to pat and admire the pretty creature, while its mother smelt suspiciously at the brown hat, and baby lazily opened one eye to see what was going on.

"Come out of that, it isn't allowed" commanded Ben, longing to do the same thing, but mindful of the proprieties and his own dignity.

Bab reluctantly tore herself away to find consolation in watching the young lions, who looked so like big puppies, and the tigers washing their faces just as puss did.

"If I stroked 'em, wouldn't they purr?" she asked, bent on enjoying herself, while Ben held her skirts lest she should try the experiment.

"You'd better not go to patting them, or you'll get your hands clawed up. Tigers do purr like fun when they are happy, but these fellers never are, and you'll only see 'em spit and snarl," said Ben, leading the way to the humpy carrels, who were peacefully chewing their cud and longing for the desert, with a dreamy, far-away look in their mournful eyes.

Here, leaning on the rope, and scientifically biting a straw while he talked, Ben played showman to his heart's content till the neigh of a horse from the circus tent beyond reminded him of the joys to come.

"We'd better hurry along and get good seats before folks begin to crowd. I want to sit near the curtain and see if any of Smitthers's lot are 'round."

"I ain't going way off there; you can't see half so well, and that big drum makes such a noise you can't hear yourself think," said Sam, who had rejoined them.

So they settled in good places where they could see and hear all that went on in the ring and still catch glimpses of white horses, bright colors, and the glitter of helmets beyond the dingy red curtains. Ben treated Bab to peanuts and pop-corn like an indulgent parent, and she murmured protestations of undying gratitude with her mouth full, as she sat blissfully between him and the congenial Billy.

Sancho, meantime, had been much excited by the familiar sights and sounds, and now was greatly exercised in his doggish mind at the unusual proceeding of his master; for he was sure that they ought to be within there, putting on their costumes, ready to take their turn. He looked anxiously at Ben, sniffed disdainfully at the strap as if to remind him that a scarlet ribbon ought to take its place, and poked peanut shells about with his paw as if searching for the letters with which to spell his famous name.

"I know, old boy, I know; but it can't be done. We've quit the busin'ess and must just look on. No larks for us this time, Sanch, so keep quiet and behave,' whispered Ben, tucking the dog away under the seat with a sympathetic cuddle of the curly head that peeped out from between his feet.

"He wants to go and cut up, don't he?" said Billy, "and so do you, I guess. Wish you were going to. Wouldn't it be fun to see Ben showing off in there?"

"I'd be afraid to have him go up on a pile of elephants and jump through hoops like these folks," answered Bab, poring over her pictured play-bill with unabated relish.

"Done it a hundred times, and I'd just like to show you what I can do. They don't seem to have any boys in this lot; shouldn't wonder if they'd take me if I asked 'em," said Ben, moving uneasily on his seat and casting wistful glances toward the inner tent where he knew he would feel more at home than in his present place.

"I heard some men say that it's against the law to have small boys now; it's so dangerous and not good for them, this kind of thing. If that's so, you're done for, Ben," observed Sam, with his most grown-up air, remembering Ben's remarks on "fat boys."

"Don't believe a word of it, and Sanch and I could go this minute and get taken on, I'll bet. We are a valuable couple, and I could prove it if I chose to," began Ben, getting excited and boastful.

"Oh, see, they're coming! - gold carriages and lovely horses, and flags and elephants, and every thing," cried Bab, giving a clutch at Ben's arm as the opening procession appeared headed by the band, tooting and banging till their faces were as red as their uniforms.

Round and round they went till every one had seen their fill, then the riders alone were left caracoling about the ring with feathers flying, horses prancing, and performers looking as tired and indifferent as if they would all like to go to sleep then and there.

"How splendid!" sighed Bab, as they went dashing out, to tumble off almost before the horses stopped.

"That's nothing! You wait till you see the bareback riding and the 'acrobatic exercises,'" said Ben, quoting from the play-bill, with the air of one who knew all about the feats to come, and could never be surprised any more.

"What are 'crowbackic exercises'?" asked Billy, thirsting for information.

"Leaping and climbing and tumbling; you'll see George! what a stunning horse!" and Ben forgot every thing else to feast his eyes on the handsome creature who now came pacing in to dance, upset and replace chairs, kneel, bow, and perform many wonderful or graceful feats, ending with a swift gallop while the rider sat in a chair on its back fanning himself, with his legs crossed, as comfortably as you please.

"That, now, is something like," and Ben's eyes shone with admiration and envy as the pair vanished, and the pink and silver acrobats came leaping into the ring.

The boys were especially interested in this part, and well they might be; for strength and agility are manly attributes which lads appreciate, and these lively fellows flew about like India-rubber balls, each trying to outdo the other, till the leader of the acrobats capped the climax by turning a double somersault over five elephants standing side by side.

"There, Sir, how's that for a jump?" asked Ben, rubbing his hands with satisfaction as his friends clapped till their palms tingled.

"We'll rig up a spring-board and try it," said Billy, fired with emulation.

"Where'll you get your elephants?" asked Sam, scornfully. for gymnastics were not in his line.

"You'll do for one," retorted Ben, and Billy and Bab joined in his laugh so heartily that a rough-looking, man who sat behind them, hearing all they said, pronounced them a "jolly set," and kept his eye on Sancho, who now showed signs of insubordination.

"Hullo, that wasn't on the bill!" cried Ben, as a parti-colored clown came in, followed by half a dozen dogs.

"I'm so glad; now Sancho will like it. There's a poodle that might be his ownty donty brother - the one with the blue ribbon," said Bab. beaming with delight as the dogs took their seats in the chairs arranged for them.

Sancho did like it only too well, for be scrambled out from under the seat in a great hurry to go and greet his friends; and, being sharply checked, sat up and begged so piteously that Ben found it very hard to refuse and order him down. He subsided for a moment, but when the black spaniel, who acted the canine clown, did something funny and was applauded, Sancho made a dart as if bent on leaping into the ring to outdo his rival, and Ben was forced to box his ears and put his feet on the poor beast, fearing he would be ordered out if he made any disturbance.

Too well trained to rebel again, Sancho lay meditating on his wrongs till the dog act was over, carefully abstaining from any further sign of interest in their tricks, and only giving a sidelong glance at the two little poodles who came out of a basket to run up and down stairs on their fore-paws, dance jigs on their hind-legs, and play various pretty pranks to the great delight of all the children in the audience. If ever a dog expressed by look and attitude, "Pooh! I could do much better than that, and astonish you all, if I were only allowed to," that dog was Sancho, as he curled himself up and affected to turn his back on an unappreciative world.

"It's too bad, when he knows motr than all those chaps put together. I'd give any thing if I could show him off as I used to. Folks always like it, and I was ever so proud of him. He's mad now because I had to cuff him, and won't take any notice of me till I make up," said Ben, regretfully eying his offended friend, but not daring to beg pardon yet.

More riding followed, and Bab was kept in a breathless state by the marvellous agility and skill of the gauzy lady who drove four horses at once, leaped through hoops, over banners and bars, sprang off and on at full speed, and seemed to enjoy it all so much it was impossible to believe that there could be any danger or exertion in it. Then two girls flew about on the trapeze, and walked on a tight rope, causing Bab to feel that she had at last found her sphere; for, young as she was, her mother often said,

"I really don't know what this child is fit for, except mischief, like a monkey."

"I'll fix the clothes-line when I get home, and show Ma how nice it is. Then, may be, she'd let me wear red and gold trousers, and climb round like these girls," thought the busy little brain, much excited by all it saw on that memorable day.

Nothing short of a pyramid of elephants with a glittering gentleman in a turban and top boots on the summit would have made her forget this new and charming plan. But that astonishing spectacle, and the prospect of a cage of Bengal tigers with a man among them, in imminent danger of being eaten before her eyes, entirely absorbed her thoughts till, just as the big animals went lumbering out, a peal of thunder caused considerable commotion in the audience. Men on the highest seats popped their heads through the openings in the tent-cover and reported that a heavy shower was coming up. Anxious mothers began to collect their flocks of children as hens do their chickens at sunset; timid people told cheerful stories of tents blown over in gales, cages upset and wild beasts let loose. Many left in haste, and the performers hurried to finish as soon as possible.

"I'm going now before the crowd comes, so I can get a lift home. I see two or three folks I know, so I'm off;" and, climbing hastily down, Sam vanished without further ceremony.

"Better wait till the shower is over. We can go and see the animals again, and get home all dry, just as well as not," observed Ben, encouragingly, as Billy looked anxiously at the billowing canvas over his head, the swaying posts before him, and heard the quick patter of drops outside, not to mention the melancholy roar of the lion which sounded rather awful through the sudden gloom which filled the strange place.

"I wouldn't miss the tigers for any thing. See, they are pulling in the cart now, and the shiny man is all ready with his gun. Will he shoot any of them, apprehension, for the sharp crack of a rifle startled her more than the loudest thunder-clap she ever heard.

"Bless you, no, child; it's only powder to make a noise and scare 'em. I wouldn't like to be in his place, though; father says you can never trust tigers as you can lions, no matter how tame they are. Sly fellers, like cats, and when they scratch it's no joke, I tell you," answered Ben, with a knowing wag of the head, as the sides of the cage rattled down, and the poor, fierce creatures were seen leaping and snarling as if they resented this display of their captivity.

Bab curled up her feet and winked fast with excitement as she watched the "shiny man" fondle the great cats, lie down among them, pull open their red mouths, and make them leap over him or crouch at his feet as be snapped the long whip. When he fired the gun and they all fell as if dead, she with difficulty suppressed a small scream and clapped her hands over her ears; but poor Billy never minded it a bit, for he was pale and quaking with the fear of "heaven's artillery" thundering overhead, and as a bright flash of lightning seemed to run down the tall tent-poles he hid his eyes and wished with all his heart that he was safe with mother.

"Afraid of thunder, Bill?" asked Ben, trying to speak stoutly, while a sense of his own responsibilities began to worry him, for how was Bab to be got home in such a pouring rain?

"It makes me sick; always did. Wish I hadn't come," sighed Billy, feeling, all too late, that lemonade and "lozengers" were not the fittest food for man, or a stifling tent the best place to be in on a hot July day, especially in a thunder-storm.

"I didn't ask you to come; you asked me; so it isn't my fault," said Ben, rather gruffly, as people crowded by without pausing to hear the comic song the clown was singing in spite of the confusion.

"Oh, I'm so tired," groaned Bab, getting up with a long stretch of arms and legs.

"You'll be tireder before you get home, I guess. Nobody asked you to Come, any way;" and Ben gazed dolefully round him, wishing he could see a familiar face or find a wiser head than his own to help him out of the scrape he was in.

"I said I wouldn't be a bother, and I won't. I'll walk right home this minute. I ain't afraid of thunder, and the rain won't hurt these old clothes. Come along," cried Bab, bravely, bent on keeping her word, though it looked much harder after the fun was all over than before.

"My head aches like fury. Don't I wish old Jack was here to take me back," said Billy, following his companions in misfortune with sudden energy, as a louder peal than before rolled overhead.

"You might as well wish for Lita and the covered wagon while you are about it, then we could all ride," answered Ben, leading the way to the outer tent, where many people were lingering in hopes of fair weather.

"Why, Billy Barton, how in the world did you get here?" cried a surprised voice as the crook of a cane caught the boy by the collar and jerked him face to face with a young farmer, who was pushing along, followed by his, wife and two or three children.

"Oh, Uncle Eben, I'm so glad you found Me! I walked over, and it's raining, and I don't feel well. Let me go with you, can't I?" asked Billy, casting himself and all his woes upon the strong arm that had laid hold of him.

"Don't see what your mother was about to let you come so far alone, and you just over scarlet fever. We are as full as ever we can be, but we'll tuck you in somehow," said the pleasant-faced woman, bundling up her baby, and bidding the two little lads "keep close to father."

"I didn't come alone. Sam got a ride, and can't you tuck Ben and Bab in too? They ain't very big, either of them," whispered Billy, anxious to serve his friends now that he was provided for himself.

"Can't do it, any way. Got to pick up mother at the corner, and that will be all I can carry. It's lifting a little; hurry along, Lizzie, and let us get out of this as quick is possible," said Uncle Eben, impatiently; for going to a circus with a young family is not an easy task, as every one knows who has ever tried it.

"Ben, I'm real sorry there isn't room for you. I'll tell Bab's mother where she is, and may be some one will come for you," said Billy, hurriedly, as he tore himself away, feeling rather mean to desert the others, though he could be of no use.

"Cut away, and don't mind us. I'm all right, and Bab must do the best she can," was all Ben had time to answer before his comrade was hustled away by the crowd pressing round the entrance with much clashing of umbrellas and scrambling of boys and men, who rather enjoyed the flurry.

"No use for us to get knocked about in that scrimmage. We'll wait a minute and then go out easy. It's a regular rouser, and you'll be as wet as a sop before we get home. Hope you'll like that?" added Ben, looking out at the heavy rain poring down as if it never meant to stop.

"Don't care a bit," said Bab, swinging on one of the ropes with a happy-go-lucky air, for her spirits were not extinguished yet, and she was bound to enjoy this exciting holiday to the very end. "I like circuses so much! I wish I lived here all the time, and slept in a wagon, as you did, and had these dear little colties to play with."

"It wouldn't be fun if you didn't have any folks to take care of you," began Ben, thoughtfully looking about the familiar place where the men were now feeding the animals, setting their refreshment tables, or lounging on the hay to get such rest as they could before the evening entertainment. Suddenly he started, gave a long look, then turned to Bab, and thrusting Sancho's strap into her hand, said, hastily:

"I see a fellow I used to know. May be he can tell me some-thing about father. Don't you stir till I come back."

Then he was off like a shot, and Bab saw him run after a man with a bucket who bad been watering the zebra. Sancho tried to follow, but was checked with an impatient, -

"No, you can't go! What a plague you are, tagging around when people don't want you."

Sancho might have answered, "So are you," but, being a gentlemanly dog, he sat down with a resigned expression to watch the little colts, who were now awake and seemed ready for a game of bo-peep behind their mammas. Bab enjoyed their funny little frisks so much that she tied the wearisome strap to a post, and crept under the rope to pet the tiny mouse-colored one who came and talked to her with baby whinnies and confiding glances of its soft, dark eyes.

"Oh, luckless Bab! why did you turn your back? Oh, too accomplished Sancho! why did you neatly untie that knot and trot away to confer with the disreputable bull-dog who stood in the entrance beckoning with friendly wavings of an abbreviated tail? Oh, much afflicted Ben! why did you delay till it was too late to save your pet from the rough man who set his foot upon the trailing strap, and led poor Sanch quickly out of sight among the crowd?

"It was Bascum, but he didn't know any thing. Why, where's Sanch?" said Ben, returning. A breathless voice made Bab turn to see Ben looking about him with as much alarm in his hot face as if the dog had been a two years' child.

"I tied him - he's here somewhere - with the ponies," stammered Bab, in sudden dismay, for no sign of a dog appeared as her eyes roved wildly to and fro.

Ben whistled, called and searched in vain, till one of the lounging men said, lazily,

"If you are looking after the big poodle you'd better go outside; I saw him trotting off with another dog."

Away rushed Ben, with Bab following, regardless of the rain, for both felt that a great misfortune had befallen them. But, long before this, Sancho had vanished, and no one minded his indignant howls as he was driven off in a covered cart.

"If he is lost I'll never forgive you; never, never, never!" and Ben found it impossible to resist giving Bab several hard shakes, which made her yellow braids fly up and down like pump handles.

"I'm dreadful sorry. He'll come back - you said he always did," pleaded Bab, quite crushed by her own afflictions, and rather scared to see Ben look so fierce, for he seldom lost his temper or was rough with the little girls.

"If he doesn't come back, don't you speak to me for a year. Now, I'm going home." And, feeling that words were powerless to express his emotions, Ben walked away, looking as grim as a small boy could.

A more unhappy little lass is seldom to be found than Bab was, as she pattered after him, splashing recklessly through the puddles, and getting as wet and muddy as possible, as a sort of penance for her sins. For a mile or two she trudged stoutly along, while Ben marched before in solemn silence, which soon became both impressive and oppressive because so unnsual, and such a proof of his deep displeasure. Penitent Bab longed for just one word, one sign of relenting; and when none came, she began to wonder how she could possibly bear it if he kept his dreadful threat and did not speak to her for a whole year.

But presently her own discomfort absorbed her, for her feet were wet and cold as well as very tired; pop-corn and peanuts were not particularly nourishing food; and hunger made her feel faint; excitement was a new thing, and now that it was over she longed to lie down and go to sleep; then the long walk with a circus at the end seemed a very different affair from the homeward trip with a distracted mother awaiting her. The shower had subsided into a dreary drizzle, a chilly east wind blew up, the hilly road seemed to lengthen before the weary feet, and the mute, blue flannel figure going on so fast with never a look or sound, added the last touch to Bab's remorseful anguish.

Wagons passed, but all were full, and no one offered a ride. Men and boys went by with rough jokes on the forlorn pair, for rain soon made them look like young tramps. But there was no brave Sancho to resent the impertinence, and this fact was sadly brought to both their minds by the appearance of a great Newfoundland dog who came trotting after a carriage. The good creature stopped to say a friendly word in his dumb fashion, looking up at Bab with benevolent eyes, and poking his nose into Ben's hand before he bounded away with his plumy tail curled over his back.

Ben started as the cold nose touched his fingers, gave the soft head a lingering pat, and watched the dog out of sight through a thicker mist than any the rain made. But Bab broke down; for the wistful look of the creature's eyes reminded her of lost Sancho, and she sobbed quietly as she glanced back longing to see the dear old fellow jogging along in the rear.

Ben heard the piteous sound and took a sly peep over his shoulder, seeing such a mournful spectacle that he felt appeased, saying to himself as if to excuse his late sternness, -

LOUISA MAY ALCOTT

"She is a naughty girl, but I guess she is about sorry enough now. When we get to that sign-post I'll speak to her, only I won't forgive her till Sanch comes back."

But he was better than his word; for, just before the post was reached, Bab, blinded by tears, tripped over the root of a tree, and, rolling down the bank, landed in a bed of wet nettles. Ben had her out in a jiffy, and vainly tried to comfort her; but she was past any consolation he could offer, and roared dismally as she wrung her tingling hands, with great drops running over her cheeks almost as fast as the muddy little rills ran down the road.

"Oh dear, oh dear! I'm all stinged up, and I want my supper; and my feet ache, and I'm cold, and every thing is so horrid!" wailed the poor child lying on the grass, such a miserable little wet bunch that the sternest parent would have melted at the sight.

"Don't cry so, Babby; I was real cross, and I'm sorry. I'll forgive you right away now, and never shake you any more," cried Ben, so full of pity for her tribulations that he forgot his own, like a generous little man.

"Shake me again, if you want to; I know I was very bad to tag and lose Sanch. I never will any more, and I'm so sorry, I don't know what to do," answered Bab, completely bowed down by this magnanimity.

"Never mind; you just wipe up your face and come along, and we'll tell Ma all about it, and she'll fix us as nice as can be. I shouldn't wonder if Sanch got home now before we did," said Ben, cheering himself as well as her by the fond hope.

"I don't believe I ever shall. I'm so tired my legs won't go, and the water in my boots makes them feel dreadfully. I wish that boy would wheel me a piece. Don't you s'pose he would? asked Bab, wearily picking herself up as a tall lad trundling a barrow came out of a yard near by.

"Hullo, Joslyn!" said Ben, recognizing the boy as one of the "hill fellows" who came to town Saturday nights for play or business.

"Hullo, Brown!" responded the other, arresting his squeaking progress with signs of surprise at the moist tableau before him.

"Where goin'?" asked Ben with masculine brevity.

"Got to carry this home, hang the old thing."

"Where to?"

"Batchelor's, down yonder," and the boy pointed to a farm-house at the foot of the next hill.

"Goin' that way, take it right along."

"What for?" questioned the prudent youth, distrusting such unusual neighborliness.

"She's tired, wants a ride; I'll leave it all right, true as I live and breathe," explained Ben, half ashamed yet anxious to get his little responsibility home as soon as possible, for mishaps seemed to thicken.

"Ho, you couldn't cart her all that way! she's most as heavy as a bag of meal," jeered the taller lad, amused at the proposition.

"I'm stronger than most fellers of my size. Try, if I ain't," and Ben squared off in such scientific style that Joslyn responded with sudden amiability, -

"All right, let's see you do it."

Bab huddled into her new equipage without the least fear, and Ben trundled her off at a good pace, while the boy retired to the shelter of a barn to watch their progress, glad to be rid of an irksome errand.

At first, all went well, for the way was down hill, and the wheel squeaked briskly round and round; Bab smiled gratefully upon her bearer, and Ben "went in on his muscle with a will," as he expressed it. But presently the road grew sandy, began to ascend, and the load seemed to grow heavier with every step.

"I'll get out now. It's real nice, but I guess I am too heavy," said Bab, as the face before her got redder and redder, and the breath began to come in puffs.

"Sit still. He said I couldn't. I'm not going to give in with him looking on," panted Ben, and he pushed gallantly up the rise, over the grassy lawn to the side gate of the Batchelors' door-yard, with his head down, teeth set, and every muscle of his slender body braced to the task.

"Did ever ye see the like of that now? Ah, ha!

"The streets were so wide, and the lanes were so narry,
He brought his wife home on a little wheelbarry,"

sung a voice with an accent which made Ben drop his load and push back his hat, to see Pat's red head looking over the fence.

To have his enemy behold him then and there was the last bitter drop in poor Ben's cup of humiliation. A shrill approving whistle from the hill was some comfort, however, and gave him spirit to help Bab out with composure, though his hands were blistered and he had hardly breath enough to issue the Command, -

"Go along home, and don't mind him."

"Nice childer, ye are, runnin' off this way, settin' the women distracted, and me wastin' me time comin' after ye when I'd be milkin' airly so I'd get a bit of pleasure the day," grumbled Pat, coming up to untie the Duke, whose Roman nose Ben had already recognized, as well as the roomy chaise standing before the door.

"Did Billy tell you about us?" asked Bab, gladly following toward this welcome refuge.

"Faith he did, and the Squire sent me to fetch ye home quiet and aisy. When ye found me, I'd jist stopped here to borry a light for me pipe. Up wid ye, b'y, and not be wastin' me time stramashin' after a spalpeen that I'd like to lay me whip over," said Pat, gruffly, as Ben came along, having left the barrow in the shed.

"Don't you wish you could? You needn't wait for me; I'll come when I'm ready," answered Ben dodging round the chaise, bound not to mind Pat, if he spent the night by the road-side in consequence.

"Bedad, and I won't then. It's lively ye are; but four legs is better than two, as ye'll find this night, me young man."

With that he whipped up and was off before Bab could say a word to persuade Ben to humble himself for the sake of a ride. She lamented and Pat chuckled, both forgetting what an agile monkey the boy was, and as neither looked back, they were unaware Master Ben was hanging on behind among the straps and springs, making derisive grimaces at his unconscious foe through the little glass in the leathern back.

At the lodge gate Ben jumped down to run before with whoops of naughty satisfaction, which brought the anxious waiters to the door in a flock; so Pat could only shake his fist at the exulting little rascal as he drove away, leaving the wanderers to be welcomed as warmly as if they were a pair of model children.

Mrs. Moss had not been very much troubled after all; for Cy had told her that Bab went after Ben, and Billy had lately reported her safe arrival among them, so, mother-like, she fed, dried, and warmed the runaways, before she scolded them.

Even then, the lecture was a mild one, for when they tried to tell the adventures which to them seemed so exciting, not to say tragical, the effect astonished them immensely, as their audience went into gales of laughter, especially at the wheel-barrow episode, which Pat insisted on telling, with grateful minuteness, to Ben's confusion. Thorny shouted, and even tender-hearted Betty forgot her tears over the lost dog to join in the familiar melody when Bab mimicked Pat's quotation from Mother Goose.

"We must not laugh any more, or these naughty children will think they have done something very clever in running away," said Miss Celia, when the fun subsided, adding, soberly, "I am displeased, but I will say nothing, for I think Ben is already punished enough."

"Guess I am," muttered Ben, with a choke in his voice as he glanced toward the empty mat where a dear curly bunch used to be with a bright eye twinkling out of the middle of it.

CHAPTER XV

BEN'S RIDE

Great was the mourning for Sancho, because his talents and virtues made him universally admired and beloved. Miss Celia advertised, Thorny offered rewards, and even surly Pat kept a sharp look-out for poodle dogs when he went to market; but no Sancho or any trace of him appeared. Ben was inconsolable, and sternly said it served Bab right when the dogwood poison affected both face and hands. Poor Bab thought so, too, and dared ask no sympathy from him, though Thorny eagerly prescribed plantain leaves, and Betty kept her supplied with an endless succession of them steeped in cream and pitying tears. This treatment was so successful that the patient soon took her place in society as well as ever, but for Ben's affliction there was no cure, and the boy really suffered in his spirits.

"I don't think it's fair that I should have so much trouble, - first losing father and then Sanch. If it wasn't for Lita and Miss Celia, I don't believe I could stand it," he said, one day, in a fit of despair, about a week after the sad event.

"Oh, come now, don't give up so, old fellow. We'll find him if he s alive, and if he isn't I'll try and get you another as good," answered Thorny, with a friendly slap on the shoulder, as Ben sat disconsolately among the beans he had been hoeing.

"As if there ever could be another half as good!" cried Ben, indignant at the idea; "or as if I'd ever try to fill his place with the best and biggest dog that ever wagged a tail! No, sir, there's only one Sanch in all the world, and if I can't have him I'll never have a dog again."

"Try some other sort of pet, then. You may have any of mine you like. Have the peacocks; do now," urged Thorny, full of boyish sympathy and good-will.

"They are dreadful pretty, but I don't seem to care about em, thank you," replied the mourner.

"Have the rabbits, all of them," which was a handsome offer on Thorny's part, for there were a dozen at least.

"They don't love a fellow as a dog does; all they care for is stuff to eat and dirt to burrow in. I'm sick of rabbits." And well he might be, for he had had the charge of them ever since they came, and any boy who has ever kept bunnies knows what a care they are.

"So am I! Guess we'll have an auction and sell out. Would Jack be a comfort to you? If he will, you may have him. I'm so well now, I can walk, or ride anything," added Thorny, in a burst of generosity.

"Jack couldn't be with me always, as Sanch was, and I couldn't keep him if I had him."

Ben tried to be grateful, but nothing short of Lita would have healed his wounded heart, and she was not Thorny's to give, or he would probably have offered her to his afflicted friend.

"Well, no, you couldn't take Jack to bed with you, or keep him up in your room, and I'm afraid he Would never learn to do any thing clever. I do wish I had something you wanted, I'd so love to give it to you."

He spoke so heartily and was so kind that Ben looked up, feeling that he had given him one of the sweetest things in the world - friendship; he wanted to tell him so, but did not know how to do it, so caught up his hoe and fell to work, saying, in a tone Thorny understood better than words, -

"You are real good to me -never mind, I won't worry about it; only it seems extra hard coming so soon after the other -"

He stopped there, and a bright drop fell on the bean leaves, to shine like dew till Ben saw clearly enough to bury it out of sight in a great flurry.

"By Jove! I'll find that dog, if he is out of the ground. Keep your spirits up, my lad, and we'll have the dear old fellow back yet."

With which cheering prophecy Thorny went off to rack his brains as to what could be done about the matter.

Half an hour afterward, the sound of a hand-organ in the avenue roused him from the brown study into which he had fallen as he lay on the newly mown grass of the lawn. Peeping over the wall, Thorny reconnoitered, and, finding the organ a good one, the man a pleasant-faced Italian, and the monkey a lively animal, he ordered them all in, as a delicate attention to Ben, for music and monkey together might suggest soothing memories of the past, and so be a comfort.

In they came by way of the Lodge, escorted by Bab and Betty, full of glee, for hand-organs were rare in those parts, and the children delighted in them. Smiling till his white teeth shone and his black eyes sparkled, the man played away while the monkey made his pathetic little bows, and picked up the pennies Thorny threw him.

"It is warm, and you look tired. Sit down and I'll get you Some dinner," said the young master, pointing to the seat which now stood near the great gate

With thanks in broken English the man gladly obeyed, and Ben begged to be allowed to make Jacko equally comfortable, explaining that he knew all about monkeys and what they liked. So the poor thing was freed from his cocked hat and uniform, fed with bread and milk, and allowed to curl himself up in the cool grass for a nap, looking so like a tired little old man in a fur coat that the children were never weary of watching him.

Meantime, Miss Celia had come out, and was talking Italian to Giacomo in a way that delighted his homesick heart. She had been to Naples, and could understand his longing for the lovely city of his birth, so they had a little chat in the language which is all Music, and the good fellow was so grateful that he played for the children to dance till they were glad to stop, lingering afterward as if he hated to set out again upon his lonely, dusty walk.

"I'd rather like to tramp round with him for a week or so. Could make enough to live on as easy as not, if I only I had Sanch to show off," said Ben, as he was coaxing Jacko into the suit which he detested. "You go wid me, yes?" asked the man, nodding and smiling, well pleased at the prospect of company, for his quick eye and what the boys let fall in their talk showed him that Ben was not one of them.

If I had my dog I'd love to," and with sad eagerness Ben told the tale of his loss, for the thought of it was never long out of his mind.

"I tink I see droll dog like he, way off in New York. He do leetle trick wid letter, and dance, and go on he head, and many tings to make laugh," said the man, when he had listened to a list of Sanch's beauties and accomplishments.

"Who had him?" asked Thorny, full of interest at once.

"A man I not know. Cross fellow what beat him when he do letters bad."

"Did he spell his name?" cried Ben, breathlessly.

"No; that for why man beat him. He name Generale, and he go spell Sancho all times, and cry when whip fall on him. Ha! yes! that name true one; not Generale?" and the man nodded, waved his hands, and showed his teeth, almost as much excited as the boys.

"It's Sanch! let's go and get him now, right off! cried Ben, in a fever to be gone.

"A hundred miles away, and no clue but this man's story? We must wait a little, Ben, and be sure before we set out," said Miss Celia, ready to do almost any thing, but not so certain as the boys. "What sort of a dog was it? A large, curly, white poodle, with a queer tail?" she asked of Giacomo.

"No, Signorina mia, he no curly, no wite; he black, smooth dog, little tail, small, so;" and the man held up one brown finger with a gesture which suggested a short, wagging tail.

"There, you see how mistaken we were. Dogs are often named Sancho, especially Spanish poodles; for the original Sancho was a Spaniard, you know. This dog is not ours, and I'm so sorry."

The boys' faces had fallen dismally as their hope was destroyed; but Ben would not give up. For him there was and could be only one Sancho in the world, and his quick wits suggested an explanation which no one else thought of.

"It may be my dog, - they color 'em as we used to paint over trick horses. I told you he was a valuable chap, and those that stole him hide him that way, else he'd be no use, don't you see? because we'd know him."

"But the black dog had no tail," began Thorny, longing to be convinced, but still doubtful.

Ben shivered as if the mere thought hurt him, as he said, in a grim tone, -

"They might have cut Sanch's off."

"Oh, no! no! they mustn't, - they wouldn't! How Could any one be so wicked?" cried Bab and Betty, horrified at the suggestion.

"You don't know what such fellows would do to make all safe, so they could use a dog to earn their living for 'em," said Ben, with mysterious significance, quite forgetting in his wrath that be had just proposed to get his own living in that way himself.

"He no your dog? Sorry I not find him for you. Addio, signorina! Grazia, signor! Buon giorno, buon giorno!" and, kissing his hand, the Italian shouldered organ and monkey, ready to go.

Miss Celia detained him long enough to give him her address, and beg him to let her know if he met poor Sanch in any of his wanderings; for such itinerant showmen often cross each other's paths. Ben and Thorny walked to the school-corner with him, getting more exact information about the black dog and his owner, for they had no intention of giving it up so soon.

That very evening, Thorny wrote to a boy cousin in New York, giving all the particulars of the case, and begging him to hunt up the man, investigate the dog, and see that the police made sure that every thing was right. Much relieved by this performance, the boys waited anxiously for a reply, and when it came found little comfort in it. Cousin Horace had done his duty like a man, but regretted that he could only report a failure. The owner of the black poodle was a suspicious character, but told a straight story, how he had bought the dog from a stranger, and exhibited him with success till he was stolen. Knew nothing of his history, and was very sorry to lose him, for he was a remarkably clever beast.

"I told my dog-man to look about for him, but he says he has probably been killed, with ever so many more; so there is an end of it, and I call it a mean shame."

"Good for Horace! I told you he'd do it up thoroughly and see the end of it," said Thorny, as he read that paragraph in the deeply interesting letter.

"May be the end of that dog, but not of mine. I'll bet he ran away; and if it was Sanch, he'll come home. You see if he doesn't!" cried Ben, refusing to believe that all was over.

"A hundred wiles off? Oh, he couldn't find you without help, smart as he is," answered Thorny, incredulously.

Ben looked discouraged, but Miss Celia cheered him up again by saying, -

"Yes, he could. My father had a friend who left a little dog in Paris; and the creature found her in Milan, and died of fatigue next day. That was very wonderful, but true; and I've no doubt that if Sanch is alive he will come home. Let us hope so, and be happy, while we wait."

"We will!" said the boys; and day after day looked for the wanderer's return, kept a bone ready in the old place if he should arrive at night, and shook his mat to keep it soft for his weary bones when he came. But weeks passed, and still no Sanch.

Something else happened, however, so absorbing that he was almost forgotten for a time; and Ben found a way to repay a part of all he owed his best friend.

Miss Celia went off for a ride one afternoon, and an hour afterward, as Ben sat in the porch reading, Lita dashed into the yard with the reins dangling about her legs, the saddle turned round, and one side covered with black mud, showing that she had been down. For a minute, Ben's heart stood still; then he flung away his book, ran to the horse, and saw at once by her heaving flanks, dilated nostrils, and wet coat, that she must have come a long way and at full speed.

"She has had a fall, but isn't hurt or frightened," thought the boy, as the pretty creature rubbed her nose against his shoulder, pawed the ground, and champed her bit, as if she tried to tell him all about the disaster, whatever it was.

"Lita, where's Miss Celia?" he asked, looking straight into the intelligent eyes, which were troubled but not wild.

Lita threw up her head, and neighed loud and clear, as if she called her mistress; and, turning, would have gone again if Ben had not caught the reins and held her.

"All right, we'll find her;" and, pulling off the broken saddle, kicking away his shoes, and ramming his hat firmly on, Ben was up like a flash, tingling all over with a sense of power as he felt the bare back between his knees, and caught the roll of Lita's eye as she looked round with an air of satisfaction.

"Hi, there! Mrs. Moss! Something has happened to Miss Celia, and I'm going to find her. Thorny is asleep; tell him easy, and I'll come back as soon as I can!"

Then, giving Lita her head, he was off before the startled woman had time to do more than wring her hands and cry out, -

"Go for the Squire! Oh, what shall we do?"

As if she knew exactly what was wanted of her, Lita went back the way she had come, as Ben could see by the fresh, irregular tracks that cut up the road where she had galloped for help. For a mile or more they went, then she paused at a pair of bars, which were let down to allow the carts to pass into the wide hay-fields beyond. On she went again, cantering across the new-mown turf toward a brook, across which she had evidently taken a leap before; for, on the further side, at a place where cattle went to drink, the mud showed signs of a fall.

"You were a fool to try there; but where is Miss Celia?" said Ben, who talked to animals as if they were people, and was understood much better than any one not used to their companionship would imagine.

Now Lita seemed at a loss, and put her head down, as if she expected to find her mistress where she had left her, somewhere on the ground. Ben called, but there was no answer; and he rode slowly along the brook-side, looking far and wide with anxious eyes.

"May be she wasn't hurt, and has gone to that house to wait," thought the boy, pausing for a last survey of the great, sunny field, which had no place of shelter in it but one rock on the other side of the little stream. As his eye wandered over it, something dark seemed to blow out from behind it, as if the wind played in the folds of a shirt, or a human limb moved. Away went Lita, and in a moment Ben had found Miss Celia, lying in the shadow of the rock, so white and motionless, he feared that she was dead. He leaped down, touched her, spoke to her; and, receiving no answer, rushed away to bring a little water in his leaky hat to sprinkle in her face, as he had seen them do when any of the riders got a fall in the circus, or fainted from exhaustion after they left the ring, where "do or die" was the motto all adopted.

In a minute, the blue eyes opened, and she recognized the anxious face bending over her, saying faintly, as she touched it, -

"My good little Ben, I knew you'd find me, - I sent Lita for you, - I'm so hurt, I couldn't come."

"Oh, where? What shall I do? Had I better run up to the house?" asked Ben, overjoyed to hear her speak, but much dismayed by her seeming helplessness, for he had seen bad falls, and had them, too.

"I feel bruised all over, and my arm is broken, I'm afraid. Lita tried not to hurt me. She slipped, and we went down. I came here into the shade, and the pain made me faint, I suppose. Call somebody, and get me home."

Then she shut her eyes, and looked so white that Ben hurried away, and burst upon old Mrs. Paine, placidly knitting at the end door, so suddenly that, as she afterward said, "It sca't her like a clap o' thunder."

"Ain't a man nowheres around. All down in the big medder gettin' in hay," was her reply to Ben's breathless demand for "everybody to come and see to Miss Celia."

He turned to mount, for he had flung himself off before Lita stopped, but the old lady caught his jacket, and asked half a dozen questions in a breath.

"Who's your folks? What's broke? How'd she fall? Where is she? Why didn't she come right here? Is it a sunstroke?"

As fast as words could tumble out of his mouth, Ben answered, and then tried to free himself; but the old lady held on, while she gave her directions, expressed her sympathy, and offered her hospitality with incoherent warmth.

"Sakes alive! poor dear! Fetch her right in. Liddy, get out the camphire; and, Melissy, you haul down a bed to lay her on. Falls is dretful uncert'in things; shouldn't wonder if her back was broke. Father's down yender, and he and Bijah will see to her. You go call 'em, and I'll blow the horn to start 'em up. Tell her we'd be pleased to see her, and it won't make a mite of trouble."

Ben heard no more, fur as Mrs. Paine turned to take down the tin horn he was up and away.

Several long and dismal toots sent Lita galloping through the grassy path as the sound of the trumpet excites a war-horse, and "father and Bijah," alarmed by the signal at that hour, leaned on their rakes to survey with wonder the distracted-looking little horseman approaching like a whirlwind.

"Guess likely grandpa's had 'nother stroke. Told 'em to send over soon 's ever it come," said the farmer, calmly.

"Shouldn't wonder ef suthing was afire some'r's," conjectured the hired man, surveying the horizon for a cloud of smoke.

Instead of advancing to meet the messenger, both stood like statues in blue overalls and red flannel shirts, till the boy arrived and told his tale.

"Sho, that's bad," said the farmer, anxiously.

"That brook always was the darndest place," added Bijah; then both men bestirred themselves helpfully, the former hurrying to Miss Cella while the latter brought up the cart and made a bed of hay to lay her on.

"Now then, boy, you go for the doctor. My own folks will see to the lady, and she'd better keep quiet up yender till we see what the matter is," said the farmer, when the pale girl was lifted in as carefully as four strong arms could do it. "Hold on," he added, as Ben made one leap to Lita's back. You'll have to go to Berryville. Dr. Mills is a master hand for broken bones and old Dr. Babcock ain't. 'Tisn't but about three miles from here to his house, and you'll fetch him 'fore there's any harm done waitin'."

"Don't kill Lita," called Miss Celia from the cart, as it began to move.

But Ben did not hear her, for he was off across the fields, riding as if life and death depended upon his speed.

"That boy will break his neck," said Mr. Paine, standing still to watch horse and rider go over the wall as if bent on instant destruction.

"No fear for Ben, he can ride any thing, and Lita was trained to leap," answered Miss Celia, falling back on the hay with a groan, for she had involuntarily raised her head to see her little squire dash away in gallant style.

"I should hope so; regular jockey, that boy. Never see any thing like it out of a race-ground," and Farmer Paine strode on, still following with his eye the figures that went thundering over the bridge, up the hill, out of sight, leaving a cloud of cloud of dust behind.

Now that his mistress was safe, Ben enjoyed that wild ride mightily, and so did the bay mare; for Lita had good blood in her, and proved it that day by doing her three miles in a wonderfully short time. People jogging along in wagons and country carry-alls stared amazed as the reckless pair went by. Women, placidly doing their afternoon sewing at the front windows, dropped their needles to run out with exclamations of alarm, sure some one was being run away with; children playing by the roadside scattered like chickens before a hawk, as Ben passed with a warning whoop, and baby-carriages were scrambled into door-yards with perilous rapidity at his approach.

But when he clattered into town, intense interest was felt in this barefooted boy on the foaming steed, and a dozen voices asked, "Who's killed?" as he pulled up at the doctor's gate.

"Jest drove off that way; Mrs. Flynn's baby's in a fit," cried a stout lady from the piazza, never ceasing to rock, though several passers-by paused to hear the news, for she was a doctor's wife, and used to the arrival of excited messengers from all quarters at all hours of the day and night.

Deigning no reply to any one, Ben rode away, wishing he could leap a yawning gulf, scale a precipice, or ford a raging torrent, to prove his devotion to Miss Celia, and his skill in horsemanship. But no dangers beset his path, and he found the doctor pausing to water his tired horse at the very trough where Bab and Sancho had been discovered on that ever-memorable day. The story was quickly told, and, promising to be there as soon as possible, Dr. Mills drove on to relieve baby Flynn's inner man, a little disturbed by a bit of soap and several buttons, upon which he had privately lunched while his mamma was busy at the wash-tub.

Ben thanked his stars, as he had already done more than once, that he knew how to take care of a horse; for he delayed by the watering-place long enough to wash out Lita's mouth with a handful of wet grass, to let her have one swallow to clear her dusty throat, and then went slowly back over the breezy hills, patting and praising the good creature for her intelligence and speed. She knew well enough that she had been a clever little mare, and tossed her head, arched her glossy neck, and ambled daintily along, as conscious and coquettish as a pretty woman, looking round at her admiring rider to return his compliments by glance of affection, and caressing sniffs of a velvet nose at his bare feet.

Miss Celia had been laid comfortably in bed by the farmer's wife and daughter; and, when the doctor arrived, bore the setting of her arm bravely. No other serious damage appeared, and bruises soon heal, so Ben was sent home to comfort Thorny with a good report, and ask the Squire to drive up in his big carry-all for her the next day, if she was able to be moved.

Mrs. Moss had been wise enough to say nothing, but quietly made what preparations she could, and waited for tidings. Bab and Betty were away berrying, so no one had alarmed Thorny, and he had his afternoon nap in peace, - an unusually long one, owing to the stillness which prevailed in the absence of the children; and when he awoke he lay reading for a while before he began to wonder where every one was. Lounging out to see, he found Ben and Lita reposing side by side on the fresh straw in the loose box, which had been made for her in the coach-house. By the pails, sponges and curry-combs lying about, it was evident that she had been refreshed by a careful washing and rubbing down, and my lady was now luxuriously resting after her labors, with her devoted groom half asleep close by.

"Well, of all queer boys you are the queerest, to spend this hot afternoon fussing over Lita, just for the fun of it!" cried Thorny, looking in at them with much amusement.

"If you knew what we'd been doing, you'd think I ought to fuss over her, and both of us had a right to rest!" answered Ben, rousing up as bright as a button; for he longed to tell his thrilling tale, and had with difficulty been restrained from bursting in on Thorny as soon as he arrived.

He made short work of the story, but was quite satisfied with the sensation it produced; for his listener was startled, relieved, excited and charmed, in such rapid succession, that he was obliged to sit upon the meal-chest and get his breath before he Could exclaim, with an emphatic demonstration of his heels against the bin, -

"Ben Brown, I'll never forget what you've done for Celia this day, or say 'bow-legs' again as long as I live

"George! I felt as if I had six legs when we were going the pace. We were all one piece, and had a jolly spin, didn't we, my beauty?" and Ben chuckled as he took Lita's head in his lap, while she answered with a gusty sigh that nearly blew him away.

Like the fellow that brought the good news from Ghent to Aix," said Thorny, surveying the recumbent pair with great admiration.

"What follow?" asked Ben, wondering if he didn't mean Sheridan, of whose ride he had heard.

"Don't you know that piece? I spoke it at school. Give it to you now; see if it isn't a rouser."

And, glad to find a vent from his excitement, Thorny mounted the meal-chest, to thunder out that stirring ballad with such spirit that Lita pricked up her ears and Ben gave a shrill "Hooray!" as the last verse ended.

"And all I remember is friends flocking round, As I sat with his head 'twixt my knees on the ground, And no voice but was praising this Roland of mine, As I poured down his throat our last measure of wine, Which (the burgesses voted by common consent) Was no more than his due who brought good news from Ghent."

CHAPTER XVI

DETECTIVE THORNTON

A few days later, Miss Celia was able to go about with her arm in a sling, pale still, and rather stiff, but so much better than any one expected, that all agreed Mr. Paine was right in pronouncing Dr. Mills "a master hand with broken bones." Two devoted little maids waited on her, two eager pages stood ready to run her errands, and friendly neighbors sent in delicacies enough to keep these four young persons busily employed in disposing of them.

Every afternoon the great bamboo lounging chair was brought out and the interesting invalid conducted to it by stout Randa, who was head nurse, and followed by a train of shawl, cushion, foot-stool and book bearers, who buzzed about like swarming bees round a new queen. When all were settled, the little maids sewed and the pages read aloud, with much conversation by the way; for one of the rules was, that all should listen attentively, and if any one did not understand what was read, he or she should ask to have it explained on the spot. Whoever could answer was invited to do so, and at the end of the reading Miss Celia could ask any she liked, or add any explanations which seemed necessary. In this way much pleasure and profit was extracted from the tales Ben and Thorny read, and much unexpected knowledge as well as ignorance displayed, not to mention piles of neatly hemmed towels for which Bab and Betty were paid like regular sewing-women.

So vacation was not all play, and the girls found their picnics, berry parties, and "goin' a visitin'," all the more agreeable for the quiet hour spent with Miss Celia. Thorny had improved wonderfully, and was getting to be quite energetic, especially since his sister's accident; for while she was laid up he was the head of the house, and much enjoyed his promotion. But Ben did not seem to flourish as he had done at first. The loss of Sancho preyed upon him sadly, and the longing to go and find his dog grew into such a strong temptation that he could hardly resist it. He said little about it; but now, and then a word escaped him which might have enlightened any one who chanced to be watching him. No one was, just then, so he brooded over this fancy, day by day, in silence and solitude, for there was no riding and driving now. Thorny was busy with his sister trying to show her that he remembered how good she had been to him when he was ill, and the little girls had their own affairs.

Miss Celia was the first to observe the change, having nothing to do but lie on the sofa and amuse herself by seeing others work or play. Ben was bright enough at the readings, because theyn he forgot his troubles; but when they were over and his various duties done, he went to his own room or sought consolation with Lita, being sober and quiet, and quite unlike the merr monkey all knew and liked so well.

"Thorny, what is the matter with Ben?" asked Miss Celia, one day, when she and her brother were alone in the "green parlor," as they called the lilac-tree walk.

"Fretting about Sanch, I suppose. I declare I wish that dog had never been born! Losing him has just spoilt Ben. Not a bit of fun left in him, and he won't have any thing I offer to cheer him up."

Thorny spoke impatiently, and knit his brows over the pressed flowers he was neatly gumming into his herbal.

"I wonder if he has any thing on his mind? He acts as if he was hiding a trouble he didn't dare to tell. Have you talked with him about it?" asked Miss Celia, looking as if she was hiding a trouble she did not like to tell.

"Oh, yes, I poke him up now and then, but he gets peppery, so I let him alone. May be he is longing for his old circus again. Shouldn't blame him much if he was; it isn't very lively here, and he's used to excitement, you know."

"I hope it isn't that. Do you think he would slip away without telling us, and go back to the old life again? "Don't believe he would. Ben isn't a bit of a sneak; that's why I like him."

"Have you ever found him sly or untrue in any way?" asked Miss Celia, lowering her voice.

"No; he's as fair and square a fellow as I ever saw. Little bit low, now and then, but he doesn't mean it, and wants to be a gentleman, only he never lived with one before, and it's all new to him. I'll get him polished up after a while."

"Oh, Thorny, there are three peacocks on the place, and you are the finest!" laughed Miss Celia, as her brother spoke in his most condescending way with a lift of the eyebrows very droll to see.

"And two donkeys, and Ben's the biggest, not to know when he is well off and happy!" retorted the "gentleman," slapping a dried specimen on the page as if he were pounding discontented Ben.

"Come here and let me tell you something which worries me. I would not breathe it to another soul, but I feel rather helpless, and I dare say you can manage the matter better than I."

Looking much mystified, Thorny went and sat on the stool at his sister's feet, while she whispered confidentially in his ear: "I've lost some money out of my drawer, and I'm so afraid Ben took it." "But it's always locked up and you keep the keys of the drawer and the little room?"

"It is gone, nevertheless, and I've had my keys safe all the time."

"But why think it is he any more than Randa, or Katy, or me?"

"Because I trust you three as I do myself. I've known the girls for years, and you have no object in taking it since all I have is yours, dear."

"And all mine is yours, of course. But, Celia, how could he do it? He can't pick locks, I know, for we fussed over my desk together, and had to break it after all."

"I never really thought it possible till to-day when you were playing ball and it went in at the upper window, and Ben climbed up the porch after it; you remember you said, 'If it had gone in at the garret gable you couldn't have done that so well; ' and he answered, 'Yes, I could, there isn't a spout I can't shin up, or a bit of this roof I haven't been over.'"

"So he did; but there is no spout near the little room window."

"There is a tree, and such an agile boy as Ben could swing in and out easily. Now, Thorny, I hate to think this of him, but it has happened twice, and for his own sake I must stop it. If he is planning to run away, money is a good thing to have. And he may feel that it is his own; for you know he asked me to put his wages in the bank, and I did. He may not like to come to me for that, because he can give no good reason for wanting it. I'm so troubled I really don't know what to do."

She looked troubled, and Thorny put his arms about her as if to keep all worries but his own away from her.

"Don't you fret, Cely, dear; you leave it to me. I'll fix him - ungrateful little scamp!"

"That is not the way to begin. I am afraid you will make him angry and hurt his feelings, and then we can do nothing."

"Bother his feelings! I shall just say, calmly and coolly: 'Now, look here, Ben, hand over the money you took out of my sister's drawer, and we'll let you off easy,' or something like that."

"It wouldn't do, Thorny; his temper would be up in a minute, and away he would go before we could find out whether he was guilty or not. I wish I knew how to manage."

Let me think," and Thorny leaned his chin on the arm of the chair, staring hard at the knocker as if he expected the lion's mouth to open with words of counsel then and there.

"By Jove, I do believe Ben took it!" he broke out suddenly; "for when I went to his room this morning to see why he didn't come and do my boots, he shut the drawer in his bureau as quick as a flash, and looked red and queer, for I didn't knock, and sort of startled him."

"He wouldn't be likely to put stolen money there. Ben is too wise for that."

"He wouldn't keep it there, but he might be looking at it and pitch it in when I called. He's hardly spoken to me since, and when I asked him what his flag was at half-mast for, he wouldn't answer. Besides, you know in the reading this afternoon he didn't listen, and when you asked what he was thinking about, he colored up and muttered something about Sanch. I tell you, Celia, it looks bad - very bad," and Thorny shook his head with a wise air.

"It does, and yet we may be all wrong. Let us wait a little and give the poor boy a chance to clear himself before we speak. I'd rather lose my money than suspect him falsely."

"How much was it?"

"Eleven dollars; a one went first, and I supposed I'd miscalculated somewhere when I took some out; but when I missed a ten, I felt that I ought not to let it pass."

"Look here, sister, you just put the case into my hands and let me work it up. I won't say any thing to Ben till you give the word; but I'll watch him, and now that my eyes are open, it won't be easy to deceive me."

Thorny was evidently pleased with the new play of detective, and intended to distinguish himself in that line; but when Miss Celia asked how he meant to begin, he could only respond with a blank expression: "Don't know! You give me the keys and leave a bill or two in the drawer, and may be I can find him out somehow."

So the keys were given, and the little dressing-room where the old secretary stood was closely watched for a day or two. Ben cheered up a trifle which looked as if he knew an eye was upon him, but otherwise he went on as usual, and Miss Celia feeling a little guilty at even harboring a suspicion of him, was kind and patient with his moods. Thorny was very funny in the unnecessary mystery and fuss he made; his affectation of careless indifference to Ben's movements and his clumsy attempts to watch every one of them; his dodgings up and down stairs, ostentatious clanking of keys, and the elaborate traps he set to catch his thief, such as throwing his ball in at the dressing-room window and sending Ben up the tree to get it, which he did, thereby proving beyond a doubt that he alone could have taken the money, Thorny thought. Another deep discovery was, that the old drawer was so shrunken that the lock could be pressed down by slipping a knife-blade between the hasp and socket.

"Now it is as clear as day, and you'd better let me speak," he said, full of pride as well as regret at this triumphant success of his first attempt as a detective.

"Not yet, and you need do nothing more. I'm afraid it was a mistake of mine to let you do this; and if it has spoiled your friendship with Ben, I shall be very sorry; for I do not think he is guilty," answered Miss Celia.

"Why not?" and Thorny looked annoyed.

"I've watched also, and he doesn't act like a deceitful boy. To-day I asked him if he wanted any money, or should I put what I owe him with the rest, and he looked me straight in the face with such honest, grateful eyes, I could not doubt him when he said 'Keep it, please, I don't need any thing here, you are all so good to me.'"

"Now, Celia, don't you be soft-hearted. He's a sly little dog, and knows my eye is on him. When I asked him what he saw in the dressing-room, after he brought out the ball, and looked sharply at him, he laughed, and said 'Only a mouse,' as saucy as you please."

"Do set the trap there, I heard the mouse nibbling last night, and it kept me awake. We must have a cat or we shall be overrun."

"Well, shall I give Ben a good blowing up, or will you?" asked Thorny, scorning such poor prey as mice, and bound to prove that he was in the right.

"I'll let you know what I have decided in the morning. Be kind to Ben, meantime, or I shall feel as if I had done you harm by letting you watch him."

So it was left for that day, and by the next, Miss Celia had made up her mind to speak to Ben. She was just going down to breakfast when the sound of loud voices made her pause and listen. It came from Ben's room, where the two boys seemed to be disputing about something.

"I hope Thorny has kept his promise," she thought, and hurried through the back entry, fearing a general explosion.

Ben's chamber was at the end, and she could see and hear what was going on before she was near enough to interfere. Ben stood against his closet door looking as fierce and red as a turkey-cock; Thorny sternly confronted him, saying in an excited tone, and with a threatening gesture: "You are hiding something in there, and you can't deny it."

"I don't."

"Better not; I insist on seeing it."

"Well, you won't."

"What have you been stealing now?"

"Didn't steal it, - used to be mine, - I only took it when I wanted it."

"I know what that means. You'd better give it back or I'll make you."

"Stop!" cried a third voice, as Thorny put out his arm to clutch Ben, who looked ready to defend himself to the last gasp, "Boys, I will settle this affair. Is there anything hidden in the closet, Ben?" and Miss Celia came between the belligerent parties with her one hand up to part them.

Thorny fell back at once, looking half ashamed of his heat, and Ben briefly answered, with a gulp as if shame or anger made it hard to speak steadily:

"Yes 'm, there is."

"Does it belong to you?"

"Yes 'm, it does."

"Where did you get it?"

"Up to Squire's."

"That's a lie!" muttered Thorny to himself.

Ben's eye flashed, and his fist doubled up in spite of him, but he restrained himself out of respect for Miss Celia, who looked puzzled, as she asked another question, not quite wure how to proceed with the investigation: "Is it money, Ben?"

"No 'm, it isn't."

"Then what can it be?"

"Meow!" answered a fourth voice from the closet; and as Ben flung open the door a gray kitten walked out, purring with satisfaction at her release.

Miss Celia fell into a chair and laughed till her eyes were full; Thorny looked foolish, and Ben folded his arms, curled up his nose, and regarded his accuser with calm defiance, while pussy sat down to wash her face as if her morning toilette had been interrupted by her sudden abduction.

"That's all very well, but it doesn't mend matters much, so you needn't laugh, Celia," began Thorny, recovering himself, and stubbornly bent on sifting the case to the bottom, now he had begun.

"Well, it would, if you'd let a feller alone. She said she wanted a cat, so I went and got the one they gave me when I was at the Squire's. I went early and took her without asking, and I had a right to," explained Ben, much aggrieved by having his surprise spoiled.

"It was very kind of you, and I'm glad to have this nice kitty. We will shut her up in my room to catch the mice that plague me," said Miss Celia, picking up the little cat, and wondering how she would get her two angry boys safely down stairs.

"The dressing-room, she means; you know the way, and you don't need keys to get in," added Thorny, with such sarcastic emphasis that Ben felt some insult was intended, and promptly resented it.

"You won't get me to climb any more trees after your balls, and my cat won't catch any of your mice, so you needn't ask me."

"Cats don't catch thieves, and they are what I'm after!"

"What do you mean by that?" fiercely demanded Ben.

"Celia has lost some money out of her drawer, and you won't let me see what's in yours; So I thought, perhaps, you'd got it!" blurted out Thorny, finding it hard to say the words, angry as he was, for the face opposite did not look like a guilty one.

For a minute, Ben did not seem to understand him, plainly as he spoke; then he turned an angry scarlet, and, with a reproachful glance at his mistress, opened the little drawer so that both could see all that it contained.

"They ain't any thing; but I'm fond of 'em they are all I've got - I was afraid he'd laugh at me that time, so I wouldn't let him look - it was father's birthday, and I felt bad about him and Sanch -" Ben's indignant voice got more and more indistinct as he stumbled on, and broke down over the last words. He did not cry, however. but threw back his little treasures as if half their sacredness was gone; and, making a strong effort at self-control, faced around, asking of Miss Celia, with a grieved look,

"Did you think I'd steal anything of yours?"

"I tried not to, Ben, but what could I do? It was gone, and you the only stranger about the place."

"Wasn't there any one to think bad of but me? he said, so sorrowfully that Miss Celia made up her mind on the spot that he was as innocent of the theft as the kitten now biting her buttons, no other refreshment being offered.

"Nobody, for I know my girls well. Yet, eleven dollars are gone, and I cannot imagine where or how for both drawer and door are always locked, because my papers and valuables are in that room."

"What a lot! But how could I get it if it was locked up?" and Ben looked as if that question was unanswerable.

"Folks that can climb in at windows for a ball, can go the same way for money, and get it easy enough when they've only to pry open an old lock!"

Thorny's look and tone seemed to make plain to Ben all that they had been suspecting, and, being innocent, he was too perplexed and unhappy to defend himself. His eye went from one to the other, and, seeing doubt in both faces, his boyish heart sunk within him; for he could prove nothing, and his first impulse was to go away at once.

"I can't say any thing, only that I didn't take the money. You won't believe it, so I'd better go back where I come from. They weren't so kind, but they trusted me, and knew I wouldn't steal a cent. You may keep my money, and the kitty, too; I don't want 'em," and, snatching up his hat, Ben would gone straight away, if Thorny had not barred his passage.

"Come, now, don't be mad. Let's talk it over, and if I 'm wrong I'll take it all back and ask your pardon," he said, in a friendly tone, rather scared at the consequences of his first attempt, though as sure as ever that he was right.

"It would break my heart to have you go in that way, Ben. Stay at least till your innocence is proved, then no one can doubt what you say now."

"Don't see how it can be proved," answered Ben, appeased by her evident desire to trust him.

"We'll try as well as we know how, and the first thing we will do is to give that old secretary a good rummage from top to bottom. I've done it once, but it is just possible that the bills may have slipped out of sight. Come, now, I can't rest till I've done all I can to comfort you and convince Thorny." Miss Celia rose as she spoke, and led the way to the dressing-room, which had no outlet except through her chamber. Still holding his hat, Ben followed with a troubled face, and Thorny brought up the rear, doggedly determined to keep his eye on "the little scamp" till the matter was satisfactorily cleared up. Miss Celia had made her proposal more to soothe the feelings of one boy and to employ the superfluous energies of the other, than in the expectation of throwing any light upon the mystery; for she was sadly puzzled by Ben's manner, and much regretted that she had let her brother meddle in the matter.

"There," she said, unlocking the door with the key Thorny reluctantly gave up to her, "this is the room and that is the drawer on the right. The lower ones have seldom been opened since we came, and hold only some of papa's old books. Those upper ones you may turn out and investigate as much as you - Bless me! here 's something in your trap," Thorny and Miss Celia gave a little skip as she nearly trod on a long, gray tall, which hung out of the bole now filled by a plump mouse.

But her brother was intent on more serious things, and merely pushed the trap aside as he pulled out the drawer with an excited gesture, which sent it and all its contents clattering to the floor.

"Confound the old thing! It always stuck so I had to give a jerk. Now, there it is, topsy-turvy," and Thorny looked Much disgusted at his own awkwardness.

"No harm done; I left nothing of value in it. Look back there, Ben, and see if there is room for a paper to get worked over the top of the drawer. I felt quite a crack, but I don't believe it is possible for things to slip out; the place was never full enough to overflow in any way."

Miss Celia spoke to Ben, who was kneeling down to pick up the scattered papers, among which were two marked dollar bills, - Thorny's bait for the thief. Ben looked into the dusty recess, and then put in his hand, saying carelessly, -

"There's nothing but a bit of red stuff."

"My old pen-wiper - Why, what's the matter?" asked Miss Celia, as Ben dropped the handful Of what looked like rubbish.

"Something warm and wiggly inside of it," answered Ben, stooping to examine the contents of the little scarlet bundle. "Baby mice! Ain't they funny? Look just like mites of young pigs. We'll have to kill 'em if you've caught their mamma," he said, forgetting his own trials in boyish curiosity about his "find."

Miss Celia stooped also, and gently poked the red cradle with her finger; for the tiny mice were nestling deeper into the fluff with small squeals of alarm. Suddenly she cried out: "Boys, boys, I've found the thief! Look here; pull out these bits and see if they won't make up my lost bills."

Down went the motherless babies as four ruthless hands pulled apart their cosey nest, and there, among the nibbled fragments, appeared enough finely printed, greenish paper, to piece out parts of two bank bills. A large cypher and part of a figure one were visible, and that accounted for the ten; but though there were other bits, no figures could be found, and they were willing to take the other bill on trust.

"Now, then, am I a thief and a liar?" demanded Ben, pointing proudly to the tell-tale letters spread forth on the table, over which all three had been eagerly bending.

"No; I beg your pardon, and I'm very sorry that we didn't look more carefully before we spoke, then we all should have been spared this pain."

"All right, old fellow, forgive and forget. I'll never think hard of you again, - on my honor I won't."

As they spoke, Miss Celia and her brother held out their hands frankly and heartily. Ben shook both, but with a difference; for he pressed the soft one gratefully, remembering that its owner had always been good to him; but the brown paw he gripped with a vengeful squeeze that made Thorny pull it away in a hurry, exclaiming, good-naturedly, in spite of both physical and mental discomfort, -

"Come, Ben, don't you bear malice; for you've got the laugh on your side, and we feel pretty small. I do, any way; for, after my fidgets, all I've caught is a mouse!"

"And her family. I'm so relieved I'm almost sorry the poor little mother is dead - she and her babies were so happy in the old pen-wiper," said Miss Celia, hastening to speak merrily, for Ben still looked indignant, and she was much grieved at what had happened.

"A pretty expensive house," began Thorny, looking about for the interesting orphans, who had been left on the floor while their paper-hangings were examined.

No further anxiety need be felt for them, however; Kitty had come upon the scene, and as judge, jury, and prisoner, turned to find the little witnesses, they beheld the last pink mite going down Pussy's throat in one mouthful.

"I call that summary justice, - the whole family executed on the spot! Give Kit the mouse also, and let us go to breakfast. I feel as if I had found my appetite, now this worry is off my mind," said Miss Celia, laughing so infectiously that Ben had to join in spite of himself, as she took his arm and led him away with a look which mutely asked his pardon over again.

"Rather lively for a funeral procession," said Thorny, following with the trap in his hand and Puss at his heels, adding, to comfort his pride as a detective:

"Well, I said I'd catch the thief, and I have, though it is rather a small one!"

CHAPTER XVII

BETTY'S BRAVERY

"Celia, I've a notion that we ought to give Ben something. A sort of peace-offering, you know; for he feels dreadfully hurt about our suspecting him," said Thorny, at dinner that day.

"I see he does, though he tries to seem as bright and pleasant as ever. I do not wonder, and I've been thinking what I could do to soothe his feelings. Can you suggest any thing? "

"Cuff-buttons. I saw some jolly ones over at Berryville, oxidized silver, with dogs' heads on them, yellow eyes, and all as natural as could be. Those, now, would just suit him for his go-to-meeting white shirts, - neat, appropriate, and in memoriam."

Miss Celia could not help laughing, it was such a boyish suggestion; but she agreed to it, thinking Thorny knew best, and hoping the yellow-eyed dogs would be as balm to Ben's wounds.

"Well, dear, you may give those, and Lita shall give the little whip with a horse's foot for a handle, if it is not gone. I saw it at the harness shop in town; and Ben admired it so much that I planned to give it to him on his birthday."

"That will tickle him immensely; and if you'd just let him put brown tops to my old boots, and stick a cockade in his hat when he sits up behind the phaeton, he'd be a happy fellow," laughed Thorny, who had discovered that one of Ben's ambitions was to be a tip-top groom."

"No, thank you; those things are out of place in America, and would be absurd in a small country place like this. His blue suit and straw hat please me better for a boy; though a nicer little groom, in livery or out, no one could desire, and you may tell him I said so."

"I will, and he'll look as proud as punch; for he thinks every word you say worth a dozen from any one else. But won't you give him something? Just some little trifle, to show that we are both eating humble pie, feeling sorry about the mouse money."

"I shall give him a set of school-books, and try to get him ready to begin when vacation is over. An education is the best present we can make him; and I want you to help me fit him to enter as well is he can. Bab and Betty began, little dears, - lent him their books and taught all they knew; so Ben got a taste, and, with the right encouragement, would like to go on, I am sure."

"That's so like you Celia! Always thinking of the best thing and doing it handsomely. I'll help like a house a-fire, if he will let me; but, all day, he's been as stiff as a poker, so I don't believe he forgives me a bit."

"He will in time, and if you are kind and patient, he will be glad to have you help him. I shall make it a sort of favor to me on his part, to let you see to his lessons, now and then. It will be quite true, for I don't want you to touch your Latin or algebra till cool weather; teaching him will be play to you."

Miss Celia's last words made her brother unbend his brows, for he longed to get at his books again, and the idea of being tutor to his "man-servant" did not altogether suit him.

"I'll tool him along at a great pace, if he will only go. Geography and arithmetic shall be my share, and you may have the writing and spelling; it gives me the fidgets to set copies', and hear children make a mess of words. Shall I get the books when I buy the other things? Can I go this afternoon?"

"Yes, here is the list; Bab gave it to me. You can go if you will come home early and have your tooth filled."

Gloom fell at once upon Thorny's beaming face, and he gave such a shrill whistle that his sister jumped in her chair, as she added, persuasively, -

"It won't hurt a bit, now, and the longer you leave it the worse it will be. Dr. Mann is ready at any time; and, once over, you will be at peace for months. Come, my hero, give your orders, and take one of the girls to support you in the trying hour. Have Bab; she will enjoy it, and amuse you with her chatter."

"As if I needed girls round for such a trifle as that!" returned Thorny with a shrug, though he groaned inwardly at the prospect before him, as most of us do on such occasions. "I wouldn't take Bab at any price; she'd only get into some scrape, and upset the whole plan. Betty is the chicken for me, - a real little lady, and as nice and purry as a kitten."

"Very well; ask her mother, and take good care of her. Let her tuck her dolly in, and she will be contented anywhere. There's a fine air, and the awning is on the phaeton, so you won't feel the sun. Start about three, and drive carefully."

Betty was charmed to go, for Thorny was a sort of prince in her eyes; and to be invited to such a grand expedition was an overwhelming honor. Bab was not surprised, for, since Sancho's loss, she had felt herself in disgrace, and been unusually meek; Ben let her "severely alone," which much afflicted her, for he was her great admiration, and had been pleased to express his approbation of her agility and courage so often, that she was ready to attempt any fool-hardy feat to recover his regard. But vainly did she risk her neck jumping off the highest beams in the barn, trying to keep her balance standing on the donkey's back, and leaping the lodge gate at a bound; Ben vouchsafed no reward by a look, a smile, a word of commendation; and Bab felt that nothing but Sancho's return would ever restore the broken friendship.

Into faithful Betty's bosom did she pour forth her remorseful lamentations, often bursting out with the passionate exclamation, "If I could only find Sanch, and give him back to Ben, I wouldn't care if I tumbled down and broke all my legs right away!" Such abandonment of woe made a deep impression on Betty; and she fell into the way of consoling her sister by cheerful prophecies, and a firm belief that the organ-man would yet appear with the lost darling.

"I've got five cents of my berry money, and I'll buy you an orange if I see any," promised Betty stepping to kiss Bab, as the phaeton came to the door, and Thorny handed in a young lady whose white frock was so stiff with starch that it crackled like paper.

"Lemons will do if oranges are gone. I like 'em to suck with lots of sugar," answered Bab, feeling that the sour sadly predominated in her cup just now.

"Don't she look sweet, the dear!" murmured Mrs. Moss, proudly surveying her youngest.

She certainly did, sitting under the fringed canopy with "Belinda," all in her best, upon her lap, as she turned to smile and nod, with a face so bright and winsome under the little blue hat, that it was no wonder mother and sister thought there never was such a perfect child as "our Betty."

Dr. Mann was busy when they arrived, but would be ready in an hour; so they did their shopping at once, having made sure of the whip as they came along. Thorny added some candy to Bab's lemon, and Belinda had a cake, which her mamma obligingly ate for her. Betty thought that Aladdin's palace could not have been more splendid than the jeweller's shop where the canine cuff-buttons were bought; but when they came to the book-store, she forgot gold, silver, and precious stones, to revel in picture-books, while Thorny selected Ben's modest school outfit. Seeing her delight, and feeling particularly lavish with plenty of money in his pocket, the young gentleman completed the child's bliss by telling her to choose whichever one she liked best out of the pile of Walter Crane's toy-books lying in bewildering colors before her.

"This one; Bab always wanted to see the dreadful cupboard, and there's a picture of it here," answered Betty, clasping a gorgeous copy of "Bluebeard" to the little bosom, which still heaved with the rapture of looking at that delicious mixture of lovely Fatimas in pale azure gowns, pink Sister Annes on the turret top, crimson tyrants, and yellow brothers with forests of plumage blowing wildly from their mushroom-shaped caps.

Very good; there you are, then. Now, come on, for the fun is over and the grind begins," said Thorny, marching away to his doom, with his tongue in his tooth, and trepidation in his manly breast.

"Shall I shut my eyes and hold your head?" quavered devoted Betty, as they went up the stairs so many reluctant feet had mounted before them.

"Nonsense, child, never mind me! You look out of window and amuse yourself; we shall not be long, I guess;" and in went Thorn silently hoping that the dentist had been suddenly called away, or some person with an excruciating toothache would be waiting to take ether, and so give our young man an excuse for postponing his job.

But no; Dr. Mann was quite at leisure, and, full of smiling interest, awaited his victim, laying forth his unpleasant little tools with the exasperating alacrity of his kind. Glad to be released from any share in the operation, Betty retired to the back window to be as far away as possible, and for half in hour was so absorbed in her book that poor Thorny might have groaned dismally without disturbing her.

"Done now, directly, only a trifle of polishing off and a look round," said Dr. Mann, at last; and Thorny, with a yawn that nearly rent him asunder, called out, -

"Thank goodness! Pack up, Bettykin."

"I'm all ready!" and, shutting her book with a start, she slipped down from the easy chair in a great hurry.

But "looking round" took time; and, before the circuit of Thorny's mouth was satisfactorily made, Betty had become absorbed by a more interesting tale than even the immortal "Bluebeard." A noise of children's voices in the narrow alley-way behind the house attracted her attention; the long window opened directly on the yard, and the gate swung in the wind. Curious as Fatima, Betty went to look; but all she saw was a group of excited boys peeping between the bars of another gate further down.

"What's the matter?" she asked of two small girls, who stood close by her, longing but not daring to approach the scene of action.

"Boys chasing a great black cat, I believe," answered one child.

"Want to come and see?" added the other, politely extending the invitation to the stranger.

The thought of a cat in trouble would have nerved Betty to face a dozen boys; so she followed at once, meeting several lads hurrying away on some important errand, to judge from their anxious countenances.

"Hold tight, Jimmy, and let 'em peek, if they want to. He can't hurt anybody now," said one of the dusty huntsmen, who sat on the wide coping of the wall, while two others held the gate, as if a cat could only escape that way.

"You peek first, Susy, and see if it looks nice," said one little girl, boosting her friend so that she could look through the bars in the upper part of the gate.

"No; it's only an ugly old dog!" responded Susy, losing all interest at once, and descending with a bounce.

"He's mad! and Jud's gone to get his gun, so we can shoot him!" called out one mischievous boy, resenting the contempt expressed for their capture.

"Ain't, neither!" howled another lad from his perch. "Mad dogs won't drink; and this one is lapping out of a tub of water."

"Well, he may be, and we don't know him, and he hasn't got any muzzle on, and the police will kill him if Jud don't," answered the sanguinary youth who had first started the chase after the poor animal, which had come limping into town, so evidently a lost dog that no one felt any hesitation in stoning him.

"We must go right home; my mother is dreadful 'fraid of mad dogs, and so is yours," said Susy; and, having satisfied their curiosity, the young ladies prudently retired.

But Betty had not had her "peep," and could not resist one look; for she had heard of these unhappy animals, and thought Bab would like to know how they looked. So she stood on tip-toe and got a good view of a dusty, brownish dog, lying on the grass close by, with his tongue hanging out while he panted, as if exhausted by fatigue and fear, for he still cast apprehensive glances at the wall which divided him from his tormentors.

His eyes are just like Sanch's," said Betty to herself, unconscious that she spoke aloud, till she saw the creature prick up his ears and half rise, as if he had been called.

"He looks as if he knew me, but it isn't our Sancho; he was a lovely dog." Betty said that to the little boy peeping in beside her; but before he could make any reply, the brown beast stood straight up with an inquiring bark, while his eyes shone like topaz, and the short tail wagged excitedly.

"Why, that's just the way Sanch used to do!" cried Betty, bewildered by the familiar ways of this unfamiliar-looking dog.

As if the repetition of his name settled his own doubts, he leaped toward the gate and thrust a pink nose between the bars, with a howl of recognition as Betty's face was more clearly seen. The boys tumbled precipitately from their perches, and the little girl fell back alarmed, yet could not bear to run away and leave those imploring eyes pleading to her through the bars so eloquently.

"He acts just like our dog, but I don't see how it can be him. Sancho, Sancho, is it really you?" called Betty, at her wits' end what to do.

"Bow, wow, wow!" answered the well-known bark, and the little tail did all it could to emphasize the sound, while the eyes were so full of dumb love and joy, the child could not refuse to believe that this ugly stray was their own Sancho strangely transformed.

All of a sudden, the thought rushed into her mind, how glad Ben would be! - and Bab would feel all happy again. "I must carry him home."

Never stopping to think of danger, and forgetting all her doubts, Betty caught the gate handle out of Jimmy's grasp, exclaiming eagerly: "He is our dog! Let me go in; I ain't afraid."

"Not till Jud comes back; he told us we mustn't," answered the astonished Jimmy, thinking the little girl as mad as the dog.

With a confused idea that the unknown Jud had gone for a gun to shoot Sanch, Betty gave a desperate pull at the latch and ran into the yard, bent on saving her friend. That it was a friend there could be no further question; for, though the creature rushed at her as if about to devour her at a mouthful, it was only to roll ecstatically at her feet, lick her hands, and gaze into her face, trying to pant out the welcome which he could not utter. An older and more prudent person would have waited to make sure before venturing in; but confiding Betty knew little of the danger which she might have run; her heart spoke more quickly than her head, and, not stopping to have the truth proved, she took the brown dog on trust, and found it was indeed dear Sanch.

Sitting on the grass, she hugged him close, careless of tumbled hat, dusty paws on her clean frock, or a row of strange boys staring from the wall.

"Darling doggy, where have you been so long?" she cried, the great thing sprawling across her lap, as if he could not get near enough to his brave little protector. "Did they make you black and beat you, dear? Oh, Sanch, where is your tail - your pretty tail?"

A plaintive growl and a pathetic wag was all the answer he could make to these tender inquiries; for never would the story of his wrongs be known, and never could the glory of his doggish beauty be restored. Betty was trying to comfort him with pats and praises, when a new face appeared at the gate, and Thorny's authoritative voice called out, -

"Betty Moss, what on earth are you doing in there with that dirty beast?"

"It's Sanch, it's Sanch! Oh, come and see! shrieked Betty, flying up to lead forth her prize. But the gate was held fast, for some one said the words, "Mad dog," and Thorny was very naturally alarmed, because he had already seen one. "Don't stay there another minute. Get up on that bench and I'll pull you over," directed Thorny, mounting the wall to rescue his charge in hot haste; for the dog did certainly behave queerly, limping hurriedly to and fro, as if anxious to escape. No wonder, when Sancho heard a voice he knew, and recognized another face, yet did not meet as kind a welcome as before.

"No, I'm not coming out till he does. It is Sanch, and I'm going to take him home to Ben," answered Betty, decidedly, as she wet her handkerchief in the rain water to bind up the swollen paw that had travelled many miles to rest in her little hand again.

"You're crazy, child. That is no more Ben's dog than I am."

"See if it isn't!" cried Betty, perfectly unshaken in her faith; and, recalling the words of command as well as she could, she tried to put Sancho through his little performance, as the surest proof that she was right. The poor fellow did his best, weary and foot-sore though he was; but when it came to taking his tail in his mouth to waltz, he gave it up, and, dropping down, hid his face in his paws, as he always did when any of his tricks failed. The act was almost pathetic now, for one of the paws was bandaged, and his whole attitude expressed the humiliation of a broken spirit.

That touched Thorny, and, quite convinced both of the dog's sanity and identity, he sprung down from the wall with Ben's own whistle, which gladdened Sancho's longing ear as much as the boy's rough caresses comforted his homesick heart.

"Now, let's carry him right home, and surprise Ben. Won't he be pleased?" said Betty, so in earnest that she tried to lift the big brute in spite of his protesting yelps.

"You are a little trump to find him out in spite of all the horrid things that have been done to him. We must have a rope to lead him, for he's got no collar and no muzzle. He has got friends though, and I'd like to see any one touch him now. Out of the way, there, boy!" Looking as commanding as a drum-major, Thorny cleared a passage, and with one arm about his neck, Betty proudly led her treasure magnanimously ignoring his late foes, and keeping his eye fixed on the faithful friend whose tender little heart had known him in spite of all disguises.

"I found him, sir," and the lad who had been most eager for the shooting, stepped forward to claim any reward that might be offered for the now valuable victim.

"I kept him safe till she came," added the jailer Jimmy, speaking for himself.

"I said he wasn't mad", cried a third, feeling that his discrimination deserved approval.

"Jud ain't my brother," said the fourth, eager to clear his skirts from all ofi-ence.

"But all of you chased and stoned him, I suppose? You'd better look out or you'll get reported to the Society for the Prevention of Cruelty to Animals."

With this awful and mysterious threat, Thorny slammed the doctor's gate in the faces of the mercenary youths, nipping their hopes in the bud, and teaching them a good lesson.

After one astonished stare, Lita accepted Sancho without demur, and they greeted one another cordially, nose to nose, instead of shaking hands. Then the dog nestled into his old place under the linen duster with a grunt of intense content, and soon fell fast asleep, quite worn out with fatigue. No Roman conqueror bearing untold treasures with him, ever approached the Eternal City feeling richer or prouder than did Miss Betty as she rolled rapidly toward the little brown house with the captive won by her own arms. Poor Belinda was forgotten in a corner, "Bluebeard" was thrust under the cushion, and the lovely lemon was squeezed before its time by being sat upon; for all the child could think of was Ben's delight, Bab's remorseful burden lifted off, "Ma's" surprise, and Miss Celia's pleasure. She could hardly realize the happy fact, and kept peeping under the cover to be sure that the dear dingy bunch at her feet was truly there.

"I'll tell you how we'll do it," said Thorny, breaking a long silence as Betty composed herself with an irrepressible wriggle of delight after one of these refreshing peeps. "We'll keep Sanch hidden, and smuggle him into Ben's old room at your house. Then I'll drive on to the barn, and not say a word, but send Ben to get something out of that room. You just let him in, to see what he'll do. I'll bet you a dollar he won't know his own dog."

"I don't believe I can keep from screaming right out when I see him, but I'll try. Oh, won't it be fun!" - and Betty clapped her hands in joyful anticipation of that exciting moment.

A nice little plan, but Master Thorny forgot the keen senses of the amiable animal snoring peacefully among his boots; and, when they stopped at the Lodge, he had barely time to say in a whisper,

"Ben's coming; cover Sanch and let me get him in quick!" before the dog was out of the phaeton like a bombshell, and the approaching boy went down as if shot, for Sancho gave one leap, and the two rolled over and over, with a shout and a bark of rapturous recognition.

"Who is hurt?" asked Mrs. Moss, running out with floury hands uplifted in alarm.

"Is it a bear?" cried Bab, rushing after her, beater in hand, for a dancing bear was the delight of her heart.

"Sancho's found! Sancho's found!" shouted Thorny, throwing up his hat like a lunatic.

"Found, found, found!" echoed Betty, dancing wildly about as if she too had lost her little wits.

"Where? how? when? who did it?" asked Mrs. Moss, clapping her dusty hands delightedly.

"It isn't; it's an old dirty brown thing," stammered Bab, as the dog came uppermost for a minute, and then rooted into Ben's jacket as if he smelt a woodchuck, and was bound to have him out directly.

Then Thorny, with many interruptions from Betty, poured forth the wondrous tale, to which Bab and his mother listened breathlessly, while the muffins burned as black as a coal, and nobody cared a bit.

"My precious lamb, how did you dare to do such a thing?" exclaimed Mrs. Moss, hugging the small heroine with mingled admiration and alarm.

"I'd have dared, and slapped those horrid boys, too. I wish I'd gone!" and Bab felt that she had for ever lost the chance of distinguishing herself.

"Who cut his tail off?" demanded Ben, in a menacing tone, as he came uppermost in his turn, dusty, red and breathless, but radiant.

"The wretch who stole him, I suppose; and he deserves to be hung," answered Thorny, hotly.

"If ever I catch him, I'll - I'll cut his nose off," roared Ben, with such a vengeful glare that Sanch barked fiercely; and it was well that the unknown "wretch" was not there, for it would have gone hardly with him, since even gentle Betty frowned, while Bab brandished the egg-beater menacingly, and their mother indignantly declared that "it was too bad!"

Relieved by this general outburst, they composed their

outraged feelings; and while the returned wanderer went from one to another to receive a tender welcome from each, the story of his recovery was more calmly told. Ben listened with his eye devouring the injured dog; and when Thorny paused, he turned to the little heroine, saying solemnly, as he laid her hand with his own on Sancho's head,

"Betty Moss, I'll never forget what you did; from this minute half of Sanch is your truly own, and if I die you shall have the whole of him," and Ben sealed the precious gift with a sounding kiss on either chubby check.

Betty was so deeply touched by this noble bequest, that the blue eyes filled and would have overflowed if Sanch had not politely offered his tongue like a red pocket-handkerchlef, and so made her laugh the drops away, while Bab set the rest off by saying gloomily, -

"I mean to play with all the mad dogs I can find; then folks will think I'm smart and give me nice things."

"Poor old Bab, I'll forgive you now, and lend you my half whenever you want it," said Ben, feeling at peace now with all mankind, including, girls who tagged.

"Come and show him to Celia," begged Thorny, eager to fight his battles over again.

"Better wash him up first; he's a sight to see, poor thing," suggested Mrs. Moss, as she ran in, suddenly remembering her muffins.

"It will take a lot of washings to get that brown stuff off. See, his pretty, pink skin is all stained with it. We'll bleach him out, and his curls will grow, and he'll be as good as ever - all but -"

Ben could not finish, and a general wail went up for the departed tassel that would never wave proudly in the breeze again.

"I'll buy him a new one. Now form the procession and let us go in style," said Thorny, cheerily, as he swung Betty to his shoulder and marched away whistling "Hail! the conquering hero comes," while Ben and his Bow-wow followed arm-in-arm, and Bab brought up the rear, banging on a milk-pan with the egg-beater.

CHAPTER XVIII

BOWS AND ARROWS

If Sancho's abduction made a stir, one may easily imagine with what warmth and interest he was welcomed back when his wrongs and wanderings were known. For several days he held regular levees, that curious boys and sympathizing girls might see and pity the changed and curtailed dog. Sancho behaved with dignified affability, and sat upon his mat in the coach-house pensively eying his guests, and patiently submitting to their caresses; while Ben and Thorny took turns to tell the few tragical facts which were not shrouded in the deepest mystery. If the interesting sufferer could only have spoken, what thrilling adventures and hair-breadth escapes he might have related. But, alas! he was dumb; and the secrets of that memorable month never were revealed.

The lame paw soon healed, the dingy color slowly yielded to many washings, the woolly coat began to knot up into little curls, a new collar, handsomely marked, made him a respectable dog, and Sancho was himself again. But it was evident that his sufferings were not forgotten; his once sweet temper was a trifle soured; and, with a few exceptions, he had lost his faith in mankind. Before, he had been the most benevolent and hospitable of dogs; now, he eyed all strangers suspiciously, and the sight of a shabby man made him growl and bristle up, as if the memory of his wrongs still burned hotly within him.

Fortunately, his gratitude was stronger than his resentment, and he never seemed to forget that he owed his life to Betty, - running to meet her whenever she appeared, instantly obeying her commands, and suffering no one to molest her when he walked watchfully beside her, with her hand upon his neck, as they had walked out of the almost fatal backyard together, faithful friends for ever.

LOUISA MAY ALCOTT

Miss Celia called them little Una and her lion, and read the pretty story to the children when they wondered what she meant. Ben, with great pains, taught the dog to spell "Betty," and surprised her with a display of this new accomplishment, which gratified her so much that she was never tired of seeing Sanch paw the five red letters into place, then come and lay his nose in her hand, as if he added, "That's the name of my dear mistress."

Of course Bab was glad to have everything pleasant and friendly again; but in a little dark corner of her heart there was a drop of envy, and a desperate desire to do something which would make every one in her small world like and praise her as they did Betty. Trying to be as good and gentle did not satisfy her; she must do something brave or surprising, and no chance for distinguishing herself in that way seemed likely to appear. Betty was as fond as ever, and the boys were very kind to her; but she felt that they both liked "little Beteinda," as they called her, best, because she found Sanch, and never seemed to know that she had done any thing brave in defending him against all odds. Bab did not tell any one how she felt, but endeavored to be amiable, while waiting for her chance to come; and, when it did arrive, made the most of it, though there was nothing heroic to add a charm.

Miss Celia's arm had been doing very well, but would, of course, be useless for some time longer. Finding that the after-noon readings amused herself as much as they did the children, she kept them up, and brought out all her old favorites enjoying a double pleasure in seeing that her young audience relished them as much as she did when a child for to all but Thorny they were brand new. Out of one of these stories came much amusement for all, and satisfaction for one of the party.

"Celia, did you bring our old bows?" asked her brother, eagerly, as she put down the book from which she had been reading Miss Edgeworth's capital story of "Waste not Want not; or, Two Strings to your Bow."

"Yes, I brought all the playthings we left stored away in uncle's garret when we went abroad. The bows are in the long box where you found the mallets, fishing-rods, and bats. The old quivers and a few arrows are there also, I believe. What is the idea now? asked Miss Celia in her turn, as Thorny bounced up in a great hurry.

"I'm going to teach Ben to shoot. Grand fun this hot weather; and by-and-by we'll have an archery meeting, and you can give us a prize. Come on, Ben. I've got plenty of whip-cord to rig up the bows, and then we'll show the ladies some first-class shooting."

"I can't; never had a decent bow in my life. The little gilt one I used to wave round when I was a Coopid wasn't worth a cent to go," answered Ben, feeling as if that painted "prodigy" must have been a very distant connection of the respectable young person now walking off arm in arm with the lord of the manor.

"Practice is all you want. I used to be a capital shot, but I don't believe I could hit any thing but a barn-door now," answered Thorny, encouragingly.

As the boys vanished, with much tramping of boots and banging of doors, Bab observed, in the young-ladyish tone she was apt to use when she composed her active little mind and body to the feminine task of needlework, -

"We used to make bows of whalebone when we were little girls, but we are too old to play so now."

"I'd like to, but Bab won't, 'cause she's most 'leven years old," said honest Betty, placidly rubbing her needle in the "ruster," as she called the family emery-bag.

"Grown people enjoy archery, as bow and arrow shooting is called, especially in England. I was reading about it the other day, and saw a picture of Queen Victoria with her bow; so you needn't be ashamed of it, Bab," said Miss Celia, rummaging among the books and papers in her sofa corner to find the magazine she wanted, thinking a new play would be as good for the girls as for the big boys.

"A queen, just think!" and Betty looked much impressed by the fact, as well as uplifted by the knowledge that her friend did not agree in thinking her silly because she preferred playing with a harmless home-made toy to firing stones or snapping a pop-gun.

"In old times, bows and arrows were used to fight great battles with; and we read how the English archers shot so well that the air was dark with arrows, and many men were killed."

"So did the Indians have 'em; and I've got some stone arrow-heads, - found 'em by the river, in the dirt!" cried Bab, waking up, for battles interested her more than queens.

"While you finish your stints I'll tell you a little story about the Indians," said Miss Celia, lying back on her cushions, while the needles began to go again, for the prospect of a story could not be resisted.

"A century or more ago, in a small settlement on the banks of the Connecticut, - which means the Long River of Pines, - there lived a little girl called Matty Kilburn. On a hill stood the fort where the people ran for protection in any danger, for the country was new and wild, and more than once the Indians had come down the river in their canoes and burned the houses, killed men, and carried away women and children. Matty lived alone with her father, but felt quite safe in the log house, for he was never far away. One afternoon, as the farmers were all busy in their fields, the bell rang suddenly, - a sign that there was danger near, - and, dropping their rakes or axes, the men hurried to their houses to save wives and babies, and such few treasures as they could. Mr. Kilburn caught up his gun with one hand and his little girl with the other, and ran as fast as he could toward the fort. But before he could reach it he heard a yell, and saw the red men coming up from the river. Then he knew it would be in vain to try to get in, so he looked about for a safe place to hide Matty till he could come for her. He was a brave man, and could fight, so he had no thought of hiding while his neighbors needed help; but the dear little daughter must he cared for first.

"In the corner of the lonely pasture which they dared not cross, stood a big hollow elm, and there the farmer hastily hid Matty, dropping her down into the dim nook, round the mouth of which young shoots had grown, so that no one would have suspected any hole was there.

"Lie still, child, till I come; say your prayers and wait for father,' said the man, as he parted the leaves for a last glance at the small, frightened face looking up at him.

"'Come soon,' whispered Matty, and tried to smile bravely, as a stout settler's girl should.

"Mr. Kilburn went away, and was taken prisoner in the fight, carried off, and for years no one knew whether he was alive or dead. People missed Matty, but supposed she was with her father, and never expected to see her again. A great while afterward the poor man came back, having escaped and made his way through the wilderness to his old home. His first question was for Matty, but no one had seen her; and when he told them where he had left her, they shook their heads as if they thought he was crazy. But they went to look, that he might be satisfied; and he was; for they found some little bones, some faded bits of cloth, and two rusty silver buckles marked with Matty's name in what had once been her shoes. An Indian arrow lay there, too, showing why she had never cried for help, but waited patiently so long for father to come and find her."

If Miss Celia expected to see the last bit of hem done when her story ended, she was disappointed; for not a dozen stitches had been taken. Betty was using her crash towel for a handkerchief, and Bab's lay on the ground as she listened with snapping eyes to the little tragedy.

"Is it true?" asked Betty, hoping to find relief in being told that it was not.

"Yes; I have seen the tree, and the mound where the fort was, and the rusty buckles in an old farmhouse where other Kilburns live, near the spot where it all happened," answered Miss Celia, looking out the picture of Victoria to console her auditors.

"We'll play that in the old apple-tree. Betty can scrooch down, and I'll be the father, and put leaves on her, and then I'll be a great Injun and fire at her. I can make arrows, and it will be fun, won't it?" cried Bab, charmed with the new drama in which she could act the leading parts.

"No, it won't! I don't like to go in a cobwebby hole, and have you play kill me, I'll make a nice fort of hay, and be all safe, and you can put Dinah down there for Matty. I don't love her any more, now her last eye has tumbled out, and you may shoot her just as much as yon like."

Before Bab could agree to this satisfactory arrangement, Thorny appeared, singing, as he aimed at a fat robin, whose red waistcoat looked rather warm and winterish that August day, -

> "So he took up his bow,
> And he feathered his arrow,
> And said, 'I will shoot
> This little cock-sparrow.'"

But he didn't," chirped the robin, flying away, with a contemptuous flirt of his rusty-black tail.

"That is exactly what you must promise not to do, boys. Fire away at your targets as much as you like, but do not harm any living creature," said Miss Celia, as Ben followed armed and equipped with her own long-unused accoutrements.

"Of course we won't if you say so; but, with a little practice, I could bring down a bird as well as that fellow you read to me about with his woodpeckers and larks and herons," answered Thorny, who had much enjoyed the article, while his sister lamented over the destruction of the innocent birds.

"You'd do well to borrow the Squire's old stuffed owl for a target; there would be some chance of your hitting him, he is so big," said his sister, who always made fun of the boy when he began to brag.

Thorny's only reply was to send his arrow straight up so far out of sight that it was a long while coming down again to stick quivering in the ground near by, whence Sancho brought it in his mouth, evidently highly approving of a game in which he could join.

"Not bad for a beginning. Now, Ben, fire away."

But Ben's experience with bows was small, and, in spite of his praiseworthy efforts to imitate his great exemplar, the arrow only turned a feeble sort of somersault and descended perilously near Bab's uplifted nose.

"If you endanger other people's life and liberty in your pursuit of happiness, I shall have to confiscate your arms, boys. Take the orchard for your archery ground; that is safe, and we can see you as we sit here. I wish I had two hands, so that I could paint you a fine, gay target;" and Miss Celia looked regretfully at the injured arm, which as yet was of little use.

"I wish you could shoot, too; you used to beat all the girls, and I was proud of you," answered Thorny, with the air of a fond elder brother; though, at the time he alluded to, he was about twelve, and hardly up to his sister's shoulder.

"Thank you. I shall be happy to give my place to Bab and Betty if you will make them some bows and arrows; they could not use those long ones."

The young gentlemen did not take the hint as quickly as Miss Celia hoped they would; in fact, both looked rather blank at the suggestion, as boys generally do when it is proposed that girls - especially small ones - shall join in any game they are playing.

"P'r'aps it would be too much trouble," began Betty, in her winning little voice.

"I can make my own," declared Bab, with an independent toss of the head.

"Not a bit; I'll make you the jolliest small bow that ever was, Belinda," Thorny hastened to say, softened by the appealing glance of the little maid.

"You can use mine, Bab; you've got such a strong fist, I guess you could pull it," added Ben, remembering that it would not be amiss to have a comrade who shot worse than he did, for he felt very inferior to Thorny in many ways, and, being used to praise, had missed it very much since he retired to private life.

"I will be umpire, and brighten up the silver arrow I sometimes pin my hair with, for a prize, unless we can find something better," proposed Miss Celia, glad to see that question settled, and every prospect of the new play being a pleasant amusement for the hot weather.

It was astonishing how soon archery became the fashion in that town, for the boys discussed it enthusiastically all that evening, formed the "William Tell Club" next day, with Bab and Betty as honorary members, and, before the week was out, nearly every lad was seen, like young Norval, "With bended bow and quiver full of arrows," shooting away, with a charming disregard of the safety of their fellow citizens. Banished by the authorities to secluded spots, the members of the club set up their targets and practised indefatigably, especially Ben, who soon discovered that his early gymnastics had given him a sinewy arm and a true eye; and, taking Sanch into partnership as picker-up, he got more shots out of an hour than those who had to run to and fro.

Thorny easily recovered much of his former skill, but his strength had not fully returned, and he soon grew tired. Bab, on the contrary, threw herself into the contest heart and soul, and tugged away at the new bow Miss Celia gave her, for Ben's was too heavy. No other girls were admitted, so the outsiders got up a club of their own, and called it "The Victoria," the name being suggested by the magazine article, which went the rounds as a general guide and reference book. Bab and Betty belonged to this club and duly reported the doings of the boys, with whom they had a right to shoot if they chose, but soon waived the right, plainly seeing that their absence would be regarded in the light of a favor.

The archery fever raged as fiercely as the base-ball epidemic had done before it, and not only did the magazine circulate freely, but Miss Edgeworth's story, which was eagerly read, and so much admired that the girls at once mounted green ribbons, and the boys kept yards of whip-cord in their pockets like the provident Benjamin of the tale.

Every one enjoyed the new play very much, and something grew out of it which was a lasting pleasure to many, long after the bows and arrows were forgotten. Seeing how glad the children were to get a new story, Miss Celia was moved to send a box of books - old and new - to the town library, which was but scantily supplied, as country libraries are apt to be. This donation produced a good effect; for other people hunted up all the volumes they could spare for the same purpose, and the dusty shelves in the little room behind the post-office filled up amazingly. Coming in vacation time they were hailed with delight, and ancient books of travel, as well as modern tales, were feasted upon by happy young folks, with plenty of time to enjoy them in peace.

The success of her first attempt at being a public benefactor pleased Miss Celia very much, and suggested other ways in which she might serve the quiet town, where she seemed to feel that work was waiting for her to do. She said little to any one but the friend over the sea, yet various plans were made then that blossomed beautifully by-and-by.

CHAPTER XIX

SPEAKING PIECES

The first of September came all too soon, and school began. Among the boys and girls who went trooping up to the "East Corner knowledge-box," as they called it, was our friend Ben, with a pile of neat books under his arm. He felt very strange, and decidedly shy; but put on a bold face, and let nobody guess that, though nearly thirteen, he had never been to school before. Miss Celia had told his story to Teacher, and she, being a kind little woman, with young brothers of her own, made things as easy for him as she could. In reading and writing he did very well, and proudly took his place among lads of his own age; but when it came to arithmetic and geography, he had to go down a long way, and begin almost at the beginning, in spite of Thorny's efforts to "tool him along fast." It mortified him sadly, but there was no help for it; and in some of the classes he had dear little Betty to console with him when he failed, and smile contentedly when he got above her, as he soon began to do, - for she was not a quick child, and plodded through First Parts long after sister Bab was flourishing away among girls much older than herself.

Fortunately, Ben was a short boy and a clever one, so he did not look out of place among the ten and eleven year olders, and fell upon his lessons with the same resolution with which he used to take a new leap, or practise patiently till he could touch his heels with his head. That sort of exercise had given him a strong, elastic little body; this kind was to train his mind, and make its faculties as useful, quick and sure, as the obedient muscles, nerves and eye, which kept him safe where others would have broken their necks. He knew this, and found much consolation in the fact that, though mental arithmetic was a hopeless task, he could turn a dozen somersaults, and come up as steady as a judge. When the boys laughed at him for saying that China was in Africa, he routed them entirely by his superior knowledge of the animals belonging to that wild country; and when "First class in reading" was called, he marched up with the proud consciousness that the shortest boy in it did better than tall Moses Towne or fat Sam Kitteridge.

Teacher praised him all she honestly could, and corrected his many blunders so quietly that he soon ceased to be a deep, distressful red during recitation, and tugged away so manfully that no one could help respecting him for his efforts, and trying to make light of his failures. So the first hard week went by, and though the boy's heart had sunk many a time at the prospect of a protracted wrestle with his own ignorance, he made up his mind to win, and went at it again on the Monday with fresh zeal, all the better and braver for a good, cheery talk with Miss Celia in the Sunday evening twilight.

He did not tell her one of his greatest trials, however, because he thought she could not help him there. Some of the children rather looked down upon him, called him "tramp" and "beggar," twitted him with having been a circus boy, and lived in a tent like a gypsy. They did not mean to be cruel, but did it for the sake of teasing, never stopping to think how much such sport can make a fellow-creature suffer. Being a plucky fellow, Ben pretended not to mind; but he did feel it keenly, because he wanted to start afresh, and be like other boys. He was not ashamed of the old life; but, finding those around him disapproved of it, he was glad to let it be forgotten, even by himself; for his latest recollections were not happy ones, and present comforts made past hardships seem harder than before.

He said nothing of this to Miss Celia; but she found it out, and liked him all the better for keeping some of his small worries to himself. Bab and Betty came over Monday afternoon full of indignation at some boyish insult Sam had put upon Ben; and, finding them too full of it to enjoy the reading, Miss Celia asked what the matter was. Then both little girls burst out in a rapid succession of broken exclamations, which did not give a very clear idea of the difficulty, -

"Sam didn't like it because Ben jumped farther than he did -"

"And he said Ben ought to be in the poor-house."

"And Ben said he ought to be in it pigpen."

"So he had! - such a greedy thing, bringing lovely big apples, and not giving any one a single bite!"

"Then he was mad, and we all laughed; and he said, 'Want to fight?'"

"And Ben said, 'No, thanky, not much fun in pounding a feather-bed.'"

"Oh, he was awfully mad then, and chased Ben up the big maple."

"He's there now, for Sam won't let him come down till he takes it all back."

"Ben won't; and I do believe he'll have to stay up all night," said Betty, distressfully.

"He won't care, and we'll have fun firing up his supper. Nut cakes and cheese will go splendidly; and may be baked pears wouldn't get smashed, he's such a good catch," added Bab, decidedly relishing the prospect.

"If he does not come by tea-time, we will go and look after him. It seems to me I have heard something about Sam's troubling him before, haven't I?" asked Miss Celia, ready to defend her protege against all unfair persecution.

"Yes,'m, Sam and Mose are always plaguing Ben. They are big boys, and we can't make them stop. I won't let the girls do it, and the little boys don't dare to, since Teacher spoke to them." answered Bab.

"Why does not Teacher speak to the big ones?

"Ben won't tell of them, or let us. He says he'll fight his own battles, and hates tell-tales. I guess he won't like to have us tell you, but I don't care, for it is too bad!" and Betty looked ready to cry over her friend's tribulations.

"I'm glad you did, for I will attend to it, and stop this sort of thing," said Miss Celia, after the children had told some of the tormenting speeches which had tried poor Ben.

Just then Thorny appeared, looking much amused. and the little girls both called out in a breath, "Did you see Ben and get him down?"

"He got himself down in the neatest way you can imagine;" and Thorny laughed at the recollection.

"Where is Sam?" asked Bab.

"Staring up at the sky to see where Ben has flown to."

"Oh, tell about it!" begged Betty.

"Well, I came along and found Ben treed, and Sam stoning him. I stopped that at once, and told the 'fat boy' to be off. He said he wouldn't till Ben begged his pardon; and Ben said he wouldn't do it, if he stayed up for a week. I was just preparing to give that rascal a scientific thrashing, when a load of hay came along, and Ben dropped on to it so quietly that Sam, who was trying to bully me, never saw him go. It tickled me so, I told Sam I guessed I'd let him off that time, and walked away, leaving him to hunt for Ben, and wonder where the dickens he had vanished to."

The idea of Sam's bewilderment amused the others as much as Thorny, and they all had a good laugh over it before Miss Celia asked, -

"Where has Ben gone now?"

"Oh, he'll take a little ride, and then slip down and race home full of the fun of it. But I've got to settle Sam. I won't have our Ben hectored by any one -"

"But yourself," put in his sister, with a sly smile, for Thorny was rather domineering at times.

"He doesn't mind my poking him up now and then, it's good for him; and I always take his part against other people. Sam is a bully, and so is Mose; and I'll thrash them both if they don't stop."

Anxious to curb her brother's pugnacious propensities, Miss Celia proposed milder measures, promising to speak to the boys herself if there was any more trouble.

"I have been thinking that we should have some sort of merry-making for Ben on his birthday. My plan was a very simple one; but I will enlarge it, and have all the young folks come, and Ben shall be king of the fun. he needs encouragement in well-doing, for he does try; and now the first hard part is nearly over, I am sure he will get on bravely. If we treat him with respect, and show our regard for him, others will follow our example; and that will be better than fighting about it."

"So it will! What shall we do to make our party tip-top?" asked Thorny, falling into the trap at once; for he dearly loved to get up theatricals, and had not had any for a long time.

"We will plan something splendid, a 'grand combination,' as you used to call your droll mixtures of tragedy, comedy, melodrama and farce," answered his sister, with her head already full of lively plots.

"We'll startle the natives. I don't believe they ever saw a play in all their lives, hey, Bab?"

"I've seen a circus."

"We dress up and do ' Babes in the Wood,'" added Betty, with dignity.

"Pho! that's nothing. I'll show you acting that will make your hair stand on end, and you shall act too. Bab will be capital for the naughty girls," began Thorny, excited by the prospect of producing a sensation on the boards, and always ready to tease the girls.

Before Betty could protest that she did not want her hair to stand up, or Bab could indignantly decline the role offered her, a shrill whistle was heard, and Miss Celia whispered, with a warning look,
-

"Hush! Ben is coming, and he must not know any thing about this yet."

The next day was Wednesday, and in the afternoon Miss Celia went to hear the children "speak pieces," though it was very seldom that any of the busy matrons and elder sisters found time or inclination for these displays of youthful oratory. Miss Celia and Mrs. Moss were all the audience on this occasion, but Teacher was both pleased and proud to see them, and a general rustle went through the school as they came in, all the girls turning from the visitors to nod at Bab and Betty, who smiled all over their round faces to see "Ma" sitting up "'side of Teacher," and the boys grinned at Ben, whose heart began to beat fast at the thought of his dear mistress coming so far to hear him say his piece.

Thorny had recommended Marco Bozzaris, but Ben preferred John Gilpin, and ran the famous race with much spirit, making excellent time in some parts and having to be spurred a little in others, but came out all right, though quite breathless at the end, sitting down amid great applause, some of which, curiously enough, seemed to come from outside; which in fact it did, for Thorny was bound to hear but would not come in, lest his presence should abash one orator at least.

Other pieces followed, all more or less patriotic and warlike, among the boys; sentimental among the girls. Sam broke down in his attempt to give one of Webster's great speeches, Little Cy Fay boldly attacked

"Again to the battle, Achaians!"

and shrieked his way through it in a shrill, small voice, bound to do honor to the older brother who had trained him even if he broke a vessel in the attempt. Billy chose a well-worn piece, but gave it a new interest by his style of delivery; for his gestures were so spasmodic he looked as if going into a fit, and he did such astonishing things with his voice that one never knew whether a howl or a growl would come next. When

"The woods against a stormy sky
Their giant branches tossed; "

Billy's arms went round like the sails of a windmill; the "hymns of lofty cheer" not only "shook the depths of the desert gloom," but the small children on their little benches, and the school-house literally rang "to the anthems of the free!" When "the ocean eagle soared," Billy appeared to be going bodily up, and the "pines of the forest roared" as if they had taken lessons of Van Amburgh's biggest lion. "Woman's fearless eye" was expressed by a wild glare; "manhood's brow, severely high," by a sudden clutch at the reddish locks falling over the orator's hot forehead, and a sounding thump on his blue checked bosom told where "the fiery heart of youth" was located. "What sought they thus far?" he asked, in such a natural and inquiring tone, with his eye fixed on Mamie Peters, that the startled innocent replied, "Dunno," which caused the speaker to close in haste, devoutly pointing a stubby finger upward at the last line.

This was considered the gem of the collection, and Billy took his seat proudly conscious that his native town boasted an orator who, in time, would utterly eclipse Edward Everett and Wendell Phillips.

Sally Folsom led off with "The Coral Grove," chosen for the express purpose of making her friend Almira Mullet start and blush, when she recited the second line of that pleasing poem,

"Where the purple mullet and gold-fish rove."

One of the older girls gave Wordsworth's "Lost Love" in a pensive tone, clasping her hands and bringing out the "O" as if a sudden twinge of toothache seized her when she ended.

"But she is in her grave, and O,
the difference to me!

Bab always chose a funny piece, and on this afternoon set them all laughing by the spirit with which she spoke the droll poem, "Pussy's Class," which some of my young readers may have read. The "meou" and the "sptzz" were capital, and when the "fond mamma rubbed her nose," the children shouted, for Miss Bab made a paw of her hand and ended with an impro-mptu purr, which was considered the best imitation ever presented to an appreciative public. Betty bashfully murmu-rred "Little White Lily," swaying to and fro as regularly as if in no other way could the rhymes be ground out of her memory.

"That is all, I believe. If either of the ladies would like to say a few words to the children, I should be pleased to have them," said Teacher, politely, pausing before she dismissed school with a song.

"Please, 'm. I'd like to speak my piece," answered Miss Celia, obeying a sudden impulse; and, stepping forward with her hat in her hand, she made a pretty courtesy before she recited Mary Howitt's sweet little ballad, "Mabel on Midsummer Day."

She looked so young and merry, and used such simple but expressive gestures, and spoke in such a clear, soft voice that the children sat as if spell-bound, learning several lessons from this new teacher, whose performance charmed them from beginning to end, and left a moral which all could understand and carry away in that last verse, -

"'Tis good to make all duty sweet,
To be alert and kind;
'Tis good, like Littie Mabel,
To have a willing mind."

Of course there was an enthusiastic clapping when Miss Celia sat down, but even while hands applauded, consciences pricked, and undone tasks, complaining words and sour faces seemed to rise up reproachfully before many of the children, as well as their own faults of elocution.

"Now we will sing," said Teacher, and a great clearing of throats ensued, but before a note could be uttered, the half-open door swung wide, and Sancho, with Ben's hat on, walked in upon his hind-legs, and stood with his paws meekly folded, while a voice from the entry sang rapidly, -

"Benny had a little dog,
His fleece was white as snow,
And everywhere that Benny went,
The dog was sure to go.

He went into the School one day,
which was against the rule;
It made the children laugh and play
To see a dog -"

Mischievous Thorny got no further, for a general explosion of laughter drowned the last words, and Ben's command "Out, you rascal!" sent Sanch to the right-about in double-quick time.

Miss Celia tried to apologize for her bad brother, and Teacher tried to assure her that it didn't matter in the least, as this was always a merry time, and Mrs. Moss vainly shook her finger at her naughty daughters; they as well as the others would have their laugh out, and only partially sobered down when the Bell rang for "Attention." They thought they were to be dismissed, and repressed their giggles as well as they could in order to get a good start for a vociferous roar when they got out. But, to their great surprise, the pretty lady stood up again and said, in her friendly way, -

"I just want to thank you for this pleasant little exhibition, and ask leave to come again. I also wish to invite you all to my boy's birthday party on Saturday week. The archery meeting is to be in the afternoon, and both clubs will be there, I believe. In the evening we are going to have some fun, when we can laugh as much as we please without breaking any of the rules. In Ben's name I invite you, and hope you will all come, for we mean to make this the happiest birthday he ever had."

There were twenty pupils in the room, but the eighty hands and feet made such a racket at this announcement that an outsider would have thought a hundred children, at least, must have been at it. Miss Celia was a general favorite because she nodded to all the girls, called the boys by their last names, even addressing some of the largest as "Mr." which won their hearts at once, so that if she had invited them all to come and be whipped they would have gone sure that it was some delightful joke. With what eagerness they accepted the present invitation one can easily imagine, though they never guessed why she gave it in that way, and Ben's face was a sight to see, he was so pleased and proud at the honor done him that he did not know where to look, and was glad to rush out with the other boys and vent his emotions in whoops of delight. He knew that some little plot was being concocted for his birthday, but never dreamed of any thing so grand as asking the whole school, Teacher and all. The effect of the invitation was seen with comical rapidity, for the boys became overpowering in their friendly attentions to Ben. Even Sam, fearing he might be left out, promptly offered the peaceful olive-branch in the shape of a big apple, warm from his pocket, and Mose proposed a trade of jack-knives which would be greatly to Ben's advantage. But Thorny made the noblest sacrifice of all, for he said to his sister, as they walked home together, -

"I'm not going to try for the prize at all. I shoot so much better than the rest, having had more practice, you know, that it is hardly fair. Ben and Billy are next best, and about even, for Ben's strong wrist makes up for Billy's true eye, and both want to win. If I am out of the way Ben stands a good chance, for the other fellows don't amount to much."

"Bab does; she shoots nearly as well as Ben, and wants to win even more than he or Billy. She must have her chance at any rate."

"So she may, but she won't do any thing; girls can't, though it 's good exercise and pleases them to try. "

"If I had full use of both my arms I'd show you that girls can do a great deal when they like. Don't be too lofty, young man, for you may have to come down," laughed Miss Celia, amused by his airs.

"No fear," and Thorny calmly departed to set his targets for Ben's practice.

"We shall see," and from that moment Miss Celia made Bab her especial pupil, feeling that a little lesson would be good for Mr. Thorny, who rather lorded it over the other young people. There was a spice of mischief in it, for Miss Celia was very young at heart, in spite of her twenty-four years, and she was bound to see that her side had a fair chance, believing that girls can do whatever they are willing to strive patiently and wisely for.

So she kept Bab at work early and late, giving her all the hints and help she could with only one efficient hand, and Bab was delighted to think she did well enough to shoot with the club. Her arms ached and her fingers grew hard with twanging the bow, but she was indefatigable, and being a strong, tall child of her age, with a great love of all athletic sports, she got on fast and well, soon learning to send arrow after arrow with ever increasing accuracy nearer and nearer to the bull's-eye.

The boys took very little notice of her, being much absorbed in their own affairs, but Betty did for Bab what Sancho did for Ben, and trotted after arrows till her short legs were sadly tired, though her patience never gave out. She was so sure Bab would win that she cared nothing about her own success, practising little and seldom hitting any thing when she tried.

CHAPTER XX

BEN'S BIRTHDAY

A superb display of flags flapped gayly in the breeze on the September morning when Ben proudly entered his teens. An irruption of bunting seemed to have broken out all over the old house, for banners of every shape and size, color and design, flew from chimney-top to gable, porch and gate-way, making the quiet place look as lively as a circus tent, which was just what Ben most desired and delighted in.

The boys had been up very early to prepare the show, and when it was ready enjoyed it hugely, for the fresh wind made the pennons cut strange capers. The winged lion of Venice looked as if trying to fly away home; the Chinese dragon appeared to brandish his forked tail as he clawed at the Burmese peacock; the double-headed eagle of Russia pecked at the Turkish crescent with one beak, while the other seemed to be screaming to the English royal beast, "Come on and lend a paw." In the hurry of hoisting the Siamese elephant got turned upside down, and now danced gayly on his head, with the stars and stripes waving proudly over him. A green flag with a yellow harp and sprig of shamrock hung in sight of the kitchen window, and Katy, the cook, got breakfast to the tune of "St. Patrick's day in the morning." Sancho's kennel was half hidden under a rustling paper imitation of the gorgeous Spanish banner, and the scarlet sun-and-moon flag of Arabia snapped and flaunted from the pole over the coach-house, as a delicate compliment to Lita, Arabian horses being considered the finest in the world.

The little girls came out to see, and declared it was the loveliest sight they ever beheld, while Thorny played "Hail Columbia" on his fife, and Ben, mounting the gate-post, crowed long and loud like a happy cockerel who had just reached his majority. He had

LOUISA MAY ALCOTT

been surprised and delighted with the gifts he found in his room on awaking and guessed why Miss Celia and Thorny gave him such pretty things, for among them was a match-box made like a mouse-trap. The doggy buttons and the horsey whip were treasures, indeed, for Miss Celia had not given them when they first planned to do so, because Sancho's return seemed to be joy and reward enough for that occasion. But he did not forget to thank Mrs. Moss for the cake she sent him, nor the girls for the red mittens which they had secretly and painfully knit. Bab's was long and thin, with a very pointed thumb, Betty's short and wide, with a stubby thumb, and all their mother's pulling and pressing could not make them look alike, to the great affliction of the little knitters. Ben, however, assured them that he rather preferred odd ones, as then he could always tell which was right and which left. He put them on immediately and went about cracking the new whip with an expression of content which was droll to see, while the children followed after, full of admiration for the hero of the day.

They were very busy all the morning preparing for the festivities to come, and as soon as dinner was over every one scrambled into his or her best clothes as fast as possible, because, although invited to come at two, impatient boys and girls were seen hovering about the avenue as early as one.

The first to arrive, however, was an uninvited guest, for just as Bab and Betty sat down on the porch steps, in their stiff pink calico frocks and white ruffled aprons, to repose a moment before the party came in, a rustling was heard among the lilacs, and out stepped Alfred Tennyson Barlow, looking like a small Robin Hood, in a green blouse with a silver buckle on his broad belt, a feather in his little cap and a bow in his hand.

"I have come to shoot. I heard about it. My papa told me what arching meant. Will there be any little cakes? I like them."

With these opening remarks the poet took a seat and calmly awaited a response. The young ladies, I regret to say, giggled, then remembering their manners, hastened to inform him that there would be heaps of cakes, also that Miss Celia would not mind his coming without an invitation, they were quite sure.

"She asked me to come that day. I have been very busy. I had measles. Do you have them here?" asked the guest, as if anxious to compare notes on the sad subject.

"We had ours ever so long ago. What have you been doing besides having measles?" said Betty, showing a polite interest.

"I had a fight with a bumble-bee."

"Who beat?" demanded Bab.

"I did. I ran away and he couldn't catch me."

"Can you shoot nicely?"

"I hit a cow. She did not mind at all. I guess she thought it was a fly."

"Did your mother know you were coming?" asked Bab, feeling an interest in runaways.

"No; she is gone to drive, so I could not ask her."

"It is very wrong to disobey. My Sunday-school book says that children who are naughty that way never go to heaven," observed virtuous Betty, in a warning tone.

"I do not wish to go," was the startling reply.

"Why not?" asked Betty, severely.

"They don't have any dirt there. My mamma says so. I am fond of dirt. I shall stay here where there is plenty of it," and the candid youth began to grub in the mould with the satisfaction of a genuine boy.

"I am afraid you're a very bad child."

"Oh yes, I am. My papa often says so and he knows all about it," replied Alfred with an involuntary wriggle suggestive of painful memories. Then, as if anxious to change the conversation from its somewhat personal channel, he asked, pointing to a row of grinning heads above the wall, "Do you shoot at those?"

Bab and Betty looked up quickly and recognized the familiar faces of their friends peering down at them, like a choice collection of trophies or targets.

"I should think you'd be ashamed to peek before the party was ready!" cried Bab, frowning darkly upon the merry young ladies.

"Miss Celia told us to come before two, and be ready to receive folks, if she wasn't down," added Betty, importantly.

"It is striking two now. Come along, girls;" and over scrambled Sally Folsom, followed by three or four kindred spirits, just as their hostess appeared.

"You look like Amazons storming a fort," she said, as the girls cattle up, each carrying her bow and arrows, while green ribbons flew in every direction.

"How do you do, sir? I have been hoping you would call again," added Miss Celia, shaking hands with the pretty boy, who regarded with benign interest the giver of little cakes.

Here a rush of boys took place, and further remarks were cut short, for every one was in a hurry to begin. So the procession was formed at once, Miss Celia taking the lead, escorted by Ben in the post of honor, while the boys and girls paired off behind, arm in arm, bow on Shoulder, in martial array. Thorny and Billy were the band, and marched before, fifing and drumming "Yankee Doodle" with a vigor which kept feet moving briskly, made eyes sparkle, and young hearts dance under the gay gowns and summer jackets. The interesting stranger was elected to bear the prize, laid out on a red pin-cushion; and did so with great dignity, as he went beside the standard bearer, Cy Fay, who bore Ben's choicest flag, snow-white, with a green wreath surrounding a painted bow and arrow, and with the letters W. T. C. done in red below.

Such a merry march all about the place, out at the Lodge gate, up and down the avenue, along the winding paths, till they halted in the orchard, where the target stood, and seats were placed for the archers while they waited for their turns. Various rules and regulations were discussed, and then the fun began. Miss Celia had insisted that the girls should be invited to shoot with the boys; and the lads consented without much concern, whispering to one another with condescending shrugs, "Let 'em try, if they like; they can't do any thing."

There were various trials of skill before the great match came off, and in these trials the young gentlemen discovered that two at least of the girls could do something; for Bab and Sally shot better than many of the boys, and were well rewarded for their exertions by, the change which took place in the faces and conversation of their mates.

"Why, Bab, you do as well as if I'd taught you myself," said Thorny, much surprised and not altogether pleased at the little girl's skill.

"A lady taught me; and I mean to beat every one of you," answered Bab, saucily, while her sparkling eyes turned to Miss Celia with a mischievous twinkle in them.

"Not a bit of it," declared Thorny, stoutly; but he went to Ben and whispered, "Do your best, old fellow, for sister has taught Bab all the scientific points, and the little rascal is ahead of Billy."

"She won't get ahead of me," said Ben, picking out his best arrow, and trying the string of his bow with a confident air which re-assured Thorny, who found it impossible to believe that a girl ever could, would, or should excel a boy in any thing he cared to try.

It really did look as if Bab would beat when the match for the prize came off; and the children got more and more excited as the six who were to try for it took turns at the bull's-eye. Thorny was umpire, and kept account of each shot, for the arrow which went nearest the middle would win. Each had three shots; and very soon the lookers-on saw that Ben and Bab were the best marksmen, and one of them would surely get the silver arrow.

Sam, who was too lazy to practise, soon gave up the contest, saying, as Thorny did, "It wouldn't be fair for such a big fellow to try with the little chaps," which made a laugh, as his want of skill was painfully evident. But Mose went at it gallantly; and, if his eye had been as true as his arms were strong, the "little chaps" would have trembled. But his shots were none of them as near as Billy's; and he retired after the third failure, declaring that it was impossible to shoot against the wind, though scarcely a breath was stirring.

Sally Folsom was bound to beat Bab, and twanged away in great style; all in vain, however, as with tall Maria Newcomb, the third girl who attempted the trial. Being a little near-sighted, she had borrowed her sister's eye-glasses, and thereby lessened her chance of success; for the pinch on her nose distracted her attention, and not one of her arrows went beyond the second ring to her great disappointment. Billy did very well, but got nervous when his last shot came, and just missed the bull's-eye by being in a hurry.

Bab and Ben each had one turn more; and, as they were about even, that last arrow would decide the victory. Both had sent a shot into the bull's-eye, but neither was exactly in the middle; so there was room to do better, even, and the children crowded round, crying eagerly, "Now, Ben!" "Now, Bab!" "Hit her up, Ben!" "Beat him, Bab!" while Thorny looked as anxious as if the fate of the country depended on the success of his man. Bab's turn came first; and, as Miss Celia examined her bow to see that all was right, the little girl said, With her eyes on her rival's excited face, -

"I want to beat, but Ben will feel so bad, I 'most hope I sha'n't."

"Losing a prize sometimes makes one happier than gaining it. You have proved that you could do better than most of them; so, if you do not beat, you may still feet proud," answered Miss Celia, giving back the bow with a smile that said more than her words.

It seemed to give Bab a new idea, for in a minute all sorts of recollections, wishes, and plans rushed through her lively little mind, and she followed a sudden generous impulse as blindly as she often did a wilful one.

"I guess he'll beat," she said, softly, with a quick sparkle of the eyes, as she stepped to her place and fired without taking her usual careful aim.

Her shot struck almost as near the centre on the right as her last one had hit on the left; and there was a shout of delight from the girls as Thorny announced it before he hurried back to Ben, whispering anxiously, -

"Steady, old Man, steady; you must beat that, or we shall never hear the last of it."

Ben did not say, "She won't get ahead of me," as he had said at the first; he set his teeth, threw off his hat, and, knitting his brows with a resolute expression, prepared to take steady aim, though his heart beat fast and his thumb trembled as he pressed it on the bowstring.

"I hope you'll beat, I truly do," said Bab, at his elbow; and, as if the breath that framed the generous wish helped it on its way, the arrow flew straight to the bull's-eye, hitting, apparently, the very spot where Bab's best shot had left a hole.

"A tie! a tie!" cried the girls, as a general rush took place toward the target.

"No, Ben's is nearest. Ben's beat! Hooray shouted the boys, throwing up their hats. There was only a hair's-breadth difference, and Bab could honestly have disputed the decision; but she did not, though for an instant she could not help wishing that the cry had been "Bab's beat! Hurrah!" it sounded so pleasant. Then she saw Ben's beaming face, Thorny's intense relief, and caught the look Miss Celia sent her over the heads of the boys, and decided, with a sudden warm glow all over her little face, that losing a prize did sometimes make one happier than winning it. Up went her best hat, and she burst out in a shrill, "Rah, rah, rah!" that sounded very funny coming all alone after the general clamor had subsided.

"Good for you, Bab! you are an honor to the club. and I'm proud of you", said Prince Thorny, with a hearty handshake; for, as his man had won, he could afford to praise the rival who had put him on his mettle, though she was a girl.

Bab was much uplifted by the royal commendation, but a few minutes later felt pleased as well as proud when Ben, having received the prize, came to her, as she stood behind a tree sucking her blistered thumb, while Betty braided up her dishevelled locks.

"I think it would be fairer to call it a tie, Bab, for it really was, and I want you to wear this. I wanted the fun of beating, but I don't care a bit for this girl's thing and I'd rather see it on you."

As he spoke, Ben offered the rosette of green ribbon which held the silver arrow, and Bab's eyes brightened as they fell upon the pretty ornament, for to her "the girl's thing" was almost as good as the victory.

"Oh no; you must wear it to show who won. Miss Celia wouldn't like it. I don't mind not getting it; I did better than all the rest, and I guess I shouldn't like to beat you," answered Bab, unconsciously putting into childish words the sweet generosity which makes so many sisters glad to see their brothers carry off the prizes of life, while they are content to know that they have earned them and can do without the praise.

But if Bab was generous, Ben was just; and though he could not explain the feeling, would not consent to take all the glory without giving his little friend a share.

"You must wear it; I shall feel real mean if you don't. You worked harder than I did, and it was only luck my getting this. Do, Bab, to please me," he persisted, awkwardly trying to fasten the ornament in the middle of Bab's' white apron.

"Then I will. Now do you forgive me for losing Sancho?" asked Bab, with a wistful look which made Ben say, heartily, -

"I did that when he came home."

"And you don't think I'm horrid?"

"Not a bit of it; you are first-rate, and I'll stand by you like a man, for you are 'most as good as a boy!" cried Ben, anxious to deal handsomely with his feminine rival, whose skill had raised her immensely in his opinion.

Feeling that he could not improve that last compliment, Bab was fully satisfied, and let him leave the prize upon her breast, conscious that she had some claim to it.

"That is where it should be, and Ben is a true knight, winning the prize that he may give it to his lady, while he is content with the victory," said Miss Celia, laughingly, to Teacher, as the children ran off to join in the riotous games which soon made the orchard ring.

"He learned that at the circus 'tunnyments,' as he calls them. He is a nice boy, and I am much interested in him; for he has the two things that do most toward making a man, patience and courage," answered Teacher, also as she watched the young knight play and the honored lady tearing about in a game of tag.

"Bab is a nice child, too," said Miss Celia; "she is as quick as a flash to catch an idea and carry it out, though very often the ideas are wild ones. She could have won just now, I fancy, if she had tried, but took the notion into her head that it was nobler to let Ben win, and so atone for the trouble she gave him in losing the dog. I saw a very sweet look on her face just now, and am sure that Ben will never know why he beat."

"She does such things at school sometimes, and I can't bear to spoil her little atonements, though they are not always needed or very wise," answered Teacher. "Not long ago I found that she had been giving her lunch day after day to a poor child who seldom had any, and when I asked her why, she said, with tears, 'I used to laugh at Abby, because she had only crusty, dry bread, and so she wouldn't bring any. I ought to give her mine and be hungry, it was so mean to make fun of her poorness."

"Did you stop the sacrifice?"

"No; I let Bab 'go halves,' and added an extra bit to my own lunch, so I could make my contribution likewise."

"Come and tell me about Abby. I want to make friends with our poor people, for soon I shall have a right to help them;" and, putting her arm in Teacher's, Miss Celia led her away for a quiet chat in the porch, making her guest's visit a happy holiday by confiding several plans and asking advice in the friendliest way.

CHAPTER XXI

CUPID'S LAST APPEARANCE

A picnic supper on the grass followed the games, and then, as twilight began to fall, the young people were marshalled to the coach-house, now transformed into a rustic theatre. One big door was open, and seats, arranged lengthwise, faced the red table-cloths which formed the curtain. A row of lamps made very good foot-lights, and an invisible band performed a Wagner-like overture on combs, tin trumpets, drums, and pipes, with an accompaniment of suppressed laughter.

Many of the children had never seen any thing like it, and sat staring about them in mute admiration and expectancy; but the older ones criticised freely, and indulged in wild speculations as to the meaning of various convulsions of nature going on behind the curtain.

While Teacher was dressing the actresses for the tragedy, Miss Celia and Thorny, who were old hands at this sort of amusement, gave a "Potato" pantomime as a side show.

Across an empty stall a green cloth was fastened, so high that the heads of the operators were not seen. A little curtain flew up, disclosing the front of a Chinese pagoda painted on pasteboard, with a door and window which opened quite naturally. This stood on one side, several green trees with paper lanterns hanging from the boughs were on the other side, and the words "Tea Garden," printed over the top, showed the nature of this charming spot.

Few of the children had ever seen the immortal Punch and Judy, so this was a most agreeable novelty, and before they could make out what it meant, a voice began to sing, so distinctly that every word was heard, -

"In China there lived a little man,
His name was Chingery Wangery Chan."

Here the hero "took the stage" with great dignity, clad in a loose
yellow jacket over a blue skirt, which concealed the hand that
made his body. A pointed hat adorned his head, and on removing
this to bow he disclosed a bald pate with a black queue in the
middle, and a Chinese face nicely painted on the potato, the lower
part of which was hollowed out to fit Thorny's first finger, while
his thumb and second finger were in the sleeves of the yellow
jacket, making a lively pair of arms. While he saluted, the song
went n, -

"His legs were short, his feet were small,
And this little man could not walk at all."

Which assertion was proved to be false by the agility with which
the "little man" danced a jig in time to the rollicking chorus, -

"Chingery changery ri co day,
Ekel tekel happy man;
Uron odesko canty oh, oh,
Gallopy wallopy China go."

At the close of the dance and chorus, Chan retired into the tea
garden, and drank so many cups of the national beverage, with
such comic gestures, that the spectators were almost sorry when
the opening of the opposite window drew all eyes in that direction.
At the lattice appeared a lovely being; for this potato had been
pared, and on the white surface were painted pretty pink checks,
red lips, black eyes, and oblique brows; through the tuft of dark
silk on the head were stuck several glittering pins, and a pink
jacket shrouded the plump figure of this capital little Chinese lady.
After peeping coyly out, so that all could see and admire, she fell
to counting the money from a purse, so large her small hands
could hardly hold it on the window seat. While she did this, the
song went on to explain, -

"Miss Ki Hi was short and squat,
She had money and he had not
So off to her he resolved to go,
And play her a tune on his little banjo."

During the chorus to this verse Chan was seen tuning his instrument in the garden, and at the end sallied gallantly forth to sing the following tender strain, -

"Whang fun li,
Tang hua ki,
Hong Kong do ra me!
Ah sin lo,
Pan to fo,
Tsing up chin leute!"

Carried away by his passion, Chan dropped his banjo, fell upon his knees, and, clasping his hands, bowed his forehead in the dust before his idol. But, alas! -

"Miss Ki Hi heard his notes of love,
And held her wash-bowl up above
It fell upon the little man,
And this was the end of Chingery Chan,"

Indeed it was; for, as the doll's basin of real water was cast forth by the cruel charmer, poor Chan expired in such strong convulsions that his head rolled down among the audience. Miss Ki Hi peeped to see what had become of her victim, and the shutter decapitated her likewise, to the great delight of the children, who passed around the heads, pronouncing a "Potato" pantomime "first-rate fun."

Then they settled themselves for the show, having been assured by Manager Thorny that they were about to behold the most elegant and varied combination ever produced on any stage. And when one reads the following very inadequate description of the somewhat mixed entertainment, it is impossible to deny that the promise made was nobly kept.

After some delay and several crashes behind the curtain, which mightily amused the audience, the performance began with the well-known tragedy of "Bluebeard;" for Bab had set her heart upon it, and the young folks had acted it so often in their plays that it was very easy to get up, with a few extra touches to scenery and costumes. Thorny was superb as the tyrant with a beard of bright blue worsted, a slouched hat and long feather, fur cloak, red hose, rubber boots, and a real sword which clanked tragically as he walked. He spoke in such a deep voice, knit his corked eye-brows, and glared so frightfully, that it was no wonder poor Fatima quaked before him as he gave into her keeping an immense bunch of keys with one particularly big, bright one, among them.

Bab was fine to see, with Miss Celia's blue dress sweeping behind her, a white plume in her flowing hair, and a real necklace with a pearl locket about her neck. She did her part capitally, especially the shriek she gave when she looked into the fatal closet, the energy with which she scrubbed the tell-tale key, and her distracted tone when she called out: "Sister Anne, O, sister Anne, do you see anybody coming?" while her enraged husband was roaring: "Will you come down, madam, or shall I come and fetch you?"

Betty made a captivating Anne, - all in white muslin, and a hat full of such lovely pink roses that she could not help putting up one hand to feel them as she stood on the steps looking out at the little window for the approaching brothers who made such a din that it sounded like a dozen horsemen instead if two.

Ben and Billy were got up regardless of expense in the way of arms; for their belts were perfect arsenals, and their wooden swords were big enough to strike terror into any soul, though they struck no sparks out of Bluebeard's blade in the awful combat which preceded the villain's downfall and death.

The boys enjoyed this part intensely, and cries of "Go it, Ben!" "Hit him again, Billy!" "Two against one isn't fair!" "Thorny's a match for 'em." "Now he's down, hurray!" cheered on the combatants, till, after a terrific struggle, the tyrant fell, and with convulsive twitchings of the scarlet legs, slowly expired while the ladies sociably fainted in each other's arms, and the brothers waved their swords and shook hands over the corpse of their enemy.

This piece was rapturously applauded, and all the performers had to appear and bow their thanks, led by the defunct Bluebeard, who mildly warned the excited audience that if they "didn't look out the seats would break down, and then there'd be a nice mess."

Calmed by this fear they composed themselves, and waited with ardor for the next play, which promised to be a lively one, judging from the shrieks of laughter which came from behind the curtain.

"Sanch 's going to be in it, I know; for I heard Ben say, 'Hold him still; he won't bite,'" whispered Sam, longing to "jounce up and down, so great was his satisfaction at the prospect, for the dog was considered the star of the company.

"I hope Bab will do something else, she is so funny. Wasn't her dress elegant?" said Sally Folsum, burning to wear a long silk gown and a feather in her hair.

"I like Betty best, she's so cunning, and she peeked out of the window just as if she really saw somebody coming," answered Liddy Peckham, privately resolving to tease mother for some pink roses before another Sunday came.

Up went the curtain at last, and a voice announced "A Tragedy in Three Tableaux." "There's Betty!" was the general exclamation, as the audience recognized a familiar face under the little red hood worn by the child who stood receiving a basket from Teacher, who made a nice mother with her finger up, as if telling the small messenger not to loiter by the way.

"I know what that is!" cried Sally; "it's 'Mabel on Midsummer Day.' The piece Miss Celia spoke; don't you know?"

"There isn't any sick baby, and Mabel had a 'kerchief pinned about her head.' I say it's Red Riding Hood," answered Liddy, who had begun to learn Mary Howitt's pretty poem for her next piece, and knew all about it.

The question was settled by the appearance of the wolf in the second scene, and such a wolf! On few amateur stages do we find so natural an actor for that part, or so good a costume, for Sanch was irresistibly droll in the gray wolf-skin which usually lay beside Miss Celia's bed, now fitted over his back and fastened neatly down underneath, with his own face peeping out at one end, and the handsome tail bobbing gayly at the other. What a comfort that tail was to Sancho, none but a bereaved bow-wow could ever tell. It reconciled him to his distasteful part at once, it made rehearsals a joy, and even before the public he could not resist turning to catch a glimpse of the noble appendage, while his own brief member wagged with the proud consciousness that though the tail did not match the head, it was long enough to be seen of all men and dogs.

That was a pretty picture, for the little maid came walking in with the basket on her arm, and such an innocent face inside the bright hood that it was quite natural the gray wolf should trot up to her with deceitful friendliness, that she should pat and talk to him confidingly about the butter for grandma, and then that they should walk away together, he politely carrying her basket, she with her hand on his head, little dreaming what evil plans were taking shape inside.

The children encored that, but there was no time to repeat it, so they listened to more stifled merriment behind the red table-cloths, and wondered whether the next scene would be the wolf popping his head out of the window as Red Riding Hood knocks, or the tragic end of that sweet child.

It was neither, for a nice bed had been made, and in it reposed the false grandmother, with a ruffled nightcap on, a white gown, and spectacles. Betty lay beside the wolf, staring at him as if just about to say, "Why, grandma, what great teeth you've got!" for Sancho's mouth was half open and a red tongue hung out, as he panted with the exertion of keeping still. This tableau was so very good, and yet so funny, that the children clapped and shouted frantically; this excited the dog, who gave a bounce and would have leaped off the bed to bark at the rioters, if Betty had not caught him by the legs, and Thorny dropped the curtain just at the moment when the wicked wolf was apparently in the act of devouring the poor little girl, with most effective growls.

They had to come out then, and did so, both much dishevelled by the late tussle, for Sancho's cap was all over one eye, and Betty's hood was anywhere but on her head. She made her courtesy prettily, however; her fellow-actor bowed with as much dignity as a short night-gown permitted, and they retired to their well-earned repose.

Then Thorny, looking much excited, appeared to make the following request: "As one of the actors in the next piece is new to the business, the company must all keep as still as mice, and not stir till I give the word. It's perfectly splendid! so don't you spoil it by making a row."

"What do you suppose it is?" asked every one, and listened with all their might to get a hint, if possible. But what they heard only whetted their curiosity and mystified them more and more. Bab's voice cried in a loud whisper, "Isn't Ben beautiful?" Then there was a thumping noise, and Miss Celia said, in an anxious tone, "Oh, do be careful," while Ben laughed out as if he was too happy to care who heard him, and Thorny bawled "Whoa!" in a way which would have attracted attention if Lita's head had not popped out of her box, more than once, to survey the invaders of her abode, with a much astonished expression.

"Sounds kind of circusy, don't it?" said Sam to Billy, who had come out to receive the compliments of the company and enjoy the tableau at a safe distance.

"You just wait till you see what's coming. It beats any circus I ever saw," answered Billy, rubbing his hands with the air of a man who had seen many instead of but one.

"Ready! Be quick and get out of the way when she goes off!" whispered Ben, but they heard him and prepared for pistols, rockets or combustibles of some sort, as ships were impossible under the circumstances, and no other "She" occurred to them.

A unanimous "O-o-o-o !" was heard when the curtain rose, but a stern "Hush!" from Thorny kept them mutely staring with all their eyes at the grand spectacle of the evening. There stood Lita with a wide flat saddle on her back, a white head-stall and reins, blue rosettes in her ears, and the look of a much-bewildered beast in her bright eyes. But who the gauzy, spangled, winged creature was, with a gilt crown on its head, a little bow in its hand, and one white slipper in the air, while the other seemed merely to touch the saddle, no one could tell for a minute, so strange and splendid did the apparition appear. No wonder Ben was not recognized in this brilliant disguise, which was more natural to him than Billy's blue flannel or Thorny's respectable garments. He had so begged to be allowed to show himself "just once," as he used to be in the days when "father" tossed him up on the bare-backed old General, for hundreds to see and admire, that Miss Celia had consented, much against her will, and hastily arranged some bits of spangled tarlatan over the white cotton suit which was to simulate the regulation tights. Her old dancing slippers fitted, and gold paper did the rest, while Ben, sure of his power over Lita, promised not to break his bones, and lived for days on the thought of the moment when he could show the boys that he had not boasted vainly of past splendors.

Before the delighted children could get their breath, Lita gave signs of her dislike to the foot-lights, and, gathering up the reins that lay on her neck, Ben gave the old cry, "Houp-la!" and let her go, as he had often done before, straight out of the coach-house for a gallop round the orchard.

"Just turn about and you can see perfectly well, but stay where you are till he comes back," commanded Thorny, as signs of commotion appeared in the excited audience.

Round went the twenty children as if turned by one crank, and sitting there they looked out into the moonlight where the shining figure flashed to and fro, now so near they could see the smiling face under the crown, now so far away that it glittered like a firefly among the dusky green. Lita enjoyed that race as heartily as she had done several others of late, and caracoled about as if anxious to make up for her lack of skill by speed and obedience. How much Ben liked it there is no need to tell, yet it was a proof of the good which three months of a quiet, useful life had done him, that even as he pranced gayly under the boughs thick with the red and yellow apples almost ready to be gathered, he found this riding in the fresh air with only his mates for an audience pleasanter than the crowded tent, the tired horses, profane men, and painted women, friendly as some of them had been to him.

After the first burst was over, he felt rather glad, on the whole, that he was going back to plain clothes, helpful school, and kindly people, who cared more to have him a good boy than the most famous Cupid that ever stood on one leg with a fast horse under him.

"You may make as much noise as you like, now; Lita's had her run and will be as quiet as a lamb after it. Pull up, Ben, and come in; sister says you'll get cold," shouted Thorny, as the rider came cantering round after a leap over the lodge gate and back again.

So Ben pulled up, and the admiring boys and girls were allowed to gather about him, loud in their praises as they examined the pretty mare and the mythological character who lay easily on her back.

He looked very little like the god of love now; for he had lost one slipper and splashed his white legs with dew and dust, the crown had slipped down upon his neck, and the paper wings hung in an apple-tree where he had left them as he went by. No trouble in recognizing Ben, now; but somehow he didn't want to be seen, and, instead of staying to be praised, he soon slipped away, making Lita his excuse to vanish behind the curtain while the rest went into the house to have a finishing-off game of blindman's-buff in the big kitchen.

"Well, Ben, are you satisfied?" asked Miss Celia, as she stayed a moment to unpin the remains of his gauzy scarf and tunic.

"Yes, 'm, thank you, it was tip-top."

"But you look rather sober. Are you tired, or is it because you don't want to take these trappings off and be plain Ben again?" she said, looking down into his face as he lifted it for her to free him from his gilded collar.

"I want to take 'em off; for somehow I don't feel respectable," and he kicked away the crown he had helped to make so carefully, adding with a glance that said more than his words: "I'd rather be 'plain Ben' than any one else, for you like to have me."

"Indeed I do; and I'm so glad to hear you say that, because I was afraid you'd long to be off to the old ways, and all I've tried to do would be undone. Would you like to go back, Ben?" and Miss Celia held his chin an instant, to watch the brown face that looked so honestly back at her.

"No, I wouldn't - unless - he was there and wanted me."

The chin quivered just a bit, but the black eyes were as bright as ever, and the boy's voice so earnest, she knew he spoke the truth, and laid her white hand softly on his head, as she answered in the tone he loved so much, because no one else had ever used it to him, -

"Father is not there; but I know he wants you, dear, and I am sure he would rather see you in a home like this than in the place you came from. Now go and dress; but, tell me first, has it been a happy birthday?"

"Oh, Miss Celia! I didn't know they could be so beautiful, and this is the beautifulest part of it; I don't know how to thank you, but I'm going to try - " and, finding words wouldn't come fast enough, Ben just put his two arms round her, quite speechless with gratitude; then, as if ashamed of his little outburst, he knelt down in a great hurry to untie his one shoe.

But Miss Celia liked his answer better than the finest speech ever made her, and went away through the moonlight, saying to herself, -

"If I can bring one lost lamb into the fold, I shall be the fitter for a shepherd's wife, by-and-by."

CHAPTER XXII

A BOY'S BARGAIN

It was some days before the children were tired of talking over Ben's birthday party; for it was a great event in their small world; but, gradually, newer pleasures came to occupy their minds, and they began to plan the nutting frolics which always followed the early frosts. While waiting for Jack to open the chestnut burrs, they varied the monotony of school life by a lively scrimmage long known as "the wood-pile fight."

The girls liked to play in the half-empty shed, and the boys, merely for the fun of teasing, declared that they should not, so blocked up the doorway as fast as the girls cleared it. Seeing that the squabble was a merry one, and the exercise better for all than lounging in the sun or reading in school during recess, Teacher did not interfere, and the barrier rose and fell almost as regularly as the tide.

It would be difficult to say which side worked the harder; for the boys went before school began to build up the barricade, and the girls stayed after lessons were over to pull down the last one made in afternoon recess. They had their play-time first; and, while the boys waited inside, they heard the shouts of the girls, the banging of the wood, and the final crash, as the well-packed pile went down. Then, as the lassies came in, rosy, breathless, and triumphant, the lads rushed out to man the breach, and labor gallantly till all was as tight as hard blows could make it.

So the battle raged, and bruised knuckles, splinters in fingers, torn clothes, and rubbed shoes, were the only wounds received, while a great deal of fun was had out of the maltreated logs, and a lasting peace secured between two of the boys.

When the party was safely over, Sam began to fall into his old way of tormenting Ben by calling names, as it cost no exertion to invent trying speeches, and slyly utter them when most likely to annoy. Ben bore it as well as he could; but fortune favored him at last, as it usually does the patient, and he was able to make his own terms with his tormentor.

When the girls demolished the wood-pile, they performed a jubilee chorus on combs, and tin kettles, played like tambourines; the boys celebrated their victories with shrill whistles, and a drum accompaniment with fists on the shed walls. Billy brought his drum, and this was such an addition that Sam hunted up an old one of his little brother's, in order that he might join the drum corps. He had no sticks, however, and, casting about in his mind for a good substitute for the genuine thing, bethought him of bulrushes.

"Those will do first-rate, and there are lots in the ma'sh, if I can only get 'em," he said to himself, and turned off from the road on his way home to get a supply.

Now, this marsh was a treacherous spot, and the tragic story was told of a cow who got in there and sank till nothing was visible but a pair of horns above the mud, which suffocated the unwary beast. For this reason it was called "Cowslip Marsh," the wags said, though it was generally believed to be so named for the yellow flowers which grew there in great profusion in the spring.

Sam had seen Ben hop nimbly from one tuft of grass to another when he went to gather cowslips for Betty, and the stout boy thought he could do the same. Two or three heavy jumps landed him, not among the bulrushes, as he had hoped, but in a pool of muddy water, where he sank up to his middle with alarming rapidity. Much scared, he tried to wade out, but could only flounder to a tussock of grass, and cling there, while he endeavored to kick his legs free. He got them out, but struggled in vain to coil them up or to hoist his heavy body upon the very small island in this sea of mud. Down they splashed again; and Sam gave a dismal groan as he thought of the leeches and water-snakes which might be lying in wait below. Visions of the lost cow also flashed across his agitated mind, and he gave a despairing shout very like a distracted "Moo!"

Few people passed along the lane, and the sun was setting, so the prospect of a night in the marsh nerved Sam to make a frantic plunge toward the bulrush island, which was nearer than the mainland, and looked firmer than any tussock round him. But he failed to reach this haven of rest, and was forced to stop at an old stump which stuck up, looking very like the moss-grown horns of the "dear departed." Roosting here, Sarn began to shout for aid in every key possible to the human voice. Such hoots and howls, whistles and roars, never woke the echoes of the lonely marsh before, or scared the portly frog who resided there in calm seclusion.

He hardly expected any reply but the astonished Caw!" of the crow, who sat upon a fence watching him with gloomy interest; and when a cheerful "Hullo, there!" sounded from the lane, he was so grateful that tears of joy rolled down his fat cheeks.

"Come on! I'm in the ma'sh. Lend a hand and get me out!" bawled Sam, anxiously waiting for his deliverer to appear, for he could only see a hat bobbing along behind the hazel-bushes that fringed the lane.

Steps crashed through the bushes, and then over the wall came an active figure, at the sight of which Sam was almost ready to dive out of sight, for, of all possible boys, who should it be but Ben, the last person in the world whom he would like to have see him in his present pitiful plight.

"Is it you, Sam? Well, you are in a nice fix!" and Ben's eyes began to twinkle with mischievous merriment, as well they might, for Sam certainly was a spectacle to convulse the soberest person. Perched unsteadily on the gnarled stump, with his muddy legs drawn up, his dismal face splashed with mud, and the whole lower half of his body as black as if he had been dipped in an inkstand, he presented such a comically doleful object that Ben danced about, laughing like a naughty will-o'-the-wisp who, having led a traveller astray then fell to jeering at him.

"Stop that, or I'll knock your head off!" roared Sam, in a rage.

"Come on and do it; I give you leave," answered Ben, sparring away derisively as the other tottered on his perch, and was forced to hold tight lest he should tumble off.

"Don't laugh, there's a good chap, but fish me out somehow, or I shall get my death sitting here all wet and cold," whined Sam, changing his tune, and feeling bitterly that Ben had the upper hand now.

Ben felt it also; and, though a very good-natured boy, could not resist the temptation to enjoy this advantage for a moment at least.

"I won't laugh if I can help it; only you do look so like a fat, speckled frog, I may not be able to hold in. I'll pull you out pretty soon; but first I'm going to talk to you, Sam," said Ben, sobering down as he took a seat on the little point of land nearest the stranded Samuel.

"Hurry up, then; I'm as stiff as a board now, and it's no fun sitting here on this knotty old thing," growled Sam, with a discontented squirm.

"Dare say not, but 'it is good for you,' as you say when you rap me over the head. Look here, I've got you in a tight place, and I don't mean to help you a bit till you promise to let me alone. Now then!" and Ben's face grew stern with his remembered wrongs as he grimly eyed his discomfited foe.

"I'll promise fast enough if you won't tell anyone about this," answered Sam, surveying himself and his surroundings with great disgust.

"I shall do as I like about that."

"Then I won't promise a thing! I'm not going to have the whole school laughing at me," protested Sam, who hated to be ridiculed even more than Ben did.

"Very well; good-night!" and Ben walked off with his hands in his pockets as coolly as if the bog was Sam's favorite retreat.

"Hold on, don't be in such a hurry!" shouted Sam, seeing little hope of rescue if he let this chance go.

"All right!" and back came Ben, ready for further negotiations.

"I'll promise not to plague you, if you'll promise not to tell on me. Is that what you want?"

"Now I come to think of it, there is one thing more. I like to make a good bargain when I begin," said Ben, with a shrewd air. "You must promise to keep Mose quiet, too. He follows your lead, and if you tell him to stop it he will. If I was big enough, I'd make you hold your tongues. I ain't, so we'll try this way."

"Yes, Yes, I'll see to Mose. Now, bring on a rail, there's a good fellow. I've got a horrid cramp in my legs," began Sam, thinking he had bought help dearly, yet admiring Ben's cleverness in making the most of his chance.

Ben brought the rail, but, just as he was about to lay it from the main-land to the nearest tussock, he stopped, saying, with the naughty twinkle in his black eyes again, "One more little thing must be settled first, and then I'll get you ashore. promise you won't plague the girls either, 'specially Bab and Betty. You pull their hair, and they don't like it."

"Don't neither! Wouldn't touch that Bab for a dollar; she scratches and bites like a mad cat," was Sam's sulky reply.

"Glad of it; she can take care of herself. Betty can't; and if you touch one of her pig-tails I'll up and tell right out how I found you snivelling in the ma'sh like a great baby. So now!" and Ben emphasized his threat with a blow of the suspended rail which splashed the water over poor Sam, quenching his last spark of resistance.

"Stop! I will! - I will!"

"True as you live and breathe!" demanded Ben, sternly binding him by the most solemn oath he knew.

"True as I live and breathe," echoed Sam, dolefully relinquishing his favorite pastime of pulling Betty's braids and asking if she was at home.

"I'll come over there and crook fingers on the bargain," said Ben, settling the rail and running over it to the tuft, then bridging another pool and crossing again till he came to the stump.

"I never thought of that way," said Sam, watching him with much inward chagrin at his own failure.

"I should think you'd written 'Look before you leap,' in your copy-book often enough to get the idea into your stupid head. Come, crook," commanded Ben, leaning forward with extended little finger. Sam obediently performed the ceremony, and then Ben sat astride one of the horns of the stump while the muddy Crusoe went slowly across the rail from point to point till he landed safely on the shore, when he turned about and asked with an ungrateful jeer, -
"Now what's going to become of you, old Look-before-you-leap?"

"Mud turtles can only sit on a stump and bawl till they are taken off, but frogs have legs worth something, and are not afraid of a little water," answered Ben, hopping away in an opposite direction, since the pools between him and Sam were too wide for even his lively legs.

Sam waddled off to the brook in the lane to rinse the mud from his nether man before facing his mother, and was just wringing himself out when Ben came up, breathless but good natured, for he felt that he had made an excellent bargain for himself and friends.

"Better wash your face; it's as speckled as a tiger-lily. Here's my handkerchief if yours is wet," he said, pulling out a dingy article which had evidently already done service as a towel.

"Don't want it," muttered Sam, gruffly, as he poured the water out of his muddy shoes.

"I was taught to say ' Thanky' when folks got me out of scrapes. But you never had much bringing up, though you do 'live in a house with a gambrel roof,'" retorted Ben, sarcastically quoting Sam's frequent boast; then he walked off, much disgusted with the ingratitude of man.

Sam forgot his manners, but he remembered his promise, and kept it so well that all the school wondered. No one could guess the secret of Ben's power over him, though it was evident that he had gained it in some sudden way, for at the least sign of Sam's former tricks Ben would crook his little finger and wag it warningly, or call out "Bulrushes!" and Sam subsided with reluctant submission, to the great amazement of his mates. When asked what it meant, Sa, turned sulky; but Ben had much fun out of it, assuring the other boys that those were the signs and password of a secret society to which he and Sam belonged, and promised to tell them all about it if Sam would give him leave, which, of course, he would not.

This mystery, and the vain endeavors to find it out caused a lull in the war of the wood-pile, and before any new game was invented something happened which gave the children plenty to talk about for a time.

A week after the secret alliance was formed, Ben ran in one evening with a letter for Miss Celia. He found her enjoying the cheery blaze of the pine-cones the little girls had picked up for her, and Bab and Betty sat in the small chairs rocking luxuriously as they took turns to throw on the pretty fuel. Miss Celia turned quickly to receive the expected letter, glanced at the writing, post-mark and stamp, with an air of delighted surprise, then clasped it close in both hands, saying, as she hurried out of the room, -

"He has come! he has come! Now you may tell them, Thorny."

"Tell its what? asked Bab, pricking up her cars at once.

"Oh, it's only that George has come, and I suppose we shall go and get married right away," answered Thorny, rubbing his hands as if he enjoyed the prospect.

"Are you going to be married? asked Betty, so soberly that the boys shouted, and Thorny, with difficulty composed himself sufficiently to explain.

"No, child, not just yet; but sister is, and I must go and see that all is done up ship-shape, and bring you home some wedding-cake. Ben will take care of you while I'm gone."

"When shall you go?" asked Bab, beginning to long for her share of cake.

"To-morrow, I guess. Celia has been packed and ready for a week. We agreed to meet George in New York, and be married as soon as he got his best clothes unpacked. We are men of our word, and off we go. Won't it be fun?"

"But when will you come back again?" questioned Betty, looking anxious.

"Don't know. Sister wants to come soon, but I'd rather have our honeymoon somewhere else, - Niagara, Newfoundland, West Point, or the Rocky Mountains," said Thorny, mentioning a few of the places he most desired to see.

"Do you like him?" asked Ben, very naturally wondering if the new master would approve of the young man-of-all-work.

"Don't I? George is regularly jolly; though now he's a minister, perhaps he'll stiffen up and turn sober. Won't it be a shame if he does?" and Thorny looked alarmed at the thought of losing his congenial friend.

"Tell about him; Miss Celia said you might", put in Bab, whose experience of "jolly" ministers had been small.

"Oh, there isn't much about it. We met in Switzerland going up Mount St. Bernard in a storm, and -"

"Where the good dogs live?" inquired Betty, hoping they would come into the story.

"Yes; we spent the night up there, and George gave us his room; the house was so full, and he wouldn't let me go down a steep place where I wanted to, and Celia thought he'd saved my life, and was very good to him. Then we kept meeting, and the first thing I knew she went and was engaged to him. I didn't care, only she would come home so he might go on studying hard and get through quick. That was a year ago, and last winter we were in New York at uncle's; and then, in the spring, I was sick, and we came here, and that's all."

"Shall you live here always when you come back? asked Bab, as Thorny paused for breath.

"Celia wants to. I shall go to college, so I don't mind. George is going to help the old minister here and see how he likes it. I'm to study with him, and if he is as pleasant as he used to be we shall have capital times, - see if we don't."

"I wonder if he will want me round," said Ben, feeling no desire to be a tramp again.

"I do, so you needn't fret about that, my hearty," answered Thorny, with a resounding slap on the shoulder which reassured Ben more than any promises.

"I'd like to see a live wedding, then we could play it with our dolls. I've got a nice piece of mosquito netting for a veil, and Belinda's white dress is clean. Do you s'pose Miss Celia will ask us to hers?" said Betty to Bab, as the boys began to discuss St. Bernard dogs with Spirit.

"I wish I could, dears," answered a voice behind them; and there was Miss Celia, looking so happy that the little girls wondered what the letter could have said to give her such bright eyes and smiling lips." I shall not be gone long, or be a bit changed when I come back, to live among you years I hope, for I am fond of the old place now, and mean it shall be home," she added, caressing the yellow heads as if they were dear to her.

"Oh, goody!" cried Bab, while Betty whispered with both arms round Miss Celia, -

"I don't think we could bear to have anybody else come here to live."

"It is very pleasant to hear you say that, and I mean to make others feel so, if I can. I have been trying a little this summer, but when I come back I shall go to work in earnest to be a good minister's wife, and you must help me."

"We will," promised both children, ready for any thing except preaching in the high pulpit.

Then Miss Celia turned to Ben, saying, in the respectful way that always made him feel at least twenty-five, -

"We shall be off to-morrow, and I leave you in charge. Go on just as if we were here, and be sure nothing will be changed as far as you are concerned when we come back."

Ben's face beamed at that; but the only way he could express his relief was by making such a blaze in honor of the occasion that he nearly roasted the company.

Next morning, the brother and sister slipped quietly away, and the children hurried to school, eager to tell the great news that "Miss Celia and Thorny had gone to be married, and were coming back to live here for ever and ever."

CHAPTER XXIII

SOMEBODY COMES

Bab and Betty had been playing in the avenue all the afternoon several weeks later, but as the shadows began to lengthen both agreed to sit upon the gate and rest while waiting for Ben, who had gone nutting with a party of boys. When they played house Bab was always the father, and went hunting or fishing with great energy and success, bringing home all sorts of game, from elephants and crocodiles to humming-birds and minnows. Betty was the mother, and a most notable little housewife, always mixing up imaginary delicacies with sand and dirt in old pans and broken china, which she baked in an oven of her own construction.

Both had worked hard that day, and were glad to retire to their favorite lounging-place, where Bab was happy trying to walk across the wide top bar without falling off, and Betty enjoyed slow, luxurious swings while her sister was recovering from her tumbles. On this occasion, having indulged their respective tastes, they paused for a brief interval of conversation, sitting side by side on the gate like a pair of plump gray chickens gone to roost.

"Don't you hope Ben will get his bag full? We shall have such fun eating nuts evenings observed Bab, wrapping her arms in her apron, for it was October now, and the air was growing keen.

"Yes, and Ma says we may boil some in our little kettles. Ben promised we should have half," answered Betty, still intent on her cookery.

"I shall save some of mine for Thorny."

"I shall keep lots of mine for Miss Celia."

"Doesn't it seem more than two weeks since she went away?"

"I wonder what she'll bring us."

Before Bab could conjecture, the sound of a step and a familiar whistle made both look expectantly toward the turn in the road, all ready to cry out in one voice, "How many have you got?" Neither spoke a word, however, for the figure which presently appeared was not Ben, but a stranger, - a man who stopped whistling, and came slowly on dusting his shoes in the way-side grass, and brushing the sleeves of his shabby velveteen coat as if anxious to freshen himself up a bit.

"It's a tramp, let's run away," whispered Betty, after a hasty look.

"I ain't afraid," and Bab was about to assume her boldest look when a sneeze spoilt it, and made her clutch the gate to hold on.

At that unexpected sound the man looked up, showing a thin, dark face, with a pair of sharp, black eyes, which surveyed the little girls so steadily that Betty quaked, and Bab began to wish she had at least jumped down inside the gate.

"How are you?" said the man with a goodnatured nod and smile, as if to re-assure the round-eyed children staring at him.

"Pretty well, thank you, sir," responded Bab, politely nodding back at him.

"Folks at home?" asked the man, looking over their heads toward the house.

"Only Ma; all the rest have gone to be married."

"That sounds lively. At the other place all the folks had gone to a funeral," and the man laughed as he glanced at the big house on the hill.

"Whh, do you know the Squire?" exclaimed Bab, much surprised and re-assured.

LOUISA MAY ALCOTT

"Come on purpose to see him. Just strolling round till he gets back," with an impatient sort of sigh.

"Betty thought you was a tramp, but I wasn't afraid. I like tramps ever since Ben came," explained Bab, with her usual candor.

"Who's Ben!" and the man came nearer so quickly that Betty nearly fell backward. "Don't you be scared, Sissy. I like little girls, so you set easy and tell me about Ben," he added, in a persuasive tone, as he leaned on the gate so near that both could see what a friendly face he had in spite of its eager, anxious look.

"Ben is Miss Celia's boy. We found him most starved in the coach-house, and he's been here ever since," answered Bab, comprehensively.

"Tell me about it. I like tramps, too," and the man looked as if he did very much, as Bab told the little story in a few childish words that were better than a much more elegant account.

"You were very good to the little feller," was all the man said when she ended her somewhat confused tale, in which she had jumbled the old coach and Miss Celia, dinner-pails and nutting, Sancho and circuses.

"'Course we were! He's a nice boy and we are fond of him, and he likes us," said Bab, heartily.

"'Specially me," put in Betty, quite at ease now, for the black eyes had softened wonderfully, and the brown face was smiling all over.

"Don't wonder a mite. You are the nicest pair of little girls I've seen this long time," and the man put a hand on either side of them, as if he wanted to hug the chubby children. But he didn't do it; he merely smiled and stood there asking questions till the two chatterboxes had told him every thing there was to tell in the most confiding manner, for he very soon ceased to seem like a stranger, and looked so familiar that Bab, growing inquisitive in her turn, suddenly said, -

"Haven't you ever been here before? It seems as if I'd seen you."

"Never in my life. Guess you've seen somebody that looks like me," and the black eyes twinkled for a minute as they looked into the puzzled little faces before him, then he said, soberly, -

"I'm looking round for a likely boy; don't you think this Ben would suite me? I want just such a lively sort of chap."

"Are you a circus man?" asked Bab, quickly.

"Well, no, not now. I'm in better business."

"I'm glad of it - we don't approve of 'em; but I do think they're splendid!"

Bab began by gravely quoting Miss Celia, and ended with an irrepressible burst of admiration which contrasted drolly with her first remark.

Betty added, anxiously: "We can't let Ben go any way. I know he wouldn't want to, and Miss Celia would feel bad. Please don't ask him."

"He can do as he likes, I suppose. He hasn't got any folks of his own, has he?"

"No, his father died in California, and Ben felt so bad he cried, and we were real sorry, and gave him a piece of Ma, 'cause he was so lonesome," answered Betty, in her tender little voice, with a pleading look which made the man stroke her smooth check and say, quite softly, -

"Bless your heart for that! I won't take him away, child, or do a thing to trouble anybody that's been good to him."

"He's coming now. I hear Sanch barking at the squirrels!" cried Bab, standing up to get a good look down the road.

The man turned quickly, and Betty saw that he breathed fast as he watched the spot where the low sunshine lay warmly on the red maple at the corner. Into this glow came unconscious Ben, whistling "Rory O'Moore," loud and Clear, as he trudged along with a heavy bag of nuts over his shoulder and the light full on his contented face. Sancho trotted before and saw the stranger first, for the sun in Ben's eyes dazzled him. Since his sad loss Sancho cherished a strong dislike to tramps, and now he paused to growl and show his teeth, evidently intending to warn this one off the premises.

"He won't hurt you -" began Bab, encouragingly; but before she could add a chiding word to the dog, Sanch gave an excited howl, and flew at the man's throat as if about to throttle him.

Betty screamed, and Bab was about to go to the rescue when both perceived that the dog was licking the stranger's face in an ecstasy of joy, and heard the man say as he hugged the curly beast, -

"Good old Sanch!" I knew he wouldn't forget master, and he doesn't"

"What's the matter?" called Ben, coming up briskly, with a strong grip of his stout stick. There was no need of any answer, for, as he came into the shadow, he saw the man, and stood looking at him as if he were a ghost.

"It's father, Benny; don't you know me?" asked the man, with an odd sort of choke in his voice, as he thrust the dog away, and held out both hands to the boy. Down dropped the nuts, and crying, "Oh, Daddy, Daddy!" Ben cast himself into the arms of the shabby velveteen coat, while poor Sanch tore round them in distracted circles, barking wildly, as if that was the only way in which he could vent his rapture.

What happened next Bab and Betty never stopped to see, but, dropping from their roost, they went flying home like startled

Chicken Littles with the astounding news that "Ben's father has come alive, and Sancho knew him right away!"

Mrs. Moss had just got her cleaning done up, and was resting a minute before setting the table, but she flew out of her old rocking-chair when the excited children told the wonderful tale, exclaiming as they ended,

"Where is he? Go bring him here. I declare it fairly takes my breath away!"

Before Bab could obey, or her mother compose herself, Sancho bounced in and spun round like an insane top, trying to stand on his head, walk upright, waltz and bark all at once, for the good old fellow had so lost his head that he forgot the loss of his tail.

"They are coming! they are coming! See, Ma, what a nice man he is," said Bab, hopping about on one foot as she watched the slowly approaching pair.

"My patience, don't they look alike! I should know he was Ben's Pa anywhere!" said Mrs. Moss, running to the door in a hurry.

They certainly did resemble one another, and it was almost comical to see the same curve in the legs, the same wide-awake style of wearing the hat, the same sparkle of the eye, good-natured smile and agile motion of every limb. Old Ben carried the bag in one hand while young Ben held the other fast, looking a little shame-faced at his own emotion now, for there were marks of tears on his cheeks, but too glad to repress the delight he felt that he had really found Daddy this side heaven.

Mrs. Moss unconsciously made a pretty little picture of herself as she stood at the door with her honest face shining and both hands ont, saying in a hearty tone, which was a welcome in itself,

"I'm real glad to see you safe and well, Mr. Brown! Come right in and make yourself to home. I guess there isn't a happier boy living than Ben is to-night."

LOUISA MAY ALCOTT

"And I know there isn't a gratefuler man living than I am for your kindness to my poor forsaken little feller," answered Mr. Brown, dropping both his burdens to give the comely woman's hands a hard shake.

"Now don't say a word about it, but sit down and rest, and we'll have tea in less'n no time. Ben must be tired and hungry, though he's so happy I don't believe he knows it," laughed Mrs. Moss, bustling away to hide the tears in her eyes, anxious to make things sociable and easy all round.

With this end in view she set forth her best china, and covered the table with food enough for a dozen, thanking her stars that it was baking day, and every thing had turned out well. Ben and his father sat talking by the window till they were bidden to "draw up and help themselves" with such hospitable warmth that every thing had an extra relish to the hungry pair.

Ben paused occasionally to stroke the rusty coat-sleeve with bread-and-buttery fingers to convince himself that "Daddy" had really come, and his father disposed of various inconvenient emotions by eating as if food was unknown in California. Mrs. Moss beamed on every one from behind the big tea-pot like a mild full moon, while Bab and Betty kept interrupting one another in their eagerness to tell something new about Ben and how Sanch lost his tail.

"Now you let Mr. Brown talk a little; we all want to hear how he 'came alive,' as you call it," said Mrs. Moss, as they drew round the fire in the "settin'-room," leaving the tea-things to take care of themselves.

It was not a long story, but a very interesting one to this circle of listeners; all about the wild life on the plains trading for mustangs, the terrible kick from a vicious horse that nearly killed Ben, sen., the long months of unconsciousness in the California hospital, the slow recovery, the journey back, Mr. Smithers's tale of the boy's disappearance, and then the anxious trip to find out from Squire Allen where he now was.

"I asked the hospital folks to write and tell you as soon as I knew whether I was on my head or my heels, and they promised; but they didn't; so I came off the minute I could, and worked my way back, expecting to find you at the old place. I was afraid you'd have worn out your welcome here and gone off again, for you are as fond of travelling as your father."

"I wanted to sometimes, but the folks here were so dreadful good to me I couldn't," confessed Ben, secretly surprised to find that the prospect of going off with Daddy even cost him a pang of regret, for the boy had taken root in the friendly soil, and was no longer a wandering thistle-down, tossed about by every wind that blew.

"I know what I owe 'em, and you and I will work out that debt before we die, or our name isn't B.B.," said Mr. Brown, with an emphatic slap on his knee, which Ben imitated half unconsciously as he exclaimed heartily, -

"That's so!" adding, more quietly, "What are you going to do now? Go back to Smithers and the old business?"

"Not likely, after the way he treated you, Sonny. I've had it Out with him, and he won't want to see me again in a hurry," answered Mr. Brown, with a sudden kindling of the eye that reminded Bab of Ben's face when he shook her after losing Sancho.

"There's more circuses than his in the world; but I'll have to limber out ever so much before I'm good for much in that line," said the boy, stretching his stout arms and legs with a curious mixture of satisfaction and regret.

"You've been living in clover and got fat, you rascal," and his father gave him a poke here and there, as Mr. Squeers did the plump Wackford, when displaying him as a specimen of the fine diet at Do-the-boys Hall. "Don't believe I could put you up now if I tried, for I haven't got my strength back yet, and we are both out of practice. It's just as well, for I've about made up my mind to quit the business and settle down somewhere for a spell, if I can get any thing to do," continued the rider, folding his arms and gazing thoughtfully into the fire.

"I shouldn't wonder a mite if you could right here, for Mr. Towne has a great boarding-stable over yonder, and he's always wanting men." Said Mrs. Moss, eagerly, for she dreaded to have Ben go, and no one could forbid it if his father chose to take him away.

"That sounds likely. Thanky, ma'am. I'll look up the concern and try my chance. Would you call it too great a come-down to have father an 'ostler after being first rider in the 'Great Golden Menagerie, Circus, and Colossem,' hey, Ben?" asked Mr. Brown, quoting the well-remembered show-bill with a laugh.

"No, I shouldn't; it's real jolly up there when the big barn is full and eighty horses have to be taken care of. I love to go and see 'em. Mr. Towne asked me to come and be stable-boy when I rode the kicking gray the rest were afraid of. I hankered to go, but Miss Celia had just got my new books, and I knew she'd feel bad if I gave up going to school. Now I'm glad I didn't, for I get on first rate and like it."

"You done right, boy, and I'm pleased with you. Don't you ever be ungrateful to them that befriended you, if you want to prosper. I'll tackle the stable business a Monday and see what's to be done. Now I ought to be walking, but I'll be round in the morning ma'am, if you can spare Ben for a spell to-morrow. We'd like to have a good Sunday tramp and talk; wouldn't we, Sonny?" and Mr. Brown rose to go with his hand on Ben's shoulder, as if loth to leave him even for the night.

Mrs. Moss saw the longing in his face, and forgetting that he was an utter stranger, spoke right out of her hospitable heart.

"It's a long piece to the tavern, and my little back bedroom is always ready. It won't make a mite of trouble if you don't mind a plain place, and you are heartily welcome."

Mr. Brown looked pleased, but hesitated to accept any further favor from the good soul who had already done so much for him and his. Ben gave him no time to speak, however, for running to a door he flung it open and beckoned, saying, eagerly, -

"Do stay, father; it will be so nice to have you. This is a tip-top room; I slept here the night I came, and that bed was just splendid after bare ground for a fortnight."

"I'll stop, and as I'm pretty well done up, I guess we may as well turn in now," answered the new guest; then, as if the memory of that homeless little lad so kindly cherished made his heart overflow in spite of him, Mr. Brown paused at the door to say hastily, with a hand on Bab and Betty's heads, as if his promise was a very earnest one, -

"I don't forget, ma'am, these children shall never want a friend while Ben Brown's alive;" then he shut the door so quickly that the other Ben's prompt "Hear, hear!" was cut short in the middle.

"I s'pose he means that we shall have a piece of Ben's father, because we gave Ben a piece of our mother," said Betty, softly.

"Of course he does, and it's all fair," answered Bab, decidedly. "Isn't he a nice man, Ma?

"Go to bed, children," was all the answer she got; but when they were gone, Mrs. Moss, as she washed up her dishes, more than once glanced at a certain nail where a man's hat had not hung for five years, and thought with a sigh what a natural, protecting air that slouched felt had.

If one wedding were not quite enough for a child's story, we might here hint what no one dreamed of then, that before the year came round again Ben had found a mother, Bab and Betty a father, and Mr. Brown's hat was quite at home behind the kitchen door. But, on the whole, it is best not to say a word about it.

LOUISA MAY ALCOTT

CHAPTER XXIV

THE GREAT GATE IS OPENED

The Browns were up and out so early next morning that Bab and Betty were sure they had run away in the night. But on looking for them, they were discovered in the coach-house criticising Lita, both with their hands in their pockets, both chewing straws, and looking as much alike as a big elephant and a small one.

"That's as pretty a little span as I've seen for a long time," said the elder Ben, as the children came trotting down the path hand in hand, with the four blue bows at the ends of their braids bobbing briskly up and down.

"The nigh one is my favorite, but the off one is the best goer, though she's dreadfully hard bitted," answered Ben the younger, with such a comical assumption of a jockey's important air that his father laughed as he said in an undertone, -

"Come, boy, we must drop the old slang since we've given up the old business. These good folks are making a gentleman of you, and I won't be the one to spoil their work. Hold on, my dears, and I'll show you how they say good-morning in California," he added, beckoning to the little girls, who now came up rosy and smiling.

"Breakfast is ready, sir," said Betty, looking much relieved to find them.

"We thought you'd run away from us," explained Bab, as both put out their hands to shake those extended to them.

"That would be a mean trick. But I'm going to run away with you," and Mr. Brown whisked a little girl to either shoulder before they knew what had happened, while Ben, remembering the day, with difficulty restrained himself from turning a series of triumphant somersaults before them all the way to the door, where Mrs. Moss stood waiting for them.

After breakfast Ben disappeared for a short time, and returned in his Sunday suit, looking so neat and fresh that his father surveyed him with surprise and pride as he came in full of boyish satisfaction in his trim array.

"Here's a smart young chap! Did you take all that trouble just to go to walk with old Daddy?" asked Mr. Brown, stroking the smooth head, for they were alone just then, Mrs. Moss and the children being up stairs preparing for church.

"I thought may be you'd like to go to meeting first," answered Ben, looking up at him with such a happy face that it was hard to refuse any thing. I'm too shabby, Sonny, else I'd go in a minute to please you."

"Miss Celia said God didn't mind poor clothes, and she took me when I looked worse than you do. I always go in the morning; she likes to have me," said Ben, turning his hat about as if not quite sure what he ought to do.

"Do you want to go?" asked his father in a tone of surprise.

"I want to please her, if you don't mind. We could have our tramp this afternoon."

"I haven't been to meeting since mother died, and it don't seem to come easy, though I know I ought to, seeing I'm alive and here," and Mr. Brown looked soberly out at the lovely autumn world as if glad to be in it after his late danger and pain.

"Miss Celia said church was a good place to take our troubles, and to be thankful in. I went when I thought you were dead, and now I'd love to go when I've got my Daddy safe again,"

No one saw him, so Ben could not resist giving his father a sudden hug, which was warmly returned as the man said earnestly, -

"I'll go, and thank the Lord hearty for giving me back my boy better'n I left him!"

For a minute nothing was heard but the loud tick of the old clock and a mournful whine front Sancho, shut up in the shed lest he should go to church without an invitation.

Then, as steps were heard on the stairs, Mr. Brown caught up his hat, saying hastily, -

"I ain't fit to go with them, you tell 'm, and I'll slip into a back seat after folks are in. I know the way." And, before Ben could reply, he was gone. Nothing was seen of him along the way, but he saw the little party, and rejoiced again over his boy, changed in so many ways for the better; for Ben was the one thing which had kept his heart soft through all the trials and temptations of a rough life.

"I promised Mary I'd do my best for the poor baby she had to leave, and I tried; but I guess a better friend than I am has been raised up for him when he needed her most. It won't hurt me to follow him in this road," thought Mr. Brown, as he came out into the highway from his stroll "across-lots," feeling that it would be good for him to stay in this quiet place, for his own as well as his son's sake.

The Bell had done ringing when he reached the green, but a single boy sat on the steps and rail to meet him, saying, with a reproachful look, -

"I wasn't going to let you be alone, and have folks think I was ashamed of my father. Come, Daddy, we'll sit together."

So Ben led his father straight to the Squire's pew, and sat beside him with a face so full of innocent pride and joy, that people would have suspected the truth if he had not already told many of them. Mr. Brown, painfully conscious of his shabby coat, was rather "taken aback," as he expressed it; but the Squire's shake of the hand, and Mrs. Allen's gracious nod enabled him to face the eyes of the interested congregation, the younger portion of which stared steadily at him all sermon time, in spite of paternal frowns and maternal tweakings in the rear.

But the crowning glory of the day came after church, when the Squire said to Ben, and Sam heard him, -

"I've got a letter for you from Miss Celia. Come home with me, and bring your father. I want to talk to him."

The boy proudly escorted his parent to the old carry-all, and, tucking himself in behind with Mrs. Allen, had the satisfaction of seeing the slouched felt hat side by side with the Squire's Sunday beaver in front, as they drove off at such an unusually smart pace, it was evident that Duke knew there was a critical eye upon him. The interest taken in the father was owing to the son at first; but, by the time the story was told, old Ben had won friends for himself not only because of the misfortunes which he had evidently borne in a manly way, but because of his delight in the boy's improvement, and the desire he felt to turn his hand to any honest work, that he might keep Ben happy and contented in this good home.

"I'll give you a line to Towne. Smithers spoke well of you, and your own ability will be the best recommendation," said the Squire, as he parted from them at his door, having given Ben the letter.

Miss Celia had been gone a fortnight, and every one was longing to have her back. The first week brought Ben a newspaper, with a crinkly line drawn round the marriages to attract attention to that spot, and one was marked by a black frame with a large hand pointing at it from the margin. Thorny sent that; but the next week came a parcel for Mrs. Moss, and in it was discovered a box of wedding cake for every member of the family, including Sancho, who ate his at one gulp, and chewed up the lace paper which covered it. This was the third week; and, as if there could not be happiness enough crowded into it for Ben, the letter he read on his way home told him that his dear mistress was coming back on the following Saturday. One passage particularly pleased him, -

"I want the great gate opened, so that the new master may go in that way. Will you see that it is done, and all made neat afterward? Randa will give you the key, and you may have out all your flags if you like, for the old place cannot look too gay for this home-coming."

Sunday though it was, Ben could not help waving the letter over his head as he ran in to tell Mrs. Moss the glad news, and begin at once to plan the welcome they would give Miss Celia, for he never called her any thing else.

During their afternoon stroll in the mellow sunshine, Ben continued to talk of her, never tired of telling about his happy summer under her roof. And Mr. Brown was never weary of hearing, for every hour showed him more plainly what a lovely miracle her gentle words had wrought, and every hour increased his gratitude, his desire to return the kindness in some humble way. He had his wish, and did his part hand-somely when he least expected to have a chance.

On Monday he saw Mr. Towne, and, thanks to the Squire's good word, was engaged for a month on trial, making himself so useful that it was soon evident he was the right man in the right place. He lived on the hill, but managed to get down to the little brown house in the evening for a word with Ben, who just now was as full of business as if the President and his Cabinet were coming.

Every thing was put in apple-pie order in and about the old house; the great gate, with much creaking of rusty hinges and some clearing away of rubbish, was set wide open, and the first creature who entered it was Sancho, solemnly dragging the dead mullein which long ago had grown above the keyhole. October frosts seemed to have spared some of the brightest leaves for this especial occasion; and on Saturday the arched gate-way was hung with gay wreaths, red and yellow sprays strewed the flags, and the porch was a blaze of color with the red woodbine, that was in its glory when the honeysuckle was leafless.

Fortunately it was a half-holiday, so the children could trim and chatter to their heart's content, and the little girls ran about sticking funny decorations where no one would ever think of looking for them. Ben was absorbed in his flags, which were sprinkled all down the avenue with a lavish display, suggesting several Fourth of Julys rolled into one. Mr. Brown had come to lend a hand, and did so most energetically, for the break-neck things he did with his son during the decoration fever would have terrified Mrs. Moss out of her wits, if she had not been in the house giving last touches to every room, while Randa and Katy set forth a sumptuous tea.

All was going well, and the train would be due in an hour, when luckless Bab nearly turned the rejoicing into mourning, the feast into ashes. She heard her mother say to Randa, "There ought to be a fire in every room, it looks so cheerful, and the air is chilly spite of the sunshine;" and, never waiting to hear the reply that some of the long-unused chimneys were not safe till cleaned, off went Bab with an apron full of old shingles, and made a roaring blaze in the front room fire-place, which was of all others the one to be let alone, as the flue was out of order.

Charmed with the brilliant light and the crackle of the tindery fuel, Miss Bab refilled her apron, and fed the fire till the chimney began to rumble ominously, sparks to fly out at the top, and soot and swallows' nests to come tumbling down upon the hearth. Then, scared at what she had done, the little mischief-maker hastily buried her fire, swept up the rubbish, and ran off, thinking no one would discover her prank if she never told.

Everybody was very busy, and the big chimney blazed and rumbled unnoticed till the cloud of smoke caught Ben's eye as he festooned his last effort in the flag line, part of an old sheet with the words "Father has come!" in red cambric letters half a foot long sewed upon it.

"Hullo! I do believe they've got up a bonfire. without asking my leave. Miss Celia never would let us, because the sheds and roofs are so old and dry; I must see about it. Catch me, Daddy, I'm coming down!" cried Ben, dropping out of the elm with no more thought of where he might light than a squirrel swinging from bough to bough.

His father caught him, and followed in haste as his nimble-footed son raced up the avenue, to stop in the gate-way, frightened at the prospect before him, for falling sparks had already kindled the roof here and there, and the chimney smoked and roared like a small volcano, while Katy's wails and Randa's cries for water came from within.

"Up there with wet blankets, while I get out the hose!" cried Mr. Brown, as he saw at a glance what the danger was.

Ben vanished; and, before his father got the garden hose rigged, he was on the roof with a dripping blanket over the worst spot. Mrs. Moss had her wits about her in a minute, and ran to put in the fireboard, and stop the draught. Then, stationing Randa to watch that the falling cinders did no harm inside, she hurried off to help Mr. Brown, who might not know where things were. But he had roughed it so long, that he was the man for emergencies, and seemed to lay his hand on whatever was needed, by a sort of instinct. Finding that the hose was too short to reach the upper part of the roof, he was on the roof in a jiffy with two pails of water, and quenched the most dangerous spots before much harm was done.

This he kept up till the chimney burned itself out, while Ben dodged about among the gables with a watering pot, lest some stray sparks should be over-looked, and break out afresh.

While they worked there, Betty ran to and fro with a dipper of water, trying to help; and Sancho barked violently, as if he objected to this sort of illumination. But where was Bab, who revelled in flurries? No one missed her till the fire was out, and the tired, sooty people met to talk over the danger just escaped.

"Poor Miss Celia wouldn't have had a roof over her head, if it hadn't been for you, Mr. Brown," said Mrs. Moss, sinking into a kitchen chair, pale with the excitement.

"It would have burnt lively, but I guess it's all right now. Keep an eye on the roof, Ben, and I'll step up garret and see if all's safe there. Didn't you know that chimney was foul, ma'am?" asked the man, as he wiped the perspiration off his grimy face.

"Randa said it was, and I 'in surprised she made a fire there," began Mrs. Moss, looking at the maid, who just then came in with a pan full of soot.

"Bless you, ma'am, I never thought of such a thing, nor Katy neither. That naughty Bab must have done it, and so don't dar'st to show herself," answered the irate Randa, whose nice room was in a mess.

"Where is the child?" asked her mother; and a hunt was immediately instituted by Betty and Sancho, while the elders cleared up.

Anxious Betty searched high and low, called and cried, but all in vain; and was about to sit down in despair, when Sancho made a bolt into his new kennel and brought out a shoe with a foot in it while a doleful squeal came from the straw within.

"Oh, Bab, how could you do it? Ma was frightened dread-fully," said Betty, gently tugging at the striped leg, as Sancho poked his head in for another shoe.

"Is it all burnt up?" demanded a smothered voice from the recesses of the kennel.

"Only pieces of the roof. Ben and his father put it out, and I helped," answered Betty, cheering up a little as she recalled her noble exertions.

"What do they do to folks who set houses afire?" asked the voice again.

"I don't know; but you needn't be afraid, there isn't much harm done, I guess, and Miss Celia will forgive you, she's so good."

"Thorny won't; he calls me a 'botheration,' and I guess I am," mourned the unseen culprit, with sincere contrition.

"I'll ask him; he is always good to me. They will be here pretty soon, so you'd better come out and be made tidy," suggested the comforter.

"I never can come out, for every one will hate me," sobbed Bab among the straw, as she pulled in her foot, as if retiring for ever from an outraged world.

"Ma won't, she's too busy cleaning up; so it's a good time to come. Let's run home, wash our hands, and be all nice when they see us. I'll love you, no matter what anybody else does," said Betty, consoling the poor little sinner, and proposing the sort of repentance most likely to find favor in the eyes of the agitated elders.

"P'raps I'd better go home, for Sanch will want his bed," and Bab gladly availed herself of that excuse to back out of her refuge, a very crumpled, dusty young lady, with a dejected face and much straw sticking in her hair.

Betty led her sadly away, for she still protested that she never should dare to meet the offended public again; but in fifteen minutes both appeared in fine order and good spirits, and naughty Bab escaped a lecture for the time being, as the train would soon be due.

At the first sound of the car whistle every one turned good-natured as if by magic, and flew to the gate smiling as if all mishaps were forgiven and forgotten. Mrs. Moss, however, slipped quietly away, and was the first to greet Mrs. Celia as the carriage stopped at the entrance of the avenue, so that the luggage might go in by way of the lodge.

"We will walk up and you shall tell us the news as we go, for I see you have some," said the young lady, in her friendly manner, when Mrs. Moss had given her welcome and paid her respects to the gentleman who shook hands in a way that convinced her he was indeed what Thorny called him, "regularly jolly," though he was a minister.

That being exactly what she came for, the good woman told her tidings as rapidly as possible, and the new-comers were so glad to hear of Ben's happiness they made very light of Bab's bonfire, though it had nearly burnt their house down.

"We won't say a word about it, for every one must be happy to-day," said Mr. George, so kindly that Mrs. Moss felt a load taken off her heart at once.

"Bab was always teasing me for fireworks, but I guess she has had enough for the present," laughed Thorny, who was gallantly escorting Bab's mother up the avenue.

"Every one is so kind! Teacher was out with the children to cheer us as we passed, and here you all are making things pretty for me," said Mrs. Celia, smiling with tears in her eyes, as they drew near the great gate, which certainly did present an animated if not an imposing appearance.

Randa and Katy stood on one side, all in their best, bobbing delighted courtesies; Mr. Brown, half hidden behind the gate on the other side, was keeping Sancho erect, so that he might present arms promptly when the bride appeared. As flowers were scarce, on either post stood a rosy little girl clapping her hands, while out from the thicket of red and yellow boughs, which made a grand bouquet in the lantern frame, came Ben's head and shoulders, as he waved his grandest flag with its gold paper "Welcome Home!" on a blue ground.

"Isn't it beautiful!" cried Mrs. Celia, throwing kisses to the children, shaking hands with her maids, and glancing brightly at the stranger who was keeping Sanch quiet.

"Most people adorn their gate-posts with stone balls, vases, or griffins; your living images are a great improvement, love, especially the happy boy in the middle," said Mr. George, eying

Ben with interest, as he nearly tumbled overboard, top-heavy with his banner.

"You must finish what I have only begun," answered Celia, adding gayly as Sancho broke loose and came to offer both his paw and his congratulations. "Sanch, introduce your master, that I may thank him for coming back in time to save my old house."

"If I'd saved a dozen it wouldn't have half paid for all you've done for my boy, ma'am," answered Mr. Brown, bursting out from behind the gate quite red with gratitude and pleasure.

"I loved to do it, so please remember that this is still his home till you make one for him. Thank God, he is no longer fatherless!" and her sweet face said even more than her words as the white hand cordially shook the brown one with a burn across the back.

"Come on, sister. I see the tea-table all ready, and I'm awfully hungry," interrupted Thorny, who had not a ray of sentiment about him, though very glad Ben had got his father back again.

"Come over, by-and-by, little friends, and let me thank you for your pretty welcome, - it certainly is a warm one;" and Mrs. Celia glanced merrily from the three bright faces above her to the old chimney, which still smoked sullenly.

"Oh, don't!" cried Bab, hiding her face.

"She didn't mean to," added Betty, pleadingly.

"Three cheers for the bride!" roared Ben, dipping his flag, as leaning on her husband's arm his dear mistress passed under the gay arch, along the leaf-strewn walk, over the threshold of the house which was to be her happy home for many years.

The closed gate where the lonely little wanderer once lay was always to stand open now, and the path where children played before was free to all comers, for a hospitable welcome henceforth awaited rich and poor, young and old, sad and gay, Under the Lilacs.

LOUISA MAY ALCOTT

Louisa May Alcott
(November 29, 1832 – March 6, 1888

Louisa May Alcott (November 29, 1832 – March 6, 1888) was an American novelist. She is best known for the novel Little Women, published in 1868. This novel is loosely based on her childhood experiences with her three sisters. Though of New England parentage and residence, she was born in Germantown, which is currently part of Philadelphia, Pennsylvania. Alcott's early education had included lessons from the naturalist Henry David Thoreau but had chiefly been in the hands of her father. She also received some instruction from writers and educators such as Ralph Waldo Emerson, Nathaniel Hawthorne, and Margaret Fuller, who were all family friends. She later described these early years in a newspaper sketch entitled "Transcendental Wild Oats", afterwards reprinted in the volume Silver Pitchers (1876), which relates the experiences of her family during their experiment in "plain living and high thinking" at Fruitlands.

LaVergne, TN USA
03 January 2011
210887LV00002B/49/P